THE DRAMATIC HISTORY OF THE WORLD

THE DRAMATIC HISTORY OF THE WORLD

Kolachelam Sreenivasa Rao

GYAN

Published by

GYAN

Gyan Publishing House
5, Ansari Road
Daryaganj, New Delhi-110002
Phone: 011-47034999, 9811692060
E-mail: books@gyanbooks.com

Distribution Network
gyanbooks.com
India, USA, Canada, UK, Australia, France

ISBN : 978-81-212-3333-0 (PB)
First Published, 1908

2nd Impression 2020

Printed at: Gyan Press, Delhi.

The Dramatic
History of the World
Author: Kolachelam Sreenivasa Rao

PREFACE.

In this little book the reader will be greatly disappointed if he opens it with a sanguine expectation of finding a regular detailed dramatical history of the world. The object of the present work is to furnish a brief summary of the origin and progress of dramatic representations from the remotest times, to show that every element that helps the formation of dramatical representation was created by highly revered sages for the harmless entertainment and the educational enlightenment of the people and to prove that the combination of several dramatic elements could only result in the attainment of a beneficial object. Ruled by immense worldly experience of human nature and guided by illimitable knowledge gained by a careful perusal of books containing ancient wisdom, the poets generally avoid such of the themes as would draw weak minds towards immorality. Dramas are the text-books for the students to study and the college professors teach them vividly. Actors perform the very same functions, but more satisfactorily by placing before you living pictures and explaining to you the thoughts of the poet in a highly entertaining manner and leaving in your mind all the vivid impressions of the drama more firmly than you could do yourself by reading, and the professor could do in a college. I feel, therefore, that there is no inherent bad influence in the actor's art. If the drama and the dramatic art have not in themselves a bad influence, what is it then that produces moral contamination on the stage? Donaldson, in his book, "The Recollections of an Actor," says, "I believe no one ever asserted that the stage was in itself immoral; and to destroy it altogether would be, to use a medical simile, to abolish a very powerful medicine because quacks have contrived to make it kill." Things which are not desirable and which are really sometimes regrettable, do happen on the stage by the wayward fancy of youths in full vigour of health, uncontrolled by experience and uncriticised by the public.

We should consider such things as superfluous overgrowths and try to crop them.

Indian theatrical representations are, unlike those of European nations after the Restoration, pure and harmless. No Indian comedy ever insulted any statesman. No Indian satire ever insulted the feelings of any respectable family. No Indian dramatic piece ever attempted to attack the King and his ministers. No Indian performance ever insultingly attacked the religious tenets of all powerful reigning Popes. No Indian dramatist ever attempted to satiate his private grudge against his rival by publicly insulting him on the stage. No Indian ever attempted to drag the dead into this world again and insult them with ludicrous arguments. No Indian dramatist ever attempted to use expressions considered indecent by the society. Educated Indians are accustomed to exaggerated descriptions of women and they do not feel them to be repulsive to good taste when they hear minute descriptions of women's face, chest, breast, lips, nose, legs or hands. This is only a question of taste and custom. Beyond this description and the use of some hackneyed expressions of love in frenzy, the Indian author knows no vice and his dramas cannot but be considered pure and harmless. He is averse to introduce characters that exhibit personal mimicry or imitate idiosyncrasies of any particular individual. His subjects are always divine beings, their heroic deeds, their love, their conduct towards each other and their virtues. In case he introduces worldly beings, he invests them with divine characteristics. Can there possibly be any harm in themes like these?

The decline of the Hindu kings must have caused the decline of the Hindu stage. A perusal of the dramatic histories of the different countries of the world leads one to believe that, like man, the stage has also the vicissitudes of life —the cyclic turns—birth, growth and decline. It must have been in this last condition in the life of the stage, when every limb was rotten, that the stigma to the noble art originated

The present century is the time for its re-birth. Nourishment is required for healthy growth. If intellectual audience by their indifference were to continue to let the stage grow wild with the nourishment given to it by uneducated and immoral bodies of people, I fear that the contamination would extend rapidly to the more refined classes also. Neither the priestly threats of hell nor the royal orders of prison could eradicate the dramatic element from the heart of the nation. It is a wonder that educated Indians are philosophically putting up with the various kinds of clowns and dancers, who sweep away our money but add nothing to our national literature. The Indian stage at present needs healthy development and growth.

It is a matter for regret that the stage, which was considered by our ancients as a religious platform, wherefrom lessons on morality and other subjects were intended to be imparted to the people by men of highest learning and knowledge, is now converted into a place where an ignorant few play like children for amusement only. It is this state of the stage our forefathers detested and they styled everyone that appeared on it as not a social being. A thirst for pure and intellectual amusement is nowhere censured. Our ancients knew that the stage educates people, in as much as it "leads, draws forth, trains and exercises the powers of the mind, the passions, the affections and dispositions, habits and manners." They also knew that, "there was no instrument so powerful, so instant and so effective as the drama." The stage really requires men of high learning, who could understand and feel what they say. P. J. Cooke in his "Handbook of Drama, its philosophy and teaching," says, "If a man feels what he is saying, he will show it in his face, in his voice and above all in his gestures. He must, if he be an actor or reciter sink himself for the time being, heart and soul, into the character he is representing. If he can do so successfully, he has every right to be called a good actor or a good elocutionist. If he cannot, he is simply a mouthing, ranting, grotesque magpie, who apes the character but who does not do it. The actor whom we cannot recognise in his different impersonations on the stage is unquestionably a conscientious actor ; and he who can be discovered in the first word he speaks is only a theatrical parrot who gets off words by rote and repeats them with much force and intelligence as that species of feathered tribe generally succeeds in doing." Now we see what amount of acting, what amount of elocution and what amount of intelligence are required to be an actor ; and what amount of learning the actor needs to understand and feel what he says. People may say that such actors are rare. Certainly rare are the Indian actors because, the timid educated people have not as yet shaken off the prejudices implanted in them by the ignorant and the dogmatic men, of the bygone generations.

The religious character of the drama assumed an artistic shape during the decline of the Hindu kingdom Its artistic character declined during the Mahomedan period into an effort to amuse their vulgar sensual taste. In a country where higher education could reach only a select few, the uneducated formed the overwhelming majority, and anything that is devoid of broad and coarse humour is denounced as worthless ; and this opinion gains a vantage ground among the masses. Attempts to please the vulgar with coarse and indecent language, must have created in the minds of the educated, a feeling of hatred. The stage which was once considered a school for the education of the masses and a moral educator, became a place for the unprincipled actors to inculcate immorality. The learned, in their rage, must have styled the actors as so many brutes. S. Jones says that " an intellectual drama can only exist by favour of intellectual public."

In the convocation address given in Madras in 1877, Colonel R. M. Macdonald said as follows :—

"We have had among us not very long ago, a Parsee gentleman who has proved that even the stage is not an impossible career for a highly educated native gentleman. The drama has in all civilized nations been a source of much intellectual entertainment and the Hindus at a very early period produced dramatic works, some of which have been the admiration of Europe. But the drama may exercise an evil, as well as a good influence, and its tendency in this Presidency has been at times so pernicious a character that I should rejoice to see some well directed effort on the part of native gentlemen of position and education, to purify and elevate the taste of their countrymen. The revival of the ancient Sanscrit drama and the creation of a modern Vernacular School are objects in no way unworthy of your ambition. If a new school of vernacular literature is to arise at all, it must be created by you or by such as you. It is sometimes said that we are premature in our expectations, that the higher education is a plant of recent growth in this Presidency, and that there has not been sufficient time for the production of any great work. Thirty or forty years may be a short period in the history of a Nation, but it is a long period in the life of a man, and the fact remains that one generation has grown up under the influence of European culture and is passing away without having left any permanent mark on the literature of the country. About 20 years ago Dr. Coldwell remarked that for the last one hundred and fifty years the Dravidian mind appeared to have sunk into a state of lethargy, scarcely any Tamil poem or treatise of any real value having appeared, except such as had been composed by European Missionaries, and he ascribed this stagnation to the natural tendency to decay and death, which is inherent in a system of slavery to great names."

I could not get much useful information about the dramatic literature in America, Africa and Australia ; so my treatment of the subject concerning the above continents is meagre. I have collected enough of information regarding the British dramatical literature but I have omitted a greater part of it, lest I should increase the size of this book. Instead of writing everything the book contains in my own simple inornate language, I have, on proper consideration, thought it prudent to furnish the information by quotations from various authors—some of whom are named and some are not—(because when I took notes and quotations I failed to take note of the name of the author and sometimes the name of the book). I am highly indebted to the English translators of classical languages, for had it not been for their exertion, I should not have had any idea of what their classical dramas were like.

In the following pages, I have attempted to trace out the historic incidents of the stage from the earliest times in the different countries of the world. With an earnest hope that my readers will excuse me for attempting to write this treatise in a foreign language, I humbly conclude this preface.

BELLARY, K. SREENIVASA RAO.
1st January 1908.

ERRATA.

Page.	Line.	For		Read.
8	10	represonted	...	represented
15	12	christian	...	Christian
40	29	miarcle	...	miracle
68	15	Puritons	...	Puritans
68	last line.	philonthrophy	...	philanthrophy
69	16	Napolian	...	Napoleon
72	1	Immeditalely	...	Immediately
73	15	Sanctury	...	Sanctuary
74	30	Natnre	...	Nature
78	6	renaiscence	...	renaissance
81	8	Supercede	...	Supersede
87	13	Reneisence	...	Renaissence
102	16	Monsienr	...	Monsieur
104	34	Maids	...	Maid's
124	11	bofore	...	before
150	1	irresistable	...	irresistible
155	26	mis	...	Miss
160	11	Windham	...	Wyndham
161	1	principle	...	principal
167	15	whatever paid	...	whatever is paid
168	6	was performed	...	were performed
171	6	best	...	lust
179	20	Partician	...	Patrician
189	1	knds	...	kinds
189	29	Nishkambha	...	Vishkambha
233	10	perforn	...	perform
Rules 3	33	ragedy	...	tragedy
„ 3	35	ight	...	sight
„ 12	7	courteous to him	...	courteous

CONTENTS.

PART I.

EUROPE.

CHAPTER I.

GREECE.

Origin of Dramas.

Eleusinian mystery.

ONE of the mystic ceremonials of the Greeks, secretly observed by them, was known as the Eleusinian mystery. They had also other mysteries containing dramatic elements which were very religiously observed. The traditional songs in them were chanted by the hierophants. One of the chief qualifications of their office was the possession of a *good voice.* On certain religious occasions, the life and the deeds of the deities presiding over the mysteries were dramatically represented by those who were initiated into the sacred secrets. The deities were represented on the stage in appropriate dresses, the parts being played by the ministers. These were known as *Mystic dramas* and they were performed secretly. I am strongly of opinion that this kind of secret dramatic divine service was the origin of the subsequent Christian mystic liturgies and still subsequent Mystery and Miracle plays. The mass which formed the central act of public worship in the Church and which was introduced by Gregory the Great, in the sixth century, was, I think, the outcome of the above pre-christian pagan service. Even before the heroic age 1184 B.C., singing and dancing were the favourite amusements of the social gatherings.

Mystic dramas.

The origin of Eleusinian Mystery.

THE Eleusinian religious performances in Greece were only the modifications of the Semitic and the Rhodian divine rites, changed subsequently to a milder form in the Christian Eucharistic ceremonies, or in other words the barbarous custom of human-sacrifice subsequently converted into goat-sacrifice, had been, during the subsequent period, changed to a sacrifice of a round cake. The rites performed during these sacramental sacrifices were more like dramatic representations. Highest ritual sacrifices in India, known as Naramedha or human-sacrifice, Aswamedha or horse-sacrifice, and Pasumedha or goat-sacrifice, resemble those sacrifices from which the Eleusinian Mysteries took their origin. The ultimate object of these sacrifices was to place the soul in Elysium in rest. The ancients had an unshaken belief in the unity of god and immortality of the soul. As I said above, only the initiated were allowed to be present at the performances of these rites at first. To exemplify the doctrines delivered to the initiated and to inculcate them more sensibly, the ancient Greeks commenced to celebrate these Mysteries by shows at stated seasons of the year. These shows exhibited a representation of Heaven, Hell, Elysium and Purgatory and all that related to the future state of the dead. I read in Cicero's Life by Middleton that these shows in Greece were represented with great pomp and machinery and that people from all countries went to Greece to witness the sacred performances. For further particulars about the origin of these rites I would refer the reader to the book "Pagan Christs" by J. M. Robertson, and to the "History of Literature of Ancient Greece" by K. O. Muller.

Indian Eleusinian Mysteries.

ARISTOTLE considers Homer to be the founder of the drama among the Greeks, not as having himself written any composition strictly of a dramatic nature but as having led the way to it by his lively representations of life and manners, both in the more serious and graver aspects and in the comic; his Iliad and Odyssey bearing the same relation to tragedy that his Margites does to comedy. The era of dramatic composition among the Greeks commenced about 590 B.C. Thespis who is said to have been the inventor of the tragic art was a contemporary of

Homer.

Thespis.

Solon, 536 B.C. Horace considers Thespis to be the inventor of the tragic art, for he says :—

" Thespis inventor of tragic art,
Carried his vagrant actors in a cart
High over the crowd the Mimic tribe appeared
And played and sang with lees of wine besmeared.
Then Aeschylus, a decent vizard used
Built a low stage, the flaming robe diffused
In language more sublime his actors rage
And in the graceful buskin tread the stage."

The poet in the heroic age was, it is said, held in the highest honour by the chiefs and heroes, because their names were immortalised by him. His presence was welcomed at all their feasts as that of a divine personage. Poet and prophet were synonymous terms with them.

Chorus.

THE two foremost races that chiefly made up the population of Greece were the Dorians and the Ionians. The Dorians were enterprising warriors. Their dance resembled the march of soldiers and their songs were battle chants. The dance and the songs formed their religious rites. Those engaged in dances and songs were known as the chorus. The functions of the chorus were detailed by Homer thus :—

" The chorus must support an actor's part
Side with the virtuous and advise with art
Bridle wild rage, the arrogant appease
And short repasts of frugal lables praise
Applaud the justice of well governed states
And peace triumphant with her open gates
Intrusted secrets let them never betray
But to the righteous gods with order pray
That fortune with returning smiles may bless
Affected worth and impious pride depress
Yet let their songs with apt coherence join
Promote the plot and aid the main design."

How many formed the chorus at first is not known. Subsequently it was reduced to fifty members. Their dance and songs were said to be very rude and irregular. When the Ionians mixed with them they added their dithyrambs or revellers' songs to the Dorian Music. These dithyrambs were usually sung by them when they celebrated the birth of Bacchus or his adventures. These songs were also irregular and unmethodical. The votaries of Bacchus used to sing and dance with musical instruments, when a goat was sacrificed to that deity. These songs were then known as goat-songs or tragedies. On highly religious occasions the hereditary worshippers of Bacchus wore goat skins, danced and sang before the altar. These songs were then known as Satyrs. The chorus danced round the altar singing and therefore came to be called the cyclic chorus. The goat-songs or tragedies and the satyr songs were, as said above, very unsystematic till the great musician and poet Arion of Corinth, who is said to have escaped being drowned, by pleasing the dolphins of the sea by his powers of music, systematised the songs a great deal. He is said to have flourished in the seventh century B.C. Another poet by name Stesichorus, who lived at or about that time, finally arranged the metrical system of choral poetry. The division of an ode into three parts, strophe, anti-strophe and epode are due to him. They resemble mostly the "pallavi," "anupallavi" and "pada" of our Indian songs. This three-fold division of the ode was made for the convenience of the dancers—the epode being the dancers' resting place. The greatest poet, whom the Greeks adored as a divine personage, was Pindar. He lived between the fifth and the sixth centuries B.C. It is said that in the hands of this poet "the legends of antiquity became potent instruments for instilling lessons of practical and political wisdom, of morality, and of generous ambition, into the minds of his people." It is said that he composed different species of choral poetry "to grace the services of

Tragedy.

Cyclic Chorus.

Arion.

Stesichorus.

Pindar.

the religion or to do honour to distinguished men of the day or simply to heighten the pleasures of a banquet." The Kings and Governments were vieing with each other to do him honour and establishing with him relations of personal and quasi-political friendship. The ancients considered poets as inspired heroes because they thought that the spirit of poetry was inspiration. They were not "so many soulless animals to denounce poetical creations as mere trash and nonsense" as some people of the present time do. The ancient Greeks classed the fine arts in the following order (1) Drama (2) Poetry (3) Eloquence (4) Music (5) Sculpture (6) Painting (7) Architecture (8) Gardening. The history of this divine poet Pindar written by F. D. Morris, is well worth perusal. We find there that, before the poet had advanced far in his poetical attempts, there were two poetesses, Corrinna of Tanagara and Myrtis. The poetess Corrinna once rebuked Pindar by a remark that "one should sow with the hand and not with the sack." It is also stated that this great poetess gained a victory over the poet Pindar in the poetical and singing contests. The daughters of Pindar inherited his talents. After his death, the Athenians honoured him as a God and worshipped his image. Even before Pindar and Corrinna there was a famous poetess in Greece called Errinna. This shows that even in ancient times the natural gift of poetry was improved by women. Jayadeva of India, who wrote the "Geeta Govinda" containing melodious love poems, Purandardass, Toolsidass and many others who wrote religious songs, can be placed in the same class as Pindar, but these are comparatively moderns. When the poet Arion of Corinth systematised the irregular songs or tragedies, they became known as or assumed the shape of lyrical tragedies.

Classification of fine arts.

Corrinna of Tanagara and Myrtis.

Errinna.

Lyrical tragedies.

Now the Greeks had enough of definitely formed choral odes, dancing, instrumental and vocal music. With these they worshipped their Gods. Sometimes they went in procession, chanting the hymns accompanied by flutes and harps, just like our Indian performers of "Rama bhajana." Subsequently these bands of worshippers discontinued, to a great extent, the habit of going in procession through the streets, but they met at a public place of resort. There, during the interval of choral odes and dance, the leaders of the chorus came forward and recited in verse the story of Bacchus, his birth and his travels, his sufferings, miracles and triumphs. This somewhat resembles the Indian "Hari katha." The dancing with choral odes may be compared to the practice in India of religious votaries, who teach the philosophy of devotion, tying bells to their legs, dancing and singing during nights and days before their patron Gods. This system of dance and choral odes connected with religion gave rise in Greece to the religious dramatical tragedies. The ancient Grecian chorus system was a peculiar one. The chorus consisting at first of fifty or more members sang and danced round the altar. This was what existed before the sixth century. During the time of Thespis in the sixth century B.C., he introduced the system of reciting the Mythological stories of dramatical nature known as episodes, during the interval of choral songs. As time went on, the chorus took the function of tragic actors as could be seen in many Grecian tragedies. The actors on the stage held dialogues with the members of the chorus in the Orchestra. I presume therefore that the chorus also formed a part of the action of the tragedy. Leaving aside the dance and the songs, the functions of the Grecian chorus resemble those of characters coming in the Indian classical dramas in the Pravesaka and Vishkambha scenes, or those of "*Sarathi*" in the native pageant dramas

Processions.

Recitals.

Rhapsodists.

THE Ionians had in their midst many minstrels known as rhapsodists. They had the gift of a good memory and were renowned for their intelligence. They recited Homeric and other epic poems so charmingly that the people were enchanted with hearing them. Sometimes they had musical accompaniments. The charm of the recitations of the rhapsodists was doubled by the introduction of new metres by a famous poet Archilochus. A few facts about this poet may not be out of place here, for, in my opinion he was the initiator of subsequent poetical satires which in many cases cost either the life of the satirist or the honour and life of the family satirised. This poet flourished between 760 and 680 B.C. He was a poet from his boyhood. He belonged to a very noble family. One Lycambes had promised him his daughter Neobule in marriage and subsequently declined to fulfil his promise. The poet left his native place Paros, in disappointment and disgust. At the feasts of "Ceres," he recited satirical verses accusing Lycambes of perjury and his daughters of leading the most abandoned lives. The effect produced by the verses was such that the father and the daughters hanged themselves. The poet, it is said, wrote these satires in iambic metre which he invented as most suitable for the flow of satires. He wrote also many poems in metres invented by him.

Archilochus.

Change worked out by Rhapsodists.

WHEN the rhapsodists who settled in Athens repeated these poems along with others, they were greatly encouraged. Subsequently when they were taken into the Athenian chorus they formed an important factor in changing some of the ancient ideas of the Athenians. Before this, the hymns and the dance of the chorus were invariably connected with Bacchus, the wine God. Now the incidents of epic and legendary poems of heroes, were merged in the ancient tragedies. The recitation of Homer and other sacred poets by the rhapsodists became common, the old choral odes continuing along with them. The recitations from epic poems contained interesting dialogues which a rhapsodist or a single actor could not conveniently prolong. To carry on a dialogue by only one actor does not only mar the pleasure of the audience but also hinders the easy flow of the recitation. The difficulty was keenly felt by the poets. In order to facilitate the purpose of the dialogue, the great poet Thespis introduced a second actor. This was in B.C. 535. Subsequently the poet Phrynicus composed dramas having no relation to Bacchus, retaining the ancient chorus as it was. This poet was the pupil of Thespis. The Athenian national vanity during this time was such that they could not bear to hear any of their disgraces or defects narrated to them. When this poet brought on the stage his tragedy of the capture of "Miletus," the audience burst into tears, and he was fined a thousand drachmae and the play was prohibited. Subsequently the poet wrote another tragedy "Phoenissae" recounting the great deeds of the Athenians and thereby pleased them. In this drama the immortal hero of Thermopylae acted the part of Choragus. It was Phrynicus that introduced female characters on the stage. He wrote nine plays in all.

Phrynicus.

Capture of Miletus.

Phoenissae.

THE famous Grecian poet Aeschylus, who flourished in the fifth century B.C., reduced the functions of the chorus and established dialogue as the principal part of the action and introduced speech by bringing in a second actor. It is said that he introduced the custom of clothing his characters in dresses pertaining and suitable to the parts they were representing. He wrote about seventy tragedies and received thirteen public prizes. A certain historian records that in his tragedy "Eumenides" he represented a certain character with such a ghastly mask on his head that he frightened several

Aeschylus.

children to death and many women into premature labour. He was the founder of the Grecian tragedy although Thespis was known as the founder of the dramatic art. Out of his numerous plays seven only are extant. They are (1) Eumenides (2) Suppliants (3) Choephori (4) The Persae (5) Agamemnon (6) Prometheus (7) The Seven against Thebes. This poet was himself an actor. Terror was the element of his plays. In dealing with religious topics he was very bold. He was once accused of having in one of his plays disclosed the Eleusinean mysteries and was only acquitted on the intervention of his brother. This famous poet was also a great soldier and won many battles. He was selected for the prize of pre-eminent bravery in the battle of Marathon. He left Athens, being annoyed at the prize for tragedies having been given to Sophocles, his rival.

Sophocles.

A further developement was found necessary, and the poet Sophocles, the contemporary and rival of Aeschylus in the prize for tragedies, worked it out. Many improvements were introduced on the Athenian stage by this poet and dramatist. He raised the number of actors present at once upon the scene from two to three. He attired the actors with splendid dresses. He commenced life as a dramatist in his sixteenth year in the full vigour of youth. Even the prince of satires, Aristophanes, who spared none from his satires could find no flaw or blemish in Sophocles. Sophocles as dramatist was held in the greatest estimation by the Athenians, and his tragedy "Antigone" filled them with such admiration that they appointed him in B.C. 440 one of the generals who accompanied Pericles in the war against Samos. The tragedy of "Antigone" is very pathetic. Antigone's reply to Creon when she was accused of having interred her brother against the king's order is really praiseworthy. Her reply that in disobeying the mortal law she implicitly obeyed the unwritten divine law is highly commendable. The sermon preached by Haemon to his father about the right use of reason is truly eloquent. This poet wrote about one hundred and thirty plays. His three tragedies "Oedipus the King," "Oedipus at Colonus" and "Antigone" contain the tragic history of Oedipus and his family. The tragedy of Oedipus embodying the story of the incestuous marriage of a mother with her own son, though such a destiny was worked out by the Gods, is horribly repugnant to the Indian taste, nay to the taste of any civilised nation. How the civilised Athenians allowed such a piece on the stage is a wonder. It must have been passed off as a work of the Gods. Even Aristotle admires 'Oedipus the King' as the only pure sample of a tragedy. Indian legendary lore contains such stories. A son is estranged in his infancy from his mother, loves her in his youth, but ultimately Gods or Fates reveal the relationship when not too late. The son undergoes the severest penance. It is a wonder that such a repugnant story is also dramatised by some other nations of Europe. Seneca of ancient Rome, Corneille of civilised France, Dryden and Lee of reformed England took this detestable theme of Oedipus for their tragedies. He is said to be a brother and a father to his sons, a son and a husband to his mother Jocasta, and a rival and murderer of his father Laius. Even the mention of the mythological story of this unfortunate family is horribly repulsive. I have read the translations of the tragedies about this unfortunate king, written by Sophocles and Euripides. The dialogue between the king and the sage Tiresias to trace out the murderer of Laius is really dramatic in Sophocles' tragedy. The sage's undaunted courage shown in his short replies to the several questions of Oedipus is praiseworthy. The scene between the king and his wife Jocasta, where he learns his previous history and the murder of Laius is thrilling. The death of Jocasta when she learnt that Oedipus was her son and not her husband and the ravings of the king are really pathetic.

Trilogy.

Oedipus.

Sophocles wrote tragedies even in his extreme old age. When one of his sons accused him of mental derangement, the poet defended himself before judges by reading his latest production "Oedipus at Colonus." The judges after reading the tragedy gave a decree that he was mentally sound. This, some say, happened after the poet passed the hundredth year of his age. In the drama called "Nausicca" or the "Washer woman," this great poet, "the respected Athenian citizen who had already perhaps been a general, appeared publicly in woman's clothes and, as, on account of the feebleness of his voice, he could not play the leading part of Nausicca, took perhaps the mute under-part of a maid for the sake of giving to the representation of his piece the slight ornament of bodily agility."

Euripides.

BETWEEN 490 and 406 B.C., there flourished another great tragic poet by name Euripides. He was a friend of Socrates, the philosopher, who, it is said, never failed attending the theatres. He was fortyfive years junior to Aeschylus and fifteen years younger than Sophocles. 'Aeschylus belonged to an earlier generation and Sophocles avoided every disturbing force as being perilous to the composure of art.' This great poet was of an analytical turn of mind and with the great force of poetical imagination wrote seventy five plays to suit the taste of the times. He was the first to bring philosophy on the stage. William Bodham Donne in his history of Euripides describes the Athenians of the time as follows:

Athenians during the period.

"The Athenians were not in general book-learned, but such knowledge as could be obtained by the eye and the ear, they possessed abundantly. . . . . These shabby folk were able to correct orators who mispronounced a word, singers when out of tune and actors who tripped in their delivery of dialogue. He who could recite the whole Iliad or Odyssey was now looked upon as little better than a busy idler. Even fools have sometimes portentous memories. Man was born to be some thing better than a parrot." (They used to say). This poet was held in high esteem by the orators, Cicero and Demosthenes, for he displayed considerable eloquence in tragedies. This tragic poet met a tragic death having been torn to pieces by a pack of hounds.

Quintilian's opinion of the three tragic poets.

Quintilian observes :—"Aeschylus, the sublime and daring; Sophocles, grave and majestic; Euripides flowing with copious stream of eloquence throughout his works." Of the seventeen tragedies that are now extant of Euripides "The Phoenician Virgins" is one. This is again a story concerning Jocasta and Oedipus and his family. Schlegel in writing about these poets observes that the style of Aeschylus "is grand, severe and not unfrequently harsh; that of Sophocles is marked by the most finished symmetry and harmonious gracefulness; that of Euripides is soft and luxuriant." Euripides was the first to make the unbridled passion of Medea and the unnatural love of Phaedra the main subject of his dramas. The verses of Euripides did high service to the Athenian soldiers in their war in Sicily. The Athenian army under the command of Nicias was defeated; the victors took a most cruel advantage of their victories and treated the Athenians with utter inhumanity. However they spared the lives of those Athenians who could repeat any verse from Euripides. Those that returned to Athens safely, kindly saluted Euripides declaring that they had been restored to their liberty by his verses.

Schlegel's opinion.

SATYR tragedies were also being performed along with tragedies but comedies were entirely left out. Up to the time of Alexander the Great there were one thousand and four hundred tragedies in Athens. During the time of Alexander and subsequently after him Alexandria became the centre of literature, and dramatical development shifted itself

Alexander.

for a great part to that capital. It is said that the dramatical art spread over Europe and Asia during the time of Alexander and his father, because they were celebrating their victories by scenic performances wherever they carried their arms. The dramatic activity in Alexandria was high, because all the tragic poets resorted to it. Seven tragic poets known as "Pleiades" wrote many tragedies during the time of Ptolemy Philadelphus between 283 and 247 B.C., and performed them on the stage. We find that a Jew by name Ezechiel composed a Greek drama about 100 B.C. This pre-christian drama is about the Scriptural narrative of Moses leading the Chosen people out of Egypt. This may be called the first mystery play. The dramatical activity in Alexandria progressed till 215 A.D., when the Roman Emperor Caracalla abolished all theatrical performances.

Ezechiel.

THE solemn nature of the old tragedies having religious rituals for their origin, exacted the reverence of the people, though in fact the subsequent tragedies changed its nature to the treatment of men and their deeds. Our idea of tragedy that it should end with death is a blunder of a very serious kind. Plato calls tragedies serious plays; "the narration of deeds of sufferings of heroes in Mythology or the narration of national calamity or of a national victory is a tragedy which in Greece has always a religious origin." Aristotle defines tragedy as "the imitation of some noble action great and complete in itself." "Tragedy" he says "aims at representing men who are above the average, comedy men who are below it." He says that "exhibiting purely a good man as falling into adversity is rather horrible than tragic, nor on the other hand would the representation of a villain receiving the retribution due to his crimes be a tragical story however moral it might be. There must be an element of undeserved calamity, and yet there must be some justice too in the

Definition of tragedy.

cause of events so that while we feel sorrow after what occurs, we shall feel also that things could not have been otherwise." He further says that "poets sometime make happy endings out of concession to the weakness of the spectators, but this is quite a mistake and that such endings are more suitable to comedy." Reginald S. Copleston, M.A., who wrote the history of Aeschylus remarks that "a sad ending is not essential to tragedy. Greatness and removedness are." A. W. Schlegel in his "Dramatic Art and Literature" defines tragedy and comedy thus :—

"Tragedy is the highest earnestness of poetry; Comedy altogether sportive. Tragedy delights in harmonious unity; Comedy flourishes in a chaotic exuberance; Tragedy by painful emotions, elevates us to the most dignified views of humanity; Comedy, on the other hand, by its jocose and depreciatory view of all things, calls forth the most petulant hilarity." Col. Hamby says "to represent a good man as the sport of malignant destiny is of itself an idea belonging to a pagan rather than a Christian age."

Stage maintained by the State.

TRAGEDIES were considered unavoidably necessary on religious and festive occasions. They were maintained at the expense of the public treasury. The priests, rulers, the educated and the uneducated held the actors of these tragedies in high esteem, conferred titles, gave prizes and granted jaghirs. The poets vied with each other for the honour of being actors. The performances took place in the day-time and lasted nearly all day. Three tragedies and a farce were performed on one occasion. Three tragedies thus performed were known as a "trilogy."

Trilogy.

The "Agamemnon," the "Choephoroe" and the "Eumenides" formed the trilogy of Aeschylus, the subject of it forming the events of the murder of Agamemnon by his wife, the revenge taken by his son Orestes and the latter's trial and deliverance.

THE Athenian theatre was so large as to hold thirty-thousand people. "The Athenian theatre was a national institution; no private speculation, but the pride and glory of a great people. It was also a religious institution and not merely a scene of national amusement."

Theatre.

FROM the Grecian religious constitution another institution sprang up which subsequently proved baneful not only to the Grecian society but also to the different nations of the world which followed its example, for the suppression of which at one time or other the priests and the rulers either severally or jointly made strenuous efforts and wisely too. While the educated and the enlightened Greeks exhibited tragical dramas in the capital town with all seriousness and religious devotion, bands of jolly companies in rural parts, on the occasion of vintage festivals in honour of their wine-god Bacchus, went about in procession carrying on their shoulders the "Phallic emblem" of Bacchus and "indulged in the ribald license of wanton mirth." Virgil describes this festival known as Ascolia as follows :—

Origin of Comedy.

"For this the malefactor goat was laid
On Bacchus' altar, and his forfeit paid.
At Athens this old comedy began
When round the streets the reeling actors ran
In country villages and crossing ways
Contending for the prizes of the plays
And glad with Bacchus, on the grassy soil
Leapt over the skins of goats besmeared with oil."

Their songs were known as Phallic songs. These songs undoubtedly contained praises of their deity with gross personal ridicule, and were connected with the celebration of festivals of Dionysus "under whose protection the comic poets enjoyed unbounded freedom and license. With this power they assailed every kind of vice and folly if it was sufficiently

Phallic Songs.

notorious to render their ridicule intelligible, and men in the highest position did not escape this kind of castigation."

WHEN Thespis ascended the tragic stage another poet of Attica by name Susarion occupied the comic stage. The latter attacked the vices and follies of the age and thus became the father of the comic art. Along with this comical feature, farcical entertainments were also in vogue. "These were entertainments completely in harmony with the drunken festivities of Dionysian carnival." This feast of Phallica was of Egyptian origin. Egyptians performed it in honour of Osiris. This was in the nature of religious ceremony at first but the inhabitants of Attica converted it into an impure celebration. It was on the "comic stage that democracy

Comic stage.

indulged in the most unbounded freedom, allowing any citizen rich or poor, high or low, to be attacked and assailed either in his public or private character with impunity." When Pericles was at the height

Cratinus.

of his power, he was subjected on the stage to the stinging blows of *Cratinus*. In his play called "Chiroues" the poet describes Pericles in the following verse :—

"Faction received old Time to her embraces
Hence came a tyrant-spawn on Earth called Pericles
In heaven the head-compellor."

When Pericles proposed to build a long wall, the poet ridiculed him in the following verse :—

"Stones upon stones the Orator has pil'd
With swelling words, but words will build no walls."

When a music-theatre in a comic figure was built by the direction of Pericles, the poet railed him in his play called "Thrattoe" in the following verse :—

"As Jove, an onion on his head he wears
As Pericles, a whole Orchestra bears
Afraid of broils and banishment no more
He trains the shell he trembled at before."

In some other place, the poet attacks Aspasia, the wife of Pericles, in the following verse :—

> " She bore this Juno, this Aspasia
> Skilled in the shameless trade and every art
> Of wantonness."

This poet who lived between 519 and 423 B.C., was a bold satirist. His direct and vigorous political satires were greatly admired by the people. He was the first poet who "made comedy a terrible weapon of personal attack and the comic poet a severe censor of public and private vice." When Aristophanes the prince of comedies and satires sneered at him with a remark that he was no better than a dotting drunkard, this satirist feeling the taunt, put forth all his strength in writing a satire called the "Bottle." In the contest, the "Bottle" won a victory over the "Clouds" of Aristophanes. Another rival of Aristophanes was the satirist Eupolis who lived between 445 and 400 B.C. This poet wrote many satires, in one of which he taunted Alcibiades with his satirical attacks for which, it is said, the Satirist was thrown into the sea. In the elegance and purity of diction this poet is equal to Aristophanes. This comic poet attacked also Cimon in the following verse :—

Eupolis.

> " He is not a villain, but a debauchee
> Whose careless heart is lost on wine and women
> The time has been, he slept in Lacedemon
> And left poor Elpinice here alone."

Another poet and comedian was Crates who is a contemporary and friend of Cratinus. He was a good author and an able actor. He acted in all satires of Cratinus. It is this author that introduced for the first time drunkards on the stage. He avoided making any political references in his comedies. Comic performances touching political matters were prohibited by a

Crates.

Introduction of drunkards.

law; but this law after a year or two was repealed. The most eminent dramatists belonged to the age of Pericles. When the comedies grew intolerably indelicate, men of letters were not wanting to reform them, by eliminating objectionable and obscene portions and introducing speeches and songs in their stead, thus making the comical language less indecent. Real comedies commenced with Aristophanes who lived at or about 425 B.C. Subsequent writers attacked his plays also as being coarse and indelicate. After reading the translations of his comedies I came to the conclusion that most of them are simply obscene. In Lysistrata which was performed before the public in 411 B.C., we see the heroine Lysistrata attempting to bring about peace. The plot is very simple and ludicrous. Women going into the assembly with the dress of their husbands and with false beards and making speeches there, may be comical, but the dialogue between the women is very coarse and obscene. His comedy "Thesmophoriazusae," wherein this poet as usual satirizes Euripides is much liked by the people. Euripides appearing before the policemen in different shapes in a short interval, to save his brother-in-law is comical. The herald's speech about the shameful acts of Grecian women indicates the immoral condition of that sex in ancient times. If what is contained in the speech of "Mnesilochus" in female dress about the state of society is true, it is no wonder that the Athenian glory was irrecoverably lost. This poet's comedy "Ecclesiazusae" resembles "Lysistrata" in plot and is more depraved. The second woman's speech is inconsistent with woman's nature. The dialogue between Blepyrus and his wife Praxagora is really shocking, and one who reads it will certainly infer that immorality in ancient Greece descended to the lowest depth. The scene where three ugly old women hunting after a beautiful youth who was in the company of a young fair lady is terribly obscene. The history of Aristophanes written

Aristophanes.

His Comedies.

by Rev. W. Lucas Collins, M.A., is well worth perusal. Aristophanes wrote his comedies during the long war between Athens and Sparta. The head of the democratic party in Athens was the orator Cleon who was the poet's great enemy. There were many abuses prevalent in the Athenian Government at the time. The dramatist was for peace but the statesman Cleon was for war. The Athenian constitution was such that "sentiments which it might have been dangerous to express in public assembly were enunciated in the most plain spoken language by the actor with impunity." Encouraged by the leaders who opposed Cleon, the dramatist said openly that he would "cut up Cleon the tanner into shoe-leather for the knights." Accordingly he wrote a comedy known as "Knights" wherein he exposed his enemy to a degree far beyond the limit of good-breeding. In this performance Aristophanes himself took the character which represented Cleon, his enemy. His other comedies were also written to expose the abuses of the Athenian Government. The language of the comedies is not free from indelicacy of expression as could be gathered from English translations, and the manner of their treatment is really shocking. His comedy "*Frogs*" wherein the satirist makes the two rival tragedians Aeschylus and Euripides try their talents even in hell (Pluto's regions) making Bacchus the arbitrator who decides in favour of Aeschylus, is carrying the spirit of satire too far. The dead are objects of reverence. Aristophanes is said to be witty at the expense of his friends and even sometimes at his own expense. He spared no pains to write satires against Euripides and his friend Socrates. There is no comedy of this poet wherein he does not satirically mention the name of Euripides. The satirist may be justified in attacking the tragical merits of Euripides, but to inveigh repeatedly against the mean origin of his birth shows shamefully bad taste. Aristophanes being descended from a noble family took advantage of it and hurled his invectives always against men of low birth, not caring for their merits in other respects. The reading of the tragedies of Euripides would lead one certainly to the belief that he is a poet of high order both intellectually and morally. He was vainly accused of being a woman hater. He hated bad women and wrote against them. Even in private gatherings Aristophanes insulted this tragedian with recitals of comical satires concerning the latter's hatred towards women. "When Dionysius, king of Syracuse, desired to learn the state and language of Athens, Plato sent him the plays of Aristophanes telling him in these he would find the best representation of Athenian character."

Rollin's opinion about the Grecians.

ROLLIN, the historian of ancient Greece, observes:—"the fondness of the Athenians for dramatical representations cannot be expressed. Their eyes, their ears, their imagination, their understanding all shared in the satisfaction. Nothing gave them so sensible a pleasure in dramatic performance, either tragic or comic as the strokes which were aimed at the affairs of the public; whether pure chance occasioned the application, or the address of the poets, who knew how to reconcile the most remote subjects with the transactions of the Republic. They entered by that means into the interests of the people, took occasion to sooth their passions, authorise their pretensions, justify, sometimes condemn their conduct; entertain them with agreeable hopes, instruct them in their duty in certain nice conjectures; in consequence of which they often not only acquired the applauses of the spectators, but credit and influence in the public affairs and councils: hence the theatre became so grateful and so interesting to the people. It was in this manner that Euripides artfully adopted his tragedy of "Palamedes" to the sentence passed against Socrates and pointed out by illustrations and examples of antiquity the innocence of a philosopher oppressed by malignity supported by power and faction."

Eubulus, Antiphanes and Alexis.

AFTER Aristophanes, lived Eubulus, Antiphanes and Alexis who wrote many comedies. Alexis who lived about 394 and 288 B.C., wrote about two hundred and fortyfive plays. He is an author of wit and elegance. He is said to have lived one hundred and six years. He was an uncle of Menander, the noble comedian. The comedies of this age concerned themselves with social themes. The satirical poison had, I suppose, taken its root in Athens and infected other countries which came under its influence.

Menander.

Menander who lived between 342 and 291 B.C., wrote many comedies for the upper classes by raising them to a gentility which the previous comedies hardly possessed. He was an intimate friend of Epicurus. His taste and sympathies were altogether with the philosophy of Epicurus. His contemporary and rival by name "Philemon" wrote for the multitude. Love intrigues became along with other social themes the fashion of comedies.

Philemon.

Three classifications of Grecian comedies.

THE Greek comedy has been divided into three distinct classes, the old, the middle and the new. The old comedy is noted for the extreme freedom and severity of its satire. The principal dramatists were Eupolis, Cratinus and Aristophanes. Cratinus, Aristophanes and other old writers of comedy used unbounded license in exposing the knave, the thief, the adulterer, the assassin or any infamous character whatsoever. . . . "The middle comedy" retained the spirit of the old, the vigorous delineation of manners and character, and banished from the drama all personal satire or abuse of living characters by name. The writers of this class were numerous. The new comedy included in point of time a period of about thirty years, from the death of Alexander the Great to the death of Menander. In this short period the Athenian state was truly a school of morals; and while "comedy lost none of its characteristic excellence in the just delineation of manners, she had the additional grace of tenderness, eloquence and decorum." Of this brilliant era the chief dramatic writers were Menander, Philemon, Diphilus, Apollodorus, Phillipides and Posilippus. In the comedies of Menander was found a "vein of most refined wit and pleasantry which never transgressed the bounds of decency and strict morality." His object was at once "the exemplary display of the charms of virtue and the chastisement of vice; and employing alternately the grave and the jocose at tempering moral example with keen and elegant satire." He exhibited the most instructive as well as the justest representation of human nature. The plays of Menander are recommended by Quintilian as a school of eloquence for the formation of a perfect orator, so admirable is the skill of the poet in painting the manners and passions in every condition and circumstance of life. Philemon was only second to him. When once in a literary prize-fight, the judges through prejudice in favour of Philemon, decreed for him, the poet Menander asked him "tell me fairly, Philemon, if you do not blush when the victory is decreed to you against me?" Menander's wonderful talent at expressing nature was such that a certain literary man exclaimed "O, Menander and Nature! which of you copied your pieces from other's work?"

Phallic songs compared with Indian songs.

WITH regard to the phallic songs from the basis of which the comedies and satires arose in Greece, I compare them with the old songs that Indians are familiar with, sung in the Holi festivals and also the kind of songs sung even now by women of the lower castes. Our people are not strangers to the obscene language used in songs that are even now sung by all classes of people in our most holy place of piligrimage, Tirupathi, when "Gangamma Jatra" is celebrated. We consider these as sanctioned by religion or custom just as Greeks considered the Phallic songs as sanctioned by the laws of Bacchus. We need not therefore wonder that ancient Greece and some other countries of Europe had this the most objectionable custom. It is not for me to conjecture when this pernicious custom originated. Suffice it to say to the disgrace of Indians that sister nations have reformed their customs while the boasted civilized Indian is still afflicted with this bane.

Functions of tragedy and comedy.

ATHENS thus enriched literature with the Drama, the highest and noblest of all poetical compositions. The two branches of tragedy and comedy were treated by the ancient Greeks as being distinct from each other ;—dancing, music, recitation of verses and speech being common to both. Both these branches of dramas were written by poets and acted by educated people in regularly built theatres, and no odium was attached to an actor. It is said about the orator Demosthenes that drama formed a part of his education. Actors were held in high esteem by the Athenians. Satyrus, the actor, was a close friend of Demosthenes. He is said to have given instructions to him in the art of giving full effect to his speeches by appropriate action. The great actors Neoptolemus and Aristodemus were employed as diplomatists and were received even in foreign countries as men of distinction. In fact, drama formed a part of the history of Athens.

Satyrus.

Drama—the history of Athens.

THUS we see in ancient Greece, both tragedy and comedy had their origin in religion and with the decline of Greece, dramas also declined and transferred their decaying splendor to Rome.

CHAPTER II.

ROME AND ITALY.

BEFORE we reach the age when the Romans improved upon the arts of Greece, we will see what history says of the existence of the native dramatic elements in Italy. It is said that 'Italy has ever been the native land of acting and scenic representation.' Let us verify this statement by facts. We read that in the rural festivities of ancient Italy, there were dances and jocular songs, speech and dialogue, containing abuse. There were also comic songs or stories recited with gesticulation and with the accompaniment of the flute. These were known in Italy as "Saturae." Long before 750 B.C., there was a very ancient order of priests known as the "Talic" who sang religious songs as they danced. When this practice was commenced, and whence this was borrowed, are not known. We found the same custom in Greece and we find it even now in India. I think this practice was also introduced into the early Church. The priests of yore led the dance on feast days, and they were therefore known as *Proesules.* We also read in the general History of Rome by Charles Merivale, D.D., a peculiar instance of Pagan superstition. It appears there was a pestilence in Italy in 365 B.C. The priests thought that it could be averted by the plays of the *Istrians* of Etruria whose entertainments had their origin in religious rituals. They were therefore invited to Rome where they performed a series of pantomimes with scenic effects. As their speech was unintelligible they went on reciting songs with gesticulations to make the people understand the story. From these the stage plays took their origin in Rome. Some of the Fathers of the early Church maintained that the

Native origin.

Comic songs.

Saturae.

Istrians.

angels always danced and a band of Apostles formed a chorus of dancers. Almost up to the fourth century A.D., there were feasts known as *Agapoe* among the primitive Christians. There was dancing at these feasts. Subsequently they became love-feasts with many abuses and they were therefore stopped. After the *Istrians* settled in Rome, they began to perform their rude scenic games and helped themselves with native *Saturae*. The combined entertainments were so pleasing to the people that they encourged them in every way.

Feasts of Agapoe.

The *Istrians* from whom the *Histrionic art* was named were, as said above, only dancers and pantomimists. The *Istrians* in the long run lost sight of the religious origin of their entertainments and commenced entertaining people with comic songs and stories with gesticulation. Sometimes a boy was made to sing while the actor accompanied his song with motions of the hand and body to convey the meaning. Hallam, in his "History of the Literature of Europe," says, "all nations probably have at all times, to a certain extent, amused themselves both with pantomime and oral representation of a feigned story; the sports of children are seldom without both, and the exclusive employment of the former, instead of being a first stage of the drama, as has been sometimes assumed, is rather a variety in the course of its progress." Up to the year 241 B.C., the Romans or the Italians had no indigenous regular drama.

Histrionic art.

Hallam's opinion of pantomimes.

DURING the first Punic War (261 to 241 B.C.) the contact between the Greeks and the Romans became closer. Sicily, which was the battle ground for the combatants for sometime, became also a theatrical centre for the representation of old Greek dramas. Theatres were already in

Influence of Grecian dramas.

existence at Segesta, Syracuse, Catania and Teormina. In these places the old Dorian comedies of Epicharmus had taken a firm root in the minds of the people. This comic poet who lived between 540 and 450 B.C., settled in Syracuse and wrote about fifty dramas on mythological, political and moral subjects. Even before his time comedy had existed at Megara in Sicily but it was little more than a low buffoonery. Epicharmus introduced a regular plot into it. The Italians were favourably impressed with the Grecian representations. Livius Andronicus who was brought to Rome as a slave and who subsequently became a school-master there, wrote many tragedies and comedies in Latin for the Romans in imitation of the Greek plays. He also improved the old Italian *Saturae* by inserting plots in them. Roman dramatic literature then assumed a fixed form. The subsequent tragic poet Ennius lived between 239 and 169 B.C. In his dramatical works "he combined the culture of Greece, the fresh feeling and inspiration of Italy, and the elevated mood of Rome." He was present at the capture of Ambrasia and dramatised it. Cicero and Lucretius were his admirers. He raised the Roman tragedy to a position of influence and dignity and died in 169 B.C.

Epicharmus.

Livius Andronicus.

Ennius.

In B.C. 154, or, at about that time, a regular theatre was built; but the Consul C. Cassius Longinus got it erased as it was in the fashion of Grecian theatre. In 54 B.C., Pompey began building a theatre and finished it in B.C. 52. This theatre, it is said, could hold forty thousand people. Two other theatres were also built shortly after. *Pacuvius*, who lived between 219 and 129 B.C., was a tragic poet who wrote many tragedies for the Romans. He was also a painter. He continued to write tragedies till his eightieth year. He is praised for the loftiness of his thoughts,

Theatre.

Pacuvius.

the vigor of his language and the extent of his knowledge. He was not an imitator of Grecian plays.

Lucius Accius.

Lucius Accius who lived between 159 and 70 B.C., wrote many tragedies. It is said that this poet was a rival of Pacuvius. His style is censured for harshness. Cicero, the greatest orator of Rome, had a great respect for his opinions.

Seneca.

Seneca who lived between 3 B.C. and 65 A.D., was a philosopher, an orator, a minister and a dramatist. He wrote eight tragedies. He was a man of great original thought and imagination though his style was considered by subsequent writers as being far from genuine. A. W. Ward, the author of Dramatic Literature, says that "Seneca borrows his subjects from the time-honoured themes of Greek mythology with a single minded preference for what may in a word be called the most sensational in the list. The horrid banquet placed by Atreus before Thyestes, the murder of Agamemnon by his adulterous wife and her paramour, the incestuous love of Phaedra, the revenge of the dischanted Medea—all these and others of the same kind are served up once more. But his pains are spent neither on the contrivance of the action nor in the evolution of its characters." The tragedies of ancient Rome treated mostly of Greek and Roman legends and not of any historical event. The rule of the Greeks that no tragic poet should write comedies was violated by the Romans. Cicero and even Julius Caesar wrote tragedies. It is said that Cicero wrote a Satyr-drama but it was not represented on the stage by the advice of his brother. The Romans did not do away with the chorus. They introduced prologues and epilogues. As there are no subsequent dramatists of note I will return to the consideration of the comedies.

I have stated already that the Italians had an indigenous comic element, or rather a farcical or satirical native element in the form of *Saturae* improved by Livius Andronicus.

Regular comedy.

These were not regular comedies or satires. The Romans borrowed also models from the Grecian comic writers. The former they called *Togatae* and the latter *Paliatae.* This distinction remained for a century or so, but in the long run Paliatae had to give way to Togatae, as the latter being native, pleased the people.

Roscius and Aesopus.

The famous Roman actors of the period were Roscius and Aesopus. Both were very great actors in tragedy as well as in comedy; but Roscius excelled in comedies and Aesopus in tragedies.

Roscius.

"Roscius is said to have played always in a vizard on account of a disfiguring obliquity of vision with which he was afflicted. It was a special tribute to his histrionic merits that the Romans disregarding this defect required him to relinquish his mask, that they might the better appreciate his exquisite oratory and delight in the music of his voice." His histrionic powers procured for him the favour of many of the Roman nobles and among others, of the Dictator Sulla, who presented him with a gold ring, the symbol of equestrian rank. Roscius enjoyed the friendship of Cicero who constantly speaks of him in terms both of admiration and affection. Roscius was considered by the Romans to have reached such perfection in his own profession that it became the fashion to call every one who became particularly distinguished in his own art, by the name of Roscius. In his younger years, Cicero received instruction from Roscius and at a later time he and Roscius often used to try which of them could express a thought with greater effect, the orator by his eloquence or the actor by his gestures. These exercises gave Roscius so high an opinion of his art that he wrote a book in which he compared eloquence and acting." In private life Roscius was so much esteemed as to be elevated to the rank of Senator. The orator Cicero practised oratory under Aesop. The teacher's love for his old student was such that he, as an actor, moved the audience in favour of Cicero and got him back to Rome from banishment. It is said that when acting his part, the actor forgot his individuality and identified himself with the character he assumed. It is also said in his life, that he killed a servant on the stage when the character he then assumed required ferocity of temper to be exhibited. This was carrying things to extremes. In India it is said that an actor assuming the character of Anjaneya (monkey-god) burnt the temporary theatre, in imitation of the real Anjaneya who had burnt the palace of the demon Ravana. In the prologue to "Henry V," Shakespeare claims the indulgence of the audience for the unavoidable feebleness of representation as compared with the force of reality :—

Aesop.

Literally realistic exhibitions.

> "Peace out our imperfections, with your thoughts
> Into a thousand parts divide one man
> And make imaginary puissance
> Think when we talk of horses, that you see them
> Printing their proud hoofs in the receiving earth.
> For 'tis your thoughts, that now must deck our kings
> Carry them here and there, jumping over time
> Turning the accomplishment of many years
> Into an hour-glass."

We read also in the dramatic histories of England that during the first performances of King Henry VIII, in the Globe theatre, a cannon was fired to announce the arrival of the king. The theatre took fire and was burnt. Thomas B. Shaw, M.A., in his "History of English Literature," observes that in the "Passion Play," to brighten the illusion of the scene, a condemned criminal was really crucified on the stage in the character of the Impenitent Thief. This sort of attempt at realism is not desirable.

THOUGH the Roman drama was "more than any other branch of Roman literature, an inheritance from Greece," the freedom of speech which was characteristic of the Grecian dramatist could not have been enjoyed by the Roman poets in the Oligarchy of Rome. The poet Naevius who is said to be a man of original imagination, lived and wrote dramas between 274 and 202 B.C.; like the Grecian Aristophanes he wrote many comedies, in one of which he attacked the family of Metallus by stating "it is fatality and not merit that has made 'Mettali' always Consuls of Rome." This irritated the noble family and caused the imprisonment of the poet under the libel laws of Rome. He was afterwards released, and immediately after this, a second offence of the same kind was committed. He was banished from the country. This example taught the subsequent Roman dramatists an effective lesson not to be disciples of Aristophanes. They therefore followed the example of mild Menander.

Naevius.

PLAUTUS began his career as a dramatist in B.C. 224 and continued up to 184 B.C. It is said that he was the first who raised conversational Latin to the dignity of a literary style. His prologues giving the action of the plot in detail are criticised by subsequent writers. The poet Terence who lived at or about 159 B.C., wrote many plays which were very popular. He is not a poet of original thought. His position in literature as a dramatist is due to the art of the famous Greek Menander, whose plays he rendered into Latin with artistic skill. He confesses this in his prologues to the dramas. His comedies, though more or less mere translations, have, it is said, far more elegance but less action than those of Plautus. In his prologues, Terence gives no explanation of the plot but appeals to the audience, informing them of the sources from which he borrowed his speeches and defending himself

Plautus.

Terence.

against the charge of unfair dealing brought against him by his rivals. In this connection I have to say that the Prologues of our Indian dramas, both ancient and modern, are those of Plautus and Terence put together. The system of writing prologues to dramas continued in England also up to the beginning of the nineteenth century. Garrick's description of prologue runs as follows :—

Prologues.

"Precede the play in mournful verse
As undertakers stalk before the house
Whose doleful march may strike the hardened mind
Wake its feeling for the dead behind."

In the prologue to his farce '*The deuce is in him*' George Coleman points out the distinction between the classical and the British forms of prefatory address :—

"Of old the prologue told the story
And laid the whole affairs before you
Came forth in simple phrase to say
Before the beginning of the play
I hapless Polydore was found
By fishermen or others drowned
Or......I as gentleman did wed
Great Agamemnon's royal daughter
Who is coming here to draw water
Thus gave at once the bards of Greece
The cream and marrow of the piece
Asking no trouble of your own
To skim the milk or crack the bone
Poets now take different ways
E'en let them find it out for Bayes."

Dutton Cook in his "*Book of the Plays*" says, "A certain solemnity of tone however was usually preserved in the prologue to tragedy—the good will and merciful consideration of the audience being still entreated for the author and his work, although considerable license was permitted to the

D. Cook. Book of Plays.

comedy-prologue. The prologues acquired more and more of dramatic nature, being divided sometimes between two or three speakers and less resembling former prologues than those inductions of which the early dramatists and especially Ben-Jonson seem to have been so unreasonably fond." Ben-Jonson in his prologue to "*The Staple of News*" asks the audience "to abstain from idle conversation and attend his play so that they may hear as well as see it."

Ben-Jonson's Staple of News.

> "......He'd have you wise
> Much rather by your ears than by your eyes
> And prays you will not prejudice his play for ill
> Because you mark it not and sit not still
> But have a longing to salute or talk."
> ....
> "Alas! what is it to his scene to know
> How many coaches in Hyde-park did show
> Last Spring? What fun to-day at Medley's was
> If Dunstan or the Phoenix best wine has?"

Lucilius.

Lucilius who lived between 178 and 102 B. C. reformed the Roman *Saturae* and systematised them with metrical verses. He was the inventor of *poetical satires.* This is entirely a legitimate development of an indigenous dramatical entertainment. The influence of this poet was such that though in his bold satires he spared none, he was spared to live by the people affected by his works. Of this poet, Dryden says :—

> "Lucilius was the man who bravely bold
> To Roman vices did this mirror hold
> Protected humble goodness from reproach
> Showed worth on foot and rascals in the coach."

Elsewhere it is stated of this poet that he was a very bold satirist :—

"Yet old Lucilius never feared the times
But lashed the city and dissected crimes
On Lupus Mutius poured his rage by name
And broke his grinders on their bleeding fame."

Africanus who lived a century before Christ wrote many comedies in imitation of Menander. Cicero had a high opinion of his acute genius and fluent style. These comedians or satirists could not in their plays allude to political matters. The state of the times and the spirit of the rulers of Rome at or about the first century before and after Christ can be gathered from the extracts given below from the life of Juvenal written by E. Walford, M.A. "We must remember that under the repressive system pursued by the Imperial Government, political satire as such was impossible. The actions of the divine descendant of Julian line might either be accepted in silence or greeted with gratitude and applause; but criticism—that is to say adverse criticism—on the political topics of the day was altogether forbidden. Where such criticism is found it is always directed against the dead, while the present occupant of the throne is never mentioned except to be praised. The laws of treason, that served to punish or prevent all attempts to break down the hedge of majesty that encircled the throne, were strained to the utmost; while those laws which protected the reputation of the private citizen were, on the principle of compensation, not so strictly enforced." The poetical lines of Juvenal given below explain briefly what is said above.

Africanus.

The state of Rome during the first century as described by Juvenal.

"Yet I must write and since these iron times
From living knaves preclude my angry rhymes
I point my pen against the guilty dead
And pour its gall on such obnoxious head."

The times in which most of the Roman satirists lived were anything but satisfactory. Most of the satirists were subjected to many untold indignities. Some lost their property, some their position in public matters, and some their lives. These Roman satires have no connection with the satires of the Greeks. Except Lucian, ancient Rome could not boast of any poet of originality of thought during the second century A.D. It is during this period women began to appear on the Roman stage. The elder Pliny speaks of an actress named Lucceia who acted for a hundred years and of another Galaria Copiola who was said to have appeared on the stage in her fourteenth year and performed right up to the one hundred and fourth year of her age. Critics, commentators and compilers darkened the age. With the decline of genius the corruption of taste commenced. A rapid downfall of learning began by the end of the second century and was almost completed by the middle of the fourth, although attempts were made to revive learning during the interval by a few of the Roman Emperors.

Pantomimes.

THE Roman multitude encouraged pantomimists who confined themselves to gesticulation and dancing, the chorus singing the text. The introduction of pantomimes, a certain historian remarks, was a sign of the general moral decay of the Roman Empire. These entertainments were encouraged by the recklessly sensual people, and the natural consequence was that they were full of audacious immorality and obscenity. Women called *Minas* took part in these performances. A celebrated *Mina* was raised to the imperial throne. "Lewdness of performances of the Minas in pantomime" made both the Christian and Pagan writers to denounce their performance as prejudicial to morality. It is during this period the females were by law prohibited from appearing on the stage.

It is said that under Augustus, comic pantomimes were brought to perfection by Pylades and Bathylus. Pylades was, it is said, banished from the country for pointing with his finger at a spectator who had offended him. He was however recalled. He was a favourite mimic and dancer of Augustus. Bathylus excelled in comic and Pylades in tragic personifications. It was the policy of Augustus "to cultivate other than political interests for the people and he passed laws for the protection and privilege of the pantomimists." Subsequently they used their freedom against the peace of the city. In the first century after Christ the Roman Emperor Domitian prohibited pantomimists and to a great measure theatres also. From the reading of Roman history it may be inferred that this Emperor had strong reasons to prohibit dramatical representations. Paris was a favourite of the Emperor. He was a good actor. He is said to have "corrupted the Empress Domitilla" for which crime he was assassinated. This instance gave cause for the justification of the charge against the actors. The soundness of this reason is however questionable. During the time of the Roman Emperors *Trajan* and *Aurelius*, the pantomimes were revived and continued. In the year 217 A.D., the cruel Emperor, Caracalla, who butchered his people as a butcher his sheep, and who massacred all the inhabitants of Alexandria in one day, prohibited dramatic representations of all kinds. After his death that very year, they were revived with redoubled energy.

Pylades and Bathylus.

Augustus.

Domitian.

Paris.

Trajan and Aurelius.

Caracalla.

THE dramatic art in Rome and in countries subject to Rome, later on dwindled into buffoonery, personal satires and pantomimes. In the year 362 A.D. when the Emperor Julian visited Antioch

Decline of dramatic art.

during the festivities of *Saturnalia* he found "the streets of the city resounding with insolent songs which derided the laws, the religion, the personal conduct and even the beard of the Emperor. He had been insulted with satires and libels." The patient Emperor left the place with disgust, composing a satire by name "*The enemy of the Beard*" and leaving it at the gates of the city. (Vide Gibbon's "Decline and fall of Rome.") The satire "The Enemy of the Beard" is also known as "*Misopogon.*" It is a "severe satire on the licentious and effeminate manners of the inhabitants of Antioch who had ridiculed Julian on account of his austere virtues and had laughed at his allowing his beard to grow in the ancient fashion." The same historian records the state of Rome in the beginning of the fifth century. He says "the tragic and comic muse of the Romans which seldom aspired beyond the imitation of Attic genius had been almost totally silent since the fall of the Republic and their place was unworthily occupied by licentious, fierce and effeminate music and splendid pageantry. The pantomime maintained its reputation from the age of Augustus to the sixth century and expressed, without use of words, the various fables of the Gods and heroes of antiquity; and the perfection of its art, which sometimes disarmed the gravity of the philosophers, always excited the applause and wonder of the people. The vast and magnificent theatres of Rome were filled by three thousand female dancers and by three thousand singers with the masters of the respective choruses." About 429 A.D., the Emperor Theodosius the younger, rescinded in Constantinople, the law which prohibited female christian proselytes from appearing on the stage; and they were, therefore, allowed to resume their profession without fear of spiritual censure. "Yet nevertheless, they, like the male followers of Thespis, lived more or less for

Julian.

The Enemy of the Beard.

centuries after, under the law of both Church and State."

THE literature of Rome, after the deplorable death of Boethius in five hundred and twenty-four decayed rapidly. For the next five centuries, learning and knowledge became the monopoly of the ecclesiastics. When Papal power reached its climax, the actors who were till then the real tormentors of the clergy, were refused the benefit of the Christian sacrament. Those who visited theatres instead of churches on Sundays or holidays were excommunicated. The ecclesiastics were all powerful. Even kings obeyed them. The ancient satires of the Greeks and the Romans were lying in unknown corners, unnoticed and uncared for. The pantomimists who were mostly professionals, left the frequented towns with their art and became strolling players, and thus kept alive the histrionic art which subsequently, after five or six centuries, proved a useful connecting link between the ancient and the modern dramatic art. This accounts for the absence of dramatic literature in Europe between the sixth and the eleventh century. India at this period was fertile in dramatic literature. The absence of this species of intellectual amusement was keenly felt by the people who by nature were ardently inclined to such amusements. They had other occupations to keep body and soul together, but there was nothing to satisfy their intellectual hunger. The clergy as a rule in every part of the world wanted to grow fat on the ignorance of the people. The erudition in people was an eye-sore to them. They thought they were the chosen few who were created by God to explain the mysteries of the Holy Bible and considered it was a contamination if

Decline of Literature.

Ecclesiastics severity.

others touched it. As time went on and as people learnt slowly the benefits of education, the clergy could no longer keep them in check. Consequently to claim the merit themselves of having improved the people by amusement, they invented miracles and mysteries both as an instruction to people in the way of pleasure and as a satisfaction to their own intellectual faculty.

Mysteries and Miracle plays.

LEARNED men must display their learning in some shape or other. The condemnation of actors at the end of the fourth century did not affect ecclesiastical actors. They were free from all condemnation because in themselves lay the making or unmaking of the laws. Like the temporal law-administrators of the civilised modern world, the clergy of old could twist the interpretation of their ordinances in the way that suited them best. We read that in the fourth century itself St. Gregory Nazienzen wrote the play called the "*Passion of Christ.*" This must have been written, (if there is any truth in the statement that he wrote it) when he was the head of the Eastern Church at Constantinople. A certain Historian observes that "Gregory, all inflamed with love of God, and zeal of his glory, applied himself to making of comedies and tragedies and the writing of all such verse; which he performed with so much wit and elegance and with such rare and admirable sentences, that the Christians found in his writings all they could desire in the heathen poets." The clergy commenced with miracle plays. "These were so called because they were generally devoted to the presentment in a tangible form so far as might be of the great deeds of the Saints and were started with the view of instructing the people more easily and effectually in the Sacred history than was possible by mere recitations of the parts of the Scripture. They did not always deal in facts but sometimes dealt in legends. The confused state

Gregory Nazienzen.

Miarcle plays defined.

of the Roman Empire may also be assigned as the reason for the absence of pure dramatic representations during this long interval. We may say generally that the five centuries from the sixth to the tenth comprise the dark age for Europe, though it cannot be affirmed that there was no literature during that period. Knowledge became scarce and ignorance prevailed in abundance. The clergy were prepossessed against secular education, so much so that Gregory the Great who was himself an eminent scholar, did not shrink, it is said, from burning all the heathen books of ancient time. He hated secular learning. Besides this, the Lombards in Europe, like the Mahomedans in India, destroyed all libraries, schools, and arts, wherever they went. Thus two elements combined to ruin ancient literature. The same was the case in India but the times were different. Even when Universities were established in or about the twelfth century in almost all the chief cities of Europe, and philosophy was discussed on the basis of reason, Italy being the seat of the Popes could not dare enter into such theological discussions. It was the object of the clergy of old everywhere to entertain ignorant people by the legends of the Saints, miracles worked by them and their martyrdoms. They feared discussion based on reason. The various sects among the Brahmins of India are attributable to the hot theological discussions once carried on between priests and laymen. The history of various countries teaches that wherever priests rule with despotism, general literature finds its shelter in oblivion. The priests, as a general rule, hate any subtle disputation on religion, since the free discussion of the subject occasions a loss of their prestige. In conclusion we are led to say that learning even in the clergy was not as satisfactory as one would expect in them, between the

Dark age.

Reasons for decline of literature.

fourth and the sixth centuries. We need not talk o1 honourable exceptions. We read in a foot-note in "The History of the Middle Ages" by Hallam, that "many of the Bishops in the general councils of Ephesus and Chalcedon could not write their names." In this connection I think I should do well to quote a few lines from Russels' 'Modern Europe' on the subject of the progress of society. He says "the first permanent step towards the revival of literature in Europe was the erection of schools under lay preceptors. Alfred and Charlemagne, those early luminaries of the modern world, had shed a temporary lustre over the ages in which they lived. They had encouraged learning both by their example and patronage and some gleams of genius began to break forth but the promising dawn did not arrive at perfect day. The schools erected by these great monarchs were confined to the churches and monasteries, and monks were almost the only instructors of youth. The contracted ideals of such men, partly arising from their mode of life, partly from their religious opinions, render them utterly unfit for the communication of liberal knowledge. Science in their hands degenerated into a barbarous jargon, and genius again sunk in the gloom of superstition. A long night of ignorance succeeded. Learning was considered as dangerous to true piety and darkness was necessary to hide the usurpations of the clergy who were then exalting themselves on the ruins of the Civil power. The ancient poets and orators were represented as seducers to the path of destruction. Virgil and Horace were the pimps of hell, Ovid a lecherous fiend and Cicero a vain disclaimer impiously elate with the talents of heathenish reasoning. Aristotle's logic alone was recommended because it was found capable of involving the simplest arguments and perplexing the plainest truths. It became the universal science. . . . But the gloom

Progress of Society by Russel.

at last began to disappear and the sceptre of knowledge was wrested from the hand of superstition. Several enlightened persons among the laity who had studied under the Arabs in Spain, undertook the education of youth about the beginning of the eleventh century in the chief cities of Italy and afterwards in those of France, England and Germany. Instruction was communicated in a more rational manner. More numerous and more useful branches of science were taught; a taste for ancient literature revived and some Latin poems were written before the close of twelfth century, not unworthy of the latter times of the Roman Empire." . . . Subsequently "the romantic became the favourite mode of composition; and as every kingdom of Europe had its valorous knights, every kingdom soon had its romances; and every romance was nearly the same. Whether the scene was laid in ancient or modern times in Spain or in Syria, the same set of ideal beings were introduced, the same kind of plot was pursued and the same manners were painted. A lady miraculously chaste and fair and a knight more than humanly brave and constant, encountering monsters and resisting the allurements of enchantresses formed the ground work of all those unnatural compositions. . . . Music is one of the first sciences that are cultivated and one of the last which are perfected in any country. The rude tale of the bard is accompanied with the wild notes of his voice and harp to atone for his want of ideas and engage attention; but as fable becomes more extensive and rich, the legendary poet disdains to court the ear with anything but the harmony of his numbers. He relies for interest solely on the powers of imagination and sentiment; and these without any adventitious aid produce their effect upon a people civilised but not corrupted. The dramatic writer in like manner obtains his end for a time, by the happy disposition of plot, the force of dialogue and the strength and variety of his characters.

But in proportion as mankind became more refined they became more effeminate and the luxury of harmony is found necessary to give to theatrical representations its proper influence. Then and not till then does the musical science attain perfection and then poetry begins to decline. Everything is sung; everything is composed to be warbled through the eunuch's throat and sense is sacrificed to sound."

THE cessation of secular dramatic performances at this period gave impetus to authors to compose refined religious dramas. The professors of the Christian church, its votaries and some ecclesiastics, wrote many tragic and comic plays, the themes for them being "the martyrdoms and miraculous conversions from the legends of Christian saints." These plays became the literary monastic dramas of the greater part of Europe. Children of the church under the care of monks or nuns and the priests themselves sometimes performed them in their cloisters. The service of the mass contained roughly the principal dramatic elements. "Reading out the portion of the Scripture by the priest formed its epical portion; the anthem and responses of the congregation formed the lyrical. The show of living pictures illustrating the gospel narrative and accompanied by songs completed the liturgical dramas." These were being performed inside the Church at first, but when the people crowded to suffocation they were obliged to come outside. The service of the mass was taken from the legends of the saints.

Monastic dramas.

IN one thousand two hundred and sixty-four, a society of clergymen was established at Rome and they presented '*The Passion of Jesus Christ*' on the stage. After the mysteries and miracles came moralities and farces. In moralities we see personified abstractions of envy, hatred, malice, flattery, falsehood and deceit. In Sanscrit we have a morality play in "Prabodha Chendrodaya."

Moralities.

The Roman clergy must have borrowed the idea of representing mysteries from the mystic dramas of the ancient Greeks who acted secretly the Eleusinian and other mysteries. Following the example of the priests, the lay associations and schools began to act plays in honour of their patron saints in or near their own halls. Comic elements in these religious plays intervened, when devils, vice and crimes were represented. Thus the dramas even when associated with the church grew more and more comical. Thus the dramatic elements once favoured and again denounced by the clergy flourished in one shape or other for a series of centuries in Rome and Italy along with the pantomimists who kept the dramatic art alive in spite of all disabilities.

Hallam on ancient Church dramas.

THE historian Hallam says "The religious dramas were doubtless fully as ancient in Italy as in any other country. It was very congenial to a people whose delight in sensible objects is so intense. It did not supersede the extemporaneous performances of mimi and histriones, who had probably never intermitted their sportive license since the days of their Oscan fathers and of whom we find mention, sometimes with severity, sometimes with toleration in ecclesiastical writers, but it came into competition with them, and thus may be said to have commenced in the thirteenth century a war of regular comedy against the lawless savages of the stage which has only been terminated in Italy within very recent recollection."

Mussato.

AT the end of the thirteenth century, many dramas having definite form were produced. "Mussato," who was compared to Aeschylus of Greece, wrote tragedies of much dramatic strength and originality. Mussato was born in 1261 and died in 1330. His play *Eccerinis* is said to be a well written piece keeping up national interest. It is a tragedy written in close imitation of Seneca.

THE fourteenth century was, though not productive of great dramatic art in Italy, considered to be an age when the revival of ancient literature and arts occupied the serious attention of the people. Dante, Petrarch, Boccacio and other eminent scholars lived in this century. The songs of troubadours which became common in Italy in the thirteenth and the fourteenth centuries, took a dramatic form most probably in the hands of Petrarch. Religious dramas were changed into regular dramas on the classical basis by eminent men of learning. An historian styles Dante and Petrarch as the morning stars of Modern European Literature. Petrarch gave purity, elegance and stability to the Italian tongue. He wrote a comedy called "*Philologia.*" In the memorable month of April 1341, Petrarch went to the Capitol and received the poet's crown from the Senator. On this grand occasion, men of letters from different parts of the country assembled at the Capitol and heard with wonder the great rhetorical declamations of this poet. This gave stimulus to the already thinking minds of the scholars there assembled to improve upon the ancient learning. Societies were formed for that purpose in Italy at first and in other parts of Europe gradually. This movement was known as the *Renaissance.* Though the movement originated in Italy, it did not achieve any useful and permanent work, compared to those achieved by other countries in Europe. The people before this were groaning under the despotism of ecclesiastical and feudal systems. All the reformations worked in Europe during the fifteenth and the sixteenth centuries are the effects direct and indirect of the Renaissance. Petrarch of Italy, who sowed the seed, is even now known as the father of the Renaissance. The seed grew into a noble tree, a thin rootlet at a point near the seed but wide spreading and extensive at the top far from it. A few of the Popes of Rome, even in the fifteenth century exercised their despotic powers to suppress literary

Petrarch.

Renaissance.

improvements. In 1468, eminent scholars of the day in Rome "formed an Academy to converse together on subjects of ancient learning." Pope Paul II arrested them on the imaginary charges of conspiracy against his life and of setting up pagan superstition against Christianity, and they were put in prison for twelve months under great torture.

DURING the fifteenth century, the development of dramatic art was slowly progressing. The dramas resembled in kind the mystery and miracle plays and were represented on certain popular festivities in Florence and other towns. Some well known poets wrote plays in imitation of the classical dramas of Plautus and Seneca. Landivio commemorated in a Latin Tragedy the captivity and death of a famous Captain. Both the mysteries and the regular dramas were being represented either in the universities or before an audience of ecclesiastics.

P. Laetus.

Pomponius Laetus re-established the theatre of Rome. Many of the Latin plays of Plautus and Terence as well as modern plays were performed before Pope Sixtus IV. During the carnival of 1484, the play of the "*History of Constantine*" was represented in the Papal palace.

Ballet.

The modern *ballet* was first introduced in Italy in 1480 and was played at Tortona before a certain duke of Milan. This Italian ballet became an amusement subsequently in all European countries on great occasions. Politian was the first great man who introduced into Italy his

Politian and Pastoral Drama.

musical drama, better known as *Pastoral Drama*. It was acted in 1483 before the court of Mantua. Politian was an eminent scholar possessing poetical gifts of a very high order. He was a scholar, a professor, a critic and a poet. He was greatly patronized by Lorenzo the Magnificent. It is said that he wrote the musical drama "*Orfeo*" in two days. In 1486 many dramas were performed by the order of Ercole at Ferrara. Profane comedies were also performed in different places.

Galleotto.

DURING the sixteenth century the drama occupied a more important position in Italy and several theatres were erected. Tragedies in the Italian language began to be written. In 1502, Galleotto's "*Sofonisba*," a tragedy written in Italian was performed.

Trissino.

In 1515 another *Sofonisba* by Trissino, in blank verse, and with famous Italian scenes was performed before Leo X.

Comedy of Masks.

THE Italian comedy of *masks* where the Pantaloon and Brighella, Harlequin and the Doctor played their parts most, with an action and dialogue, ever new and ever natural, pleased the masses in the fifteenth and the sixteenth centuries. This comedy of mask was not an invention. The Italian mind had the seed sown there when the "*Mimes*" and the "*Histriones*" had the field entirely in their possession. These mask comedies extended their sway to England, to France, and to Germany. As society grew more and more refined, these rude mask comedies began to lose their vitality. *Extemporaneous comedies* also highly amused the Italian populace. A scholar and actor by name Scala was the man who proposed and succeeded in this kind of performance. The plot in detail is given out, reserving the dialogue for the ingenuity of the performers. If all the actors are scholars possessing ready wit, this system of performance is certainly praiseworthy; however the dialogue cannot be as pleasing as that written before hand after much thought and skill. Such extemporaneous comedies will be a treat to an educated audience if well performed by educated actors.

Extemporaneous comedy.

Ariosto.

Comedies and burlesques and satires by Ariosto were also being performed in Italy. Ariosto is known as the father of modern comedies and his models are said to be master-pieces. In the effective drawing of character he displayed his genius. A prose comedy by name "*Mandragona*" of Machieval was acted before Pope Leo X at Rome. The historian Hallam in his *Literatnre of Europe* says "the comedies of Italy of the sixteenth century resemble more those of Aristophanes than the pleasant freedom of Plautus." It is during this century that pastoral dramas were also brought into existence. In 1554 a pastoral drama of "Beccari" was acted at the court of Ferrara. "*Aminta*" by Tasso was also performed with great success. This was acted at Ferrara in 1573. "This celebrated poem is quite simple in plot; but its design is allegorical, and the Arcadia presented by it is a reflexion of the Ferrara Court, the poet himself appearing as one of the shepherds (*Tirsi*). Adorned with choral lyrics of great beauty, the *Aminta* is substantially an allegorical treatment of a social and moral problem, applied so subtly as to touch the minds of its audience without apparent effort. Yet the conduct of the personages, who uniformly neither speak nor think of ought but the passion of love is wholly artificial; and the charm of the poem lies not in the interest of its action but in the ardour and sweetness of its sentiment."

Melodrama.

THE *Melodrama* or *the Italian opera*, was also a wonderful invention of the sixteenth century. The musical science and skill of the Italians which were dormant during the fifteenth and the beginning of the sixteenth centuries, revived during the latter half of the sixteenth century. Even the church music was changed in 1560. Ottavio Rinuccini a poet of considerable genius was its first author.

Rinuccini.

In 1590 a famous pastoral drama of "*Pastor Fido*" by Guarini was enacted, and it was applauded by the audience. It was a popular tragic love story. This drama was most probably produced in rivalry of Tasso's Aminta. "Founded on a tragic love story, it largely adds to and complicates the intrigue and introduces a comic element partly with a satirical intention, one of the most charming scenes leads to one of the most touching situations; while in the end a tragic complication is happily solved." The following is from Russel's Modern Europe, Vol. II. "Genius in the meantime continued to advance with giant strides in Italy. A succession of great poets followed Dante in the highest work of the muse; at length appeared *Ariosto* and *Tasso* the glory of the sixteenth century and whose celebrated works are supposed to contain all that is excellent in poetry. "*The Orlando*" of Ariosto is a wonderful production. It is formed upon Gothic plan, if it can be said to have any, and consequently is wild and extravagant; but it comprehends so many and such various beauties that whether considered as a whole or in parts it commands our highest admiration.

Tasso. "*The Jerusalem*" of *Tasso* is a more classical performance. It is constructed after the Grecian model; and adds to an instructing and happily constructed fable, a number of striking and well known characters all operating to one end, together with a profession of beautiful machinery, affecting situations, sublime images and bold descriptions."

THE seventeenth century is a period of decadence. However some tragedies of renown were written during this period. The "*Adams*" which furnished the idea to the "Paradise Lost" was written at this period. It was denominated a sacred representation and was performed on the stage. The tragedies of the seventeenth century were taken from ecclesiastical legends. In the passion for the Melodrama the Italians "lost all relish for the graver tone of tragedy." The great tragic actor Cotta left the stage in disgust at the apathy of the public towards the higher forms of drama.

Goldoni. A complete reformation of literature and the stage was worked in the eighteenth century by a poet named *Goldoni*, of considerable ability and originality and of wonderful dramatic genius,

He wrote one hundred and fifty comedies. He knew most of the vernaculars of Italy. He was also a scholar in Greek, Latin and French. He was invited by Louis XVI to France where he wrote a French comedy. It was a great success. He was paid a present ot 6,000 francs besides an annual pension of 1,200 francs. He died in 1793 at the age of eighty six. Till his death, it is said, he was writing comedies. In his youth, this dramatist tried his skill in tragedies but they were not very successful. He was also a lawyer. Italian comedy was in its decay when Goldoni undertook to reform it. The conventional buffoonery and the rampant immorality which had become the fashion of the stage during the seventeenth century, were completely removed by this famous dramatist.

"THE Studies of the Eighteenth Century in Italy" by Vernon Lee contains a vast information about the musical attainments of the Italians and how the *mask comedy* and *the realistic comedy* came into existence. He says that the "new comedy owed its existence to the old. . . The old comedy of masks was essentially a comedy of action. The illiterate artisans, boatmen, labourers and bravos, the violent or business-like nobles wanted to be interested by action and amused by buffoonery. It was Carlo Goldoni that brought realistic comedy into existence." Goldoni's rival, Carlo Gozzi, was the inventor of the "*Venetian Fairy Comedy*." Thus we see that "out of old venerable comedy of masks originated two forms of comedy in Italy—the realistic comedy of Goldoni, and the fantastic comedy of Carlo Gozzi." The author of the book entitled "Studies of the Eighteenth Century in Italy" says in the introduction that "Italy in the last century got her philosophy and philosophic poetry, like her dress and her furniture, from Paris and London; but Italy in the last century got her drama and her comedy neither from Paris nor from London, but from her own

Realistic and Fantastic dramas.

intellectual soil where they had been germinating for centuries; it gave her own spontaneous national music to the whole of Europe." Carlo Gozzi also wrote many plays in pure Italian. He borrowed his themes from Neapolitan and Oriental fairy tales. At the end of the seventeenth century, an Academy of the Arcadians had been established at Rome. It produced its effect in the eighteenth century. It is to the exertion and severe criticisms of this institution that the chorus which till then ruled supreme on the stage was removed. *Maffei* a noble and a famous author wrote a tragedy entitled "Merope" which obtained the most brilliant success ever obtained in dramatic literature. The tragedy is devoid of love intrigue. It was imitated by the French and the English. Mathew Arnold and George Jaffreys have written this tragedy in English. Alfiori also wrote many plays. He hated the restrictions of the French, introduced by Voltaire. In all his tragedies he showed his love of freedom in treating the subject. His dramas are said to abound in soliloquies, which when coming out of a naturally gifted Italian actor with force of declamation, highly pleased the audience. An historian remarks that "the art of tragic writing at the present day probably stands higher in Italy than in any other European country; if the tragic muse were to be depicted with the features of a living artist, it is those of Adelaide Ristori which she would amuse." The actress Adelaide Ristori enchanted the whole of Europe and America in the nineteenth century. She was a highly educated lady.

Removal of chorus.

Maffei.

Alfiori.

Adelaide Ristori.

THUS in Italy and Rome we see highly learned people encouraging dramatic performances in spite of the commands of the Popes. Even religious rites were taught from the stage.

CHAPTER III.

FRANCE.

FRANCE, before the seventh century, was, like all other countries of Europe except Greece and Rome, almost devoid of learning. Like other countries in the world it had its priests and poets with whom most naturally literary compositions begin. History narrates that between the eighth and nineth centuries, it was rare to find a layman in France, who could read and write. Before the songs of the troubadours, France had cantilinae or songs composed in a vulgar language. In the nineth century Charlemagne established numerous schools where arithmetic, grammar, theology and higher classics were taught. Before the tenth century, history says, there were songs celebrating the martyrdom of *St. Eulalis.* Before the eleventh century, the French were already imitating Latin compositions, and by the end of that century, they had their own language perfected. In the eleventh century there were songs and poems composed by William, Duke of Guienne, in a literary manner. Victor Spiers in his book entitled, the "History and Literature of France," says, "The French Theatre like that of Greece has its origin in religion. The divine service already contained the germs of the drama; high mass, which comprises both action and dialogue, is in itself a dramatic performance; so, in singing the Passion, the words of Gospel are divided among three priests, which produces a more striking effect and partially suggested the mysteries." During this period, the French attempted dramatic performances.

Literature.

Cantilinae songs.

Charlemagne.

Religious dramas.

Fabliaux.

IN the twelfth century they had their *fabliaux* which contain a recital, generally comic, of a real or possible incident occurring in ordinary human life. Most of the subsequent plays—comedies, satires, soties or farces—are taken from the fabliaux. Roman de Renart or the History of "Reynard the Fox" served as a vehicle of satirical comment on the vices and weaknesses of people in general and also the corruption of the Church and the State. "Roman de la Rosa" is a satire in verse wherein gallantry and raillery are treated in an allegorical spirit. It is said that one Guyot-de-Provins was a satirist of a very high order whose Bible, as he called his book, contains a strong satire on the time. During the twelfth century we already see the mystery plays of the "Foolish Virgins," of "Adam," of "St. Nicholas" and many kinds of farces performed. There may not have been any regular dramatic representations openly performed during this period in the face of its condemnation by the Pope; dramatical elements, notwithstanding, survived. There were the strolling pantomimists representing plays in the rural parts and occasionally in towns on festive occasions.

Roman de Renart.

Roman de la Rosa.

Guyot-de-Provins.

Mysteries.

THE Pope could not take away the music from the people and the imaginative faculty from the poets. There was no prohibition against dancing. The people were advancing in every way. The Popes thought it wise to loosen the reins. As the clergy thought themselves the guardians of Virtue, they composed sacred dramas. Some of the miracle plays and farces formed, it is said, a portion of fabliaux thrown into dialogue. Then came moralities, soties etc., which are said to be a development of fabliaux. Morality plays often combined in themselves the personifications of the devil,

Moralities and Soties.

vice, anger, hatred, jealousy when exhibited on the stage.

Comedy. Soties.

In this representation a rude form of comedy took its origin. Soties or sharp satires appealed to the feelings of the people and were in favour till the sixteenth century; and many noble men, emperors and princes, joined in the soties. The soties are satirical plays in which political and social subjects were treated with the greatest license. Rutebeuf who was at first a wandering jongleur or a miscellaneous entertainer rose to secure to himself a place among the poets and moralists of his country. "The numerous works of this versatile genius include a typical example of the satirical debate of the period." His compositions were mostly of dramatic kind.

THE French scriptural theatre was in full swing in the fourteenth century and its effect lasted up to the fifteenth and half of the sixteenth centuries. In 1313 Phillip the Fair gave a most sumptuous entertainment at Paris. Edward II and his Queen Isabella went from England with a large retinue of nobility. The religious plays were performed for eight days.

Mysteries and Miracles.

IN 1402 the Mystery of the Conception, Passion and Resurrection of Christ was performed at St. Maur. In the Mystery of the Passion, it is said, that "eighty-seven characters were introduced the first day. Heaven, Earth and Hell combined to people the stage. Several scenes were written for singing, and some for choruses." Commencing with scriptural themes the Parisians went to the legends of saints. It is recorded that in one of the miracle plays, St. Barbara was hung up by the heels on the stage, teased and torn with pincers. On the stage, this world was exhibited with heaven above and hell below. The Mystery of the Passion was performed on the entrance of the kings of France and England into Paris, upon a raised scaffolding of one hundred paces in length.

THE growth of drama in France was considerably hindered by the conflict between King Louis XII and Pope Julius II. It is said that by the encouragement given by the King, satires were directed against the Holy See.

Gringore.

The poet Gringore who wrote for pantomimes, composed a satire under the patronage of the king and caused it to be performed on the stage. It is said to be a satire against the clergy. Subsequently the "Inquisition to some extent succeeded in repressing the audacity of the actors." In the reign of Francis I, the performance of a grand mystery of the Acts of the Apostles was proclaimed and acted at Paris for many successive days before a large assemblage of nobility and the clergy. By the side of these religious plays romantic and realistic plays and satires were also acted. Gringore was a renowned dramatist of the time.

Classical study.

CLASSICAL studies were introduced into France in the fourteenth century by *Clemangis*, but the improvement in that direction was not perceptible till the end of the fifteenth century. During the latter half of that century, printing was introduced into France. The study of Greek was keenly cultivated. The mystery and miracle plays which pleased the Parisians for more than two centuries were prohibited as indecent and profane by the Parliament in 1548. For four years France had no dramatical representation. Jodelle came forward as the true father of the French theatre. He held a distinguished place in the French theatre as a reformer. His tragedy "Cleopatra Captive" was performed by himself with six other poets known as the "Pleiades" of French literature. Ronsard who established a classical school of poetry in Paris was one of the seven scholars who formed

Printing.

Jodelle.

Ronsard.

the French *Pleiade.* This tragedy as also his comedy *La Reveontre* were performed before Henry II in 1552. His comedy *Eugene* is considered to be very immoral and licentious. It contains also a satire on the clergy. Subsequently the dramatist Bounyn introduced regular tragedy. In Robert Garnier, the French tragedy reached the greatest height in nobility and dignity of style. He wrote eight tragedies. Subjects for his plays were taken from mythology and ancient history.

Bounyn.

Robert Garnier.

In the seventeenth century the Italian ballet was in full swing in France, and Catherine de Medici spent incredible sums on the dresses and scenery for representation. Under her patronage a poet by name Baif performed many allegorical, moral and ludicrous ballets. The Royal families of France took an active part in these amusements. In a ballet performance of 1681 there appeared among the dancers Madame La Dauphine, the Princesse de Conti and Mdlle de Nantes, the Prince and many Dukes. Louis XIV frequently figured in ballets. The King encouraged the nobility and the courtiers to take parts in these ballets. "It is our pleasure," he said, "that all gentlemen and ladies may sing in the said pieces and representations of our Royal Academy, without being considered on that account to derogate from their letters of nobility or from their privileges, rights and immunities." The ballet dancers were very powerful in France. They influenced princes, ministers and people. "Poets were their slaves and oftentimes philosophers were caught in their toils." Ballets and ballet de action became so fashionable in Europe that the Parisian dancers were sent for from different countries. Even the great Mr. Batterton and his company had to send for some of the French dancers to introduce foreign novel-

Italian ballet. Its influence.

Louis XIV and Ballets.

ties in England and thus to please the English people.

Ballet dancers in England.

The ballet dancers of France often visited England and achieved extraordinary successes. In 1734 Mdlle Salle appeared in London

Mdlle Salle.

with her company, and played the part of *Ariadne* in a ballet called "*Bacchus and Ariadne.*" It is stated that "the beauty of her dances, attitudes and gestures and her skill in depicting by movements grief, anger, love and despair," obtained the warmest approval of the audience. "She was patronised by the King, Queen and Royal family, and her *benefit* produced an overflow and something more; tickets were sold at most exorbitant prices and the people fought for places both with swords and fists. There are stories, too, of purses full of gold being flung upon the stage, with showers of bonbons—not ordinary sugar plums but rouleaux of guineas tightly wrapped up in bank-notes. The dancer is said to have profited by her benefit to the extent of some ten thousand pounds."

THE poet Larivey wrote many comedies taking incidents from real life as themes. These

Larivey and his comedies.

comedies, it is said, are higly licentious both in their incidents and language. Italians naturalized in France greatly influenced the growth of comedy there.

Belleau.

Belleau, another dramatist, who formed the Pleiade above mentioned, also wrote comedies and performed them on the stage. As there was no regular theatre in France during the sixteenth century, the plays were performed either in Colleges or in private houses.

Effect of civil and religious wars.

The great civil and religious wars in France in the sixteenth century, had the effect of improving the literature by eminent scholars settling in Paris and thus creating a new phase of national life in the people. The French tired of wars and suffering, wished for amusements to direct their attention from the effects thereof. Even in the troublesome days, the French had their street dialogues. Till the beginning of the seventeenth century the French tragedies maintained the classical chorus which was a reminiscence of the old miracle plays. Till the end of the sixteenth century, dramas were performed on the stage "to a select and refined literary audience," but in the seventeenth century the dramatists and the actors appealed to the people and felt it had the public for a Judge.

A. Hardy and his plavs

ALEXANDER Hardy (1560–1631), a great dramatist and a distinguished actor, wrote about eight-hundred dramas. His comedies and burlesque farces were represented on the stage. It is said that his plays paid no regard to decency either in the language or the circumstances. Few persons of rank, especially ladies, attended the theatres. It is said that a majority of his dramas are not presentable. Many of his plays are imitations of Spanish dramas. Victor Spiers observes that this dramatist was a "manufacturer of plays rather than a poet: one week was enough for him to invent, write and bring out a tragedy with his own company. The chief interest of his plays is in the plot. He knew exactly how to seize on an interesting situation and had the instinct of effect."

Opinion of Victor Spiers.

Cardinal Richelieu.

CARDINAL Richelieu came into power in 1624. He was a great patron of literature and dramas. He would never miss a good performance and often shed tears when a hero or heroine was beset with troubles. Under his patronage there were many poets, of whom, Rotrou the great dramatist, was one. Under his suggestions the dramatist Rotrou wrote many tragedies and comedies. Heroic love and love intrigues formed themes for the comic writers. Richelieu built a large room in his own palace for the representation of a tragedy suspected to be of his own composition. He encouraged dramatists

Rotrou.

and actors. Much of the indecency of language and action was checked by his supervision. Many plays were performed in his palace.

Corneille.

Corneille whose name as a dramatist shines in glory in the French literature, was a great reformer of the stage. Respectable women often went to witness his performances. He admitted nothing licentious in his comedies. He was well connected with the literary men of his time. His tragic characters and tragic passions are really admirable. He was one of the five poets patronised by Cardinal Richelieu. His independence was too high to allow him to submit to the Cardinal in the matter of the ideas to be introduced into the plays. He commenced with comedies and highly pleased the Parisians. In 1636 his drama "*Cid*" took Paris by storm. Cardinal Richelieu out of ill-will caused many criticisms to be written on it, but all the criticisms perished in the ocean of popular praise. Many of his plays (*Horace, Cinna and Polyeucte*) are master-pieces. His women are said to be more heroic than his men. In the Polyeucte the chivalry of Severus, the devotion of Pauline and the martyrdom of Polyeucte are much admired. I quote below a few lines extracted from the tragedy as translated by Thomas Constable in the book known as "*The Great French Triumvirate.*"

Cid.

Horace, Cinna and Polyeucte.

(*a*) "The fruit of rivalry is ever hate."
(*b*) "Weak reason naught when headlong passion reigns."
(*c*) "Words, oaths, are but the tools wherewith all men deceive."
(*d*) "I know that words are wind, I know that wind is naught."
(*e*) "Who loves a lie can never follow truth."
(*f*) "The part that is diseased—that part we bleed, so is the state from knaves and caitiffs freed."

He was known as the father of French tragedy and comedy. In his declining age he joined with Moliere in producing an opera "*Psyche.*" His popularity gradually waned before his rising rival *Racine.*

Racine.

Racine came into prominence as a tragic writer when Corneille was in his decline. He was a friend of Moliere and Boileau and some other men of letters. He was favoured by the King, Louis XIV. His first play was performed by Moliere's company at the palace Royal in 1664. There was a rupture between Moliere and Racine in 1665, for, the latter allowed his play to be acted by a rival company. Racine was hostile to Corneille also. He was an effective tragedian. His "*Iphigenie*" is a master-piece of pathos. His "*Phedre*" is a marvellous representation of human agony. In his tragedy, "*Athaliah,*" the ambition, avarice, and revenge of an old woman are vividly depicted, though in her last days she was terribly afraid of a dreamy phantom. The author describes her state of mind as follows—"Mistress of all beside, but mastered now by fear." In France, Racine is regarded as the greatest of all masters of tragic pathos. Under Corneille and Racine the French tragic art took a definite form and ruled the dramatical literature of Europe for sometime. The chorus was almost removed from the stage. Corneille, Racine and other dramatists of the period, who wrote tragedies were inclined either to Spanish pomposity or Italian affectation or both. When Voltaire was asked "why he did not write a commentary on Racine, as he had composed one on Corneille," he replied, "It is done already: one has but to write at the foot of each page, *Beautiful, Pathetic, Harmonious* and *Sublime.*" During this period there was a great actor by name *Baron* who was so proud as to say "once in a century we might see a Caesar, but that two thousand years were requisite to produce a Baron." It is said that he was a highly talented actor though sometimes he was carried away by vanity. His father Baron was also said to be a good actor. When "playing the part of Don Diego, in The Cid" his sword fell from his hand as the piece required and kicking it from him in indignation, he, unfortunately, struck against the point of it, by which his little toe was pierced. The wound was at first treated as a trifle, but it developed into a gangrene afterwards and the amputation of the leg was declared to be necessary. Nothing, however, could induce Baron to submit to the operation. "No, no," said he, "what would a theatrical monarch be without a leg?" And so preferring death to the loss of professional fame, he calmly awaited his fate.

Alison's opinion on French tragedies.

SIR Archibald Alison, in his history of Europe, says, "the theatre Francais had, for above a century, been to the Parisians what the Forum was to the Athenians, a great arena in which political and moral sentiments of the most elevated kind were inculcated and arguments, the most admirable, urged on the opposite sides of every great public question. The people listened to the inimitable declamations of Corneille or Racine with the same admiration which the Greek citizens felt when witnessing the oratorical contests of Aeschylus and Demosthenes. The grandeur of thought, the elevation of sentiment, the heroism of character which were so nobly portrayed in these dramas, unavoidably acquired a vast influence over the public mind."

Moliere.

MOLIERE, whom even the Englishmen place by the side of the immortal Shakespere, flourished between 1622 and 1693. He was a man of education—honoured and distinguished—a graduate, an advocate and a dramatist. He determined to be an actor "at a period when the theatre was no greater national institution holding a high place in the life of an age." Though he met with reverses for a series of years—reverses of a very serious nature—he combatted against them heroically and came out successfully. He acquired enduring and inexhaustible fame. The elegance and purity of the French language had degenerated in the years between 1650 and 1660, into exaggeration and absurdity. "All that was natural was rejected and nothing admired but what was enigmatic, subtle, and replete with mannerism." Moliere with his comedies, satires and farces, injured the courtiers, nobility, priests and medical men and there was therefore a strong opposition against him. Though Louis XIV loved him as a friend and granted him a royal pension, he was obliged by the tide of the opinion of the clergy and the courtiers to suppress one or two of his comedies. A comedy known as "*Hypocrites*" was represented on the stage. Clergymen were offended at this. One Pierre Roules, cure of St. Barthelamy, attacked the dramatist with a pamphlet, an extract from which is given below. "A man, rather a demon clad in human flesh and dressed as a man, a more confirmedly impious libertine than ever existed in former ages, had been wicked and abominable enough to produce from out of his diabolical intelligence, a play already to be made public by being put upon the stage, to the derision of the whole church and in contempt of the most sacred character and most divine function, in contempt of all that is most holy in the church." The appreciation of Moliere's drama was such that though King Louis XIV prohibited the public representation of some of his plays yet he enjoyed them in private. Much interesting information about this actor—the greatest dramatist of France—may be gathered from his life by Mrs. Oliphant and E. Tarver, M.A. It appears to me that the abovenamed play is known as "*Tartuffe*." The introduction to this play written by Thomas Constable containing the charges of the clergy and Moliere's defence, is worth perusal. I quote below a few lines extracted from the "*Tartuffe*" and also from his comedy known as "*Misanthrophe.*"

Hypocrites.

(*a*) "Those who to vice are most disposed to pander,
Are of all men the most inclined to slander."

(*b*) "When lovers sigh no more, when beauty ends,
'Tis sweet to see how piety befriends."

(c) "The saint in silence gives the heart's devotion,
The pseudo-saint is all trumpet and commotion."
(d) "All are not virtuous who virtues claim,
Profession with performance not the same."
(e) "If thus with highest Heaven were bargains made,
Then must religion sink into a trade."
(f) "But if I seem to deviate from duty,
Fault lies not in me but in your beauty."
(g) "When there is no scandal, we need not repent,
What is done in silence is quite innocent."
(h) "Where is your religion now? This but a cheat,
Temptation comes—religion beats retreat."
(i) "Is all religion nothing but a joke?
Is piety but a convenient cloak?"
(j) "Bottle your wrath my friend—yes, cork your rage,
My honour is worthless, you have won by tricks.
Who feeds the ass, endures the donkey's kicks."

Select lines from the "MISANTHROPE" of Moliere.

(a) "I thought my friend was mine, but now I find,
He is the impartial friend of all mankind."
(b) "Chicanery and plots his daily food."
(c) "Extremes are folly :—in the golden mean,
In moderation, is true wisdom seen."
(d) "On my side reason, equity are clear,
Yet to that side I'd add the Judge's ear."
(e) "........... they can use their sting,
And fairest name in foulest mud can fling."
(f) "He is strangely gifted, he can multiply,
Nothing by nothing to infinity.
His words are mountains, tho' their meaning nill."
(g) "I do not say that you are the creator
Of these reports, but you are the incubator."

O. Elton's opinion of Moliere.

Oliver Elton in his book entitled "*The Augustan Age*" says, of the comedies of Moliere, the following :—

"The history of comedy before his day does not belong to this book. But it may be remembered that between 1650 and 1660, there were four chief kinds none of which

Moliere ignored and none of which was alone strong enough to solve the anarchy prevailing in the comic art. (1) Popular farce had a long and deep history in France and depended not only on infinite colouring and unclothed jesting but on a certain definite pungency and narrative point, comparable with those of the fableaux. Moliere's fund of this kind of drama was inexhaustible. (2) He also drew from the farce and show of the Italian type. (3) The comedy of extravagant burlesque or the heroic-comic drama was tolerably rife. (4) He turned comedy into the representation of character and into the criticism of life." Moliere's comedies exercised some influence on English literature also. His "L'Etroudi" was rendered by Dryden into English with the name of "Sir Martin Marr-All"; his "Le Depet Amoureux" was translated by John Vanbrugh and it was known as "The Mistake"; his "Le Misanthrope," was converted into the comedy "The Plain Dealer" by William Wycherley; Henry Fielding translated his "Le Medecin Malgre Lui" styling it as "The Mock Doctor"; his "L'Avare" became "The Miser" in Henry Fieldings' hand; and his "Le Tartufe" was rendered into English by Colley Cibber, with the name of "The Non-Juror."

Voltaire.

THE writing of satirical comedies attacking the politics of the day, brought indescribable miseries on the authors of all countries. Voltaire, the greatest French writer, was imprisoned for a year or so for his mischievous tendency to write satire against the Regent. Though he was thus punished, his merit was acknowledged. He wrote a tragedy when in jail. After his release, his tragedy was acted before the court and the very Regent who sentenced him to imprisonment, gave him a thousand crowns and also a small pension. His tragedy (Oedipus) was acted for forty nights. This poet maintained that "the time occupied in the action should be the same as that of representation." About the *"three unities"* in tragedy, the author of the History and Literature of France observes :—

Three unities.

"It is not astonishing that the conception of a grand unity in drama should have found favour with the minister whose one aim in his Home Policy had ever been the unity of France. He crushed the Protestants as a political party because they formed a state within the Estate; and he crushed the nobility who wished to establish themselves as feudal potentates in their dominions as independent from the crown; these two obstacles to the unity of France were obstacles to her greatness. The *three unities* therefore pleased Richelieu who decided that Mariet should set the example. "The Cardinal put these rules of unity into practice and he made them absolute rules for the drama, and had them propounded as such by the dramatic theorists who gratuitously place them under the shield and authority of Aristotle." This appears to be the hardest rule in dramaturgy. Even the Indian dramatists who are very technical in the observance of rules, would find it very difficult to follow. If such a rule is enforced, the interest of the play will certainly be diminished. When Voltaire extolled Addison's "Cato" as the first English tragedy reasonable, *i.e.*, the first in which the rules had been observed with perfect obedience to them as based upon reason, Dennis remarked that "by observing the unity of place, the author had only contrived to render the action impossible. For, in order to accomodate his incidents to the rules, Addison was obliged to exclude much that was essential to the action, while he included much that is not only non-essential but disturbing." It is a fortunate feature that no dramatist of any country has strictly followed the example of this great man. Macaulay says "First in celebrity and in absurdity stand the dramatic unities of place and time. No human being has been able to find anything that could, even by courtesy, be called an argument for these unities. All the greatest masterpieces of dramatic art have been composed in direct violation of unities and could never have been composed if the unities had not been violated." Voltaire composed twenty-six tragedies and many comedies; in the latter, with all his learning, he did not succeed. *Adrienne le Counreur* was the finest and the best actress of the age. It is said that she was a woman of a warm and generous heart. She was the first example of a French actress who combined professional renown with consideration in society. She was the dear and intimate friend of Voltaire, and she was the heroine in most of his tragedies. Her education was so complete that her letters, it is said, would tend to refine the French language. Sir Walter Scott ascribes to Voltaire the sole merit of introducing correct costumes." Thus dramatical progress took unusually rapid strides during the time of Louis XIV (1654–1715).

Quinault and Lully. Lyrical Opera.

QUINAULT who is known as the chief inventor of lyrical operas wrote many plays in partnership with the musician Lully. This lyrical dramatist helped Moliere and Corneille in their "*Psyche*" (1671). Even a century did not pass before the French dramatical tone became vulgar. The state of the dramatic literature and the contrast in the stage between the seventeenth and the eighteenth centuries are well described by the historian Thiers. He says, "in the seventeenth century, France arrayed in all brilliancy of youth and glory had been seen excelling in the highest degree in the tragic representation of the passions of man and in the comic representation of his oddities, giving lustre to the pulpit, by a grave, energetic, sublime eloquence unknown to the world, which has never heard it and which will never hear it again. She had been seen in the eighteenth century, suddenly changing her taste, her genius, her creed, forsaking art for polemics, attacking the alter, the throne, all the social

Decline.

Thiers' opinion.

institutions, acrimonious, vehement, immoral too in the literature which occı pies itself in depicting the human heart."

THE reason for the French society growing reckless and immoral in the beginning of the eighteenth century was that Loius XIV in his old age grew very religious and insisted upon his subjects being religious too. They pretended to be pious to please the king. Piety became a fashion and not a reality. When the king died, the people went many steps below the standard of morality which had ruled the nation before piety was forced upon them. It was but a natural re-action. It is the case with every nation where a new theory is forced upon them. English society would not have been reckless and immoral after the Restoration, had it not been for the fanaticism of the Puritons who tried with threats to make the English nation religious and even over-religious and had it not been for the restraint put upon all amusements which the people naturally wished to enjoy. Extreme relaxation is the natural effect of extreme restraint. Morality and religion must be a natural growth in man. One must prepare one's mind to receive the seeds usefully. This preparation of mind, man makes by his experience in the world. Nothing can be forced upon him with advantage. When Louis XIV died, restraint disappeared and the people grew licentious and impudent. It took a long time for them to undeistand their degraded position and to reform themselves. If reformation had been forced upon them at that time, they would have gone to oblivion. Morality and religion are the natural privileges of men and people do not like others to force upon them the things which belong to them by birth right.

Reasons for decline.

THE eighteenth century had also innumerable tragic and comic plays. *Diderot* (1713–1784), an eminent and enterprising scholar, sought the help of the stage for social reform and also for the spread of Gospel philonthrophy. He wrote many

Diderot.

dramas and acted them on the stage. Melodrama encouraged by Vondevilles and Rousseau, was also in vogue at this period. Chenier (1764–1811) wrote, an historic drama with a political moral. He wrote also many satires. It is during this period, the end of the eighteenth century, that the tragic writer Talma distinguished himself as an actor. In the play entitled "Mahamet" he took also an active part. He was noted as an exponent of strong and concentrated passion. He was the "advocate of realism in scenery and costume." He had a voice of great beauty and power and was well fitted for highest tragic part. He had at first a certain degree of thickness of utterance which he gradually conquered and became possessed of matchless elocution. This famous actor and tragic writer enjoyed the intimacy of Napolian. Rhetorical tendency was the great national feature of French tragedy. Voltaire was its prime cause. Victor Hugo and Alexander Dumas followed in his footsteps more or less. During the first half of the nineteenth century, there lived a tragic actress by name Rachel. George Henry Lewes calls her the "panther of the stage." Scorn, triumph, rage, lust, and merciless malignity, she could represent in symbols of irresistable power. "Her elocution, it is said, was musical and artistically graduated to the fluctuations of the meaning."

Chenier.

Talma—the actor.

V. Hugo & A. Dumas.

Rachel—the actress.

ROMANTIC movement which took its origin in Germany in the latter part of the eighteenth century, had its effect in France in the nineteenth century. The artistic rules framed by Boileau for the guidance of classical tragedy were gradually done away with. The three unities of action, time and place were not cared for as they would hamper not only the flow of the imagination of the dramatist but also the free action of the actor on the stage. The rule that the heroes and heroines of Classical Tragedy should be kings and queens, princes and

Romantic movement.

princesses, was greatly slackened. Much attention was paid to the costumes of the age to which the characters of the drama belonged. Some of the tenets of the Romantic School are given below, as taken from the "History and Literature of France." While the Classicists with Boileau considered reason as supreme and clearness and precision as essential qualities, the Romanticists upheld the claims of imagination and fancy and aimed at high colouring, contrast and effect. The Classicists sought the models of their art and the sources of their inspiration in the master-pieces of antiquity; the Romanticists seek inspiration in modern foreign literature; for pagan mythology, they substitute the Christian Arts of the middle ages; the rule of the Three Unities they throw to the winds; they bring the action upon the stage and flood it with duels, suicides, and murders, thus introducing the sensational melodrama upon the tragic stage; they surround their characters with exact local colouring and represent with minute historical fidelity the costumes and scenery of the time of the play."

Reasons for the three unities.

VICTOR HUGO was considered the champion of this Romantic movement. He, with his companions, like most reformers, went too far. War between the Classical School and the Romantic School was actually declared and fought out on the night of the 25th February 1830, when "Hernani" of Victor Hugo was performed on the stage. "At the first infringement of the classical rules, a storm of hisses broke out, followed and covered by the noisy applause of the poet's well wishers. Every line of the piece was fought through to the end. Every evening the same battle ensued, amid the jeers and hisses of the classicists and the enthusiastic counter-applause of the young Romanticists who ridiculed and insulted their foes and went so far as to stop the carpers' mouths with their hands, and free fights ensued. Nevertheless, Victor Hugo won the day. Though

Romantic School.

Classical School.

his drama is, even more than his other works, marred by his excessive love of contrast, his generous efforts undoubtedly rendered an inestimable service to France by shaking off the trammels of the artificial Three Unities and the exaggerated pomposity of the settled style.

Reformation.

In the nineteenth century many dramatists wrote plays on romantic subjects, and the French theatrical activity was in its progressive career. Alexander Dumas (younger) undertook to reform society by means of the stage and many other dramatists joined him in that attempt.

Mme Sarah Bernhardt.

I cannot close the history of histrionic development in France without introducing to my Indian readers, the greatest genius—the greatest actress, the greatest artist the world ever produced. She is Mme Sarah Bernhardt. Her life written by Jules Huret and translated into the English language by G. A. Raper is worth reading. When her friend asked her to give the most memorable events of her brilliant career, she narrated as follows :—" My dear friend, you are asking for nothing less than a full confession, but I have no hesitation in answering. I am proud and thoroughly happy at the prospect of the fete that is to be given me. . . . . For twenty-nine years past I have given to the public the vibrations of my soul, the pulsations of my heart and the tears of my eyes. . . . . I have struggled like no other human being has struggled. . . . . I have ardently longed to climb the topmost pinnacle of my art. I have not yet reached it. . . . . I have journeyed across the ocean, carrying with me my ideal of art and the genius of my nation has triumphed. I have planted the French language in the heart of foreign literature and this is my proudest achievement. . . . Here is a typical incident. When I arrived in Australia, the French residents were dominated by the Germans. Our Consul was neither liked nor esteemed. Immeditately upon my arrival I was received by the Mayor in his robes of office. His wife and children offered me flowers and a military band played the national anthems of France and England. I owed this polite attention to orders from England. The effect was immediately felt and this semi-royal reception was much to the benefit of my countrymen at Sydney and Melbourne. . . . . In Hungary, the towns in which I was to perform were decorated with French flags, in spite of orders from the Austrian Government. . . . . And now, after having finished my confession, I can still find one little circumstance in my own favour. Five months ago, I refused an offer of a million francs to perform in Germany. If there be any carping critics to say the fete about to be given me is out of proportion to my talents, tell them I am the militant doyenne of a grand inspiring, elevating form of art. Tell them French courtesy was never more manifest than when, desiring to honour the art of interpretation and raise the interpreter to the level of other creative artists, it selected a woman."

CHAPTER IV.

SPAIN AND PORTUGAL.

Origin.

IN Spain, the dramatic element-proper, not to speak of musical dances and pantomimes which must have been coeval with the very existence of the nation itself, is traced to a period in the middle of the twelfth century. The oldest play known as the mystery of the Magician kings was, it is said, a short semi-liturgical play acted in the Church of Toledo. The existence of regulations made between 1252 and 1257, shows that the religious plays were being enacted on festival days. Buffoonery entering into these performances gave them a secular character and brought down the censure of the clergy. Alfonso the Wise, then made a rule that those dramas which commemorate the principal episodes of the life of Christ should be enacted by the clergy in the Sanctury only.

Liturgical play.

IN the festival "Corpus Christi" instituted by Urban IV in 1264, the dramatical representation became a custom to explain the eucharistic mystery. In this connection it may be said that religion and morality may be taught to the illiterate masses impressively through the stage. This is instruction by means of pleasure. Subsequent secular dramas were only the developments of religious plays.

Drama to explain eucharistic mystery.

IT is an acknowledged fact that the Spaniards have always been a poetical people. A deep enthusiasm, strong passions and original imagination are visible everywhere. The historian of Spanish literature says "the energy, the fancy which earlier produced the beautiful ballads of Spain, the force of national character which drove the Moors from

Nature of Spanish people.

Toledo, Seville and Granada ,called forth, in the seventeenth century a dramatic literature which grew out of the national genius and the condition of the mass of the people. . . .

Nature of Spanish dramas.

The Spanish drama in its most heroic forms was still a popular entertainment. The purpose was not only to please all classes but to please all equally." "To blend military valour with strongest feelings of devotion and of love were the themes of Spanish dramas and the chivalrous enthusiasm pervaded all their actions." The Spanish poet Enzina wrote many comedies. Some denominated his plays as sacred and profane "*Eclogues.*" These were performed before distinguished persons on festival days.

First dialogue comedy.

DURING the latter half of the sixteenth century attempts were made in Spain to form a national theatre. Torres Naharro and Lope-de-Rueda were its real founders. The former was the inventor of Spanish comedy. He wrote eight comedies. Lope-de-Rueda, it is said, is remarkable for ingenuity of invention. Their plays were mostly comedies of intrigue which are the type of the classic stage. In Spain also at one time when the dramas were gross as well as audacious in tone, the Church had to interfere for their suppression. The immortal Cervantes (1585) reformed dramatic literature and created romantic dramas on classical models. His tragedy "Neumancia" was pronounced to be a drama of extraordinary power. Lope-de-Vega one of the most astonishing geniuses the world has known, wrote about one thousand and five-hundred plays, besides three-hundred dramatic works and a vast series of other literary compositions. He was called by Cervantes "a prodigy of Nature." His invention is as unparallelled in the history of poetry, as the talent which enabled him to compose regular

Regular comedies.

Lope-de-Rueda.

Cervantes. Neumancia.

Lope-de-Vega a prodigy of natnre.

and well constructed verse with as much ease as prose. He required only four and twenty hours to write a versified drama of three acts abounding in intrigues, prodigies and interesting situations. In some instances he composed a play in the short space of three or four hours. Hallam in his history of the "Literature of Europe" gives a fine description of the extraordinary abilities of this wonderful poet of the seventeenth century.

Ruiz-de-Alarcon.

Ruiz-de-Alarcon also wrote many dramas containing a distinctive element of moral purpose.

Tirso-de-Molina.

Tirso-de-Molina was also an author of many comedies containing graceful and easy dialogue. He was considered to be very ingenious in the construction of plots.

Zorilla.

Franciso-de-Rojos Zorilla also was the author of many comedies containing well constructed plots.

A. Moreto.

Augustin Moreto who died in 1669 wrote many plays which were greatly imitated by the French.

Philip IV.

Philip IV of Spain was himself a dramatist. The greatest and famous dramatist and a warrior, by name Calderon wrote about one hundred and thirty dramas. His plays are largely used. It is said that between

Number of dramas.

1590 and 1681 thirty-thousand plays were written in Spain.

Subjects of dramas.

There was no subject which the Spanish dramatists did not treat. Bible legends of martyrs, national traditions, the deeds of heroes in foreign and native histories, the daily incidents of common life, duels and murders, etc., formed themes for dramas.

Calderon.

Henry VIII, etc.

Calderon's historic poems "Henry VIII," "Semiramis" and "Constant Prince" are really worth reading. The stories are given in abstract with certain extracts in the "Calderon" by E. J. Hassal. Some ideas there may be repugnant to Indian taste but the dramas are on the whole very beautifully written.

Decline.

THE end of the seventeenth century witnessed the decline and decay of the spirit of Spain and its national art. The authors had to degrade themselves to the level of the audience. Burlesque poetry reigned supreme.

Opinions on the Spanish dramas by Dryden.

BEFORE leaving Spain, I shall say a few words about the general character of the Spanish dramas. Dryden in his poem, "The Art of Poetry," says of Spain,—

"A Spanish poet may with good event
In one day's space whole ages represent.
There oft, the hero of the wandering stage
Begins a child and ends the play of age."

This criticism on the Spanish dramas holds good of the stories of Indian dramas also. Even some of the English dramas are so. We need not therefore pay much attention to the want of unity of time in the Spanish dramatists. The division into acts and scenes covers this defect. An Englishman who had seen Spanish performances wrote that the pleasing elegance of nature is disfigured by a combination of pedants in the seventeenth century, "who losing sight of every beautiful idea, contemning at the same time the rules of art, made way for their inspired vagaries." Then he classifies the dramatists under three heads: *viz.*, those that violated all the laws of the drama and introduced innumerable defects on the stage; those who added to the then existing glaring improprieties, a ridiculous bombast and affectation which became superlatively intolerable and absurd; and thirdly those who out of their false zeal for the chastity of the muses, introduced a greater purity of diction but by their awkward and ignorant presumption substituted obscure and unknown expressions to a new and turgid dialect." The above is the sum and substance of the remarks of an English traveller in 1778. These defects are found in the dramas of all the nations at one time or other

RICHARD Ford, author of "The Gatherings from Spain," observes, that the fantastic zeal of Spaniards for bull-fights and other spectacles of amphitheatral nature tended to the decline of Spanish drama and the country which once supplied dramatic plots to many European nations has been now borrowing them from other countries.

Bull fights and other spectacles. Chief causes of decline.

SPAIN had no women on the stage before the sixteenth century or at any rate, before France had its influence on the country and its people.

PORTUGAL.

THE ancient inhabitants of the dominions which made up subsequently what is now known as Portugal, had the fortunes and the misfortunes of foreign invasions which were then only too many and too varied. From the original Turanians, they had the epic poem known as "Aravia." From the Celtic people who succeeded the Turanians they had their lyric poem "Guayade." From the Roman conquerors they were possessed of "Cantor-de-ladino." They also derived "Chacones" or dance songs from the Visigoths. From the Arab conquerors they inherited sensuous songs of love. Thus the influence of its conquerors gave the country the above species of poetry till the beginning of the twelfth century when the Provincals settled in Portugal exercised much influence upon the poetic lyric art of the people. The celebrated troubadour Marcabrum lived in Portugal about this time, (1146). The king Alfonso Henriques was himself a poet. Piere Vidal and Piere Valeria and other poets who by their songs raised the feeling of the Christians to crusade against the Moors, lived in Portugal in the beginning of the thirteent' century. Alfonso III with his nobles lived in France for some time and returned home imbued with the northern sentiments. The nobles, most of them poets, became known as

The mixed character of the poetry.

Troubadour influence

"Trouveres." The first Portuguese gesta was written by one of these nobles. Alfonso III was also a great poet. During the reign of Diniz (1279–1325) literature took a firm root under the influence of both southern and Provencal poets. Diniz was himself a poet of high renown. The renaiscence movement of Italy produced its effect in Portugal in founding Dantesque or allegorical school in the sixteenth century. The Poetry of Portugal where all men were singers was admirable before the twelfth century. The Portuguese troubadours were proverbially good singers. From the twelfth to fourteenth century the Portuguese like the Spanish people amused themselves with the love and war songs of troubadours. There were many poets who filled the literature with songs of these species. During the latter part of the fifteenth century a poet by name Gil Vicente wrote many miracle plays for the people and also comedies of various kinds. This poet holds also honourable position in Spanish literature. On the occasion of the birth of John III in June 1502, he produced and took a leading part in the performance of a pastoral drama. He wrote many comedies, tragedies, tragic-comedies, farces and autos. This famous poet was said to be the first who introduced regular dramas. A drama of his was performed at Lisbon in 1504. Historians deny to him this claim for praise—however, he was said to be a comic writer of great reputation. His contemporaries were Antonio Prestes, George Pinto and others. They also wrote many plays. George Farreira-de-Vasconcellos wrote many dramas amongst which his Eufrozina is quite up to the modern standard of excellence. Camoens wrote several plays. During the seventeenth century the Spanish influence on Portuguese literature was irressistable and all the serious plays were written in the Castilian dialect while the lighter pieces were written in Portuguese.

Diniz.

Gil Vicente and other poets.

Camoens.

CHAPTER V.

GREAT BRITAIN.

WE learn from History, that the Britains, even before B.C. 55 were gifted with imaginative faculty, skill in music and a taste for literature. The ancient Britons though known as a people of the woods, had all the learning which nature bestows on man. They may not have possessed the artificial alphabet or letters but the deficiency in this respect must have helped them to strengthen their intellectual faculty. We also read that the ancient bards were singing poems of unusual length, containing the deeds of their pagon Gods and heroes.

The ancient Britains.

WE observe in Charles Coote's History of England that the attachment of the islanders to their own language rendered them averse for some time to the acquisition of the Latin tongue notwithstanding the efforts of the Governor Agricola to educate them in Latin. The historian observes "though we have reason to imagine that during the Roman government in Britain there were many natives of distinguished genius, learning and merit, we read of very few Britons approaching that character." Pictorical History of England, Vol. I, says, that Ireland even before the sixth century had old schools in one of which St. Gildas studied. Aneurin who was converted to Christianity was a bard of great fame and wrote the "History of Britain" and an "Epistle to the Tyrants of Britain." Nennius and St. Columbanus were the great authors who lived in the middle of the sixth century and from the writings of the latter it is inferred that Ireland had, even at

Aneurin.

Nennius and St. Columbanus.

that early period, a splendid library. Between the seventh and the eighth centuries lived the Venerable Bede who wrote the Ecclesiastical History of England. Eddius a well known author who lived at this period is said to have taught singing in the Churches of Northumberland. Many of the poets and authors that were patronised by Charlemagne were Irish.

Venerable Bede. Eddius.

THE Saxons of old were gifted with vocal music and they had also instrumental music to help them. Besides bells, they had horns, trumpets, flutes, drums, cymbals, viols, lyres and harps. They had organs as well. The following extract is taken from the Pictorial History of England to show how the Anglo-Saxons of old amused themselves during festivals. "The gleemen were the most important characters in the Anglo-Saxon festivals. They were mimics, dancers, tumblers and performers of sleight of hand tricks, and the rudiments of the Drama are to be traced to some of the performances by which they amused the people. Some of their dances appear to have demanded great exertion and skill. One of these was a sort of war-dance by two men in martial dresses. They were armed each with a sword and a shield and went through a mock combat to the sound of music—the musicians were a man playing upon a horn and a female dancing round the combatants." Elsewhere it is recorded that "the mimic with his antic personifications added enjoyment to the luxuries of the feast. To these may be added the dramatic exhibitions." The same author speaking of the manners and customs of the people between 1066 and 1216 says, "plays founded upon romantic, historical or passing events were already represented before the nobles and citizens; but these primitive attempts

Instrumental music.

Amusements of Saxons.

Rudiments of drama.

Plays.

were so completely in accordance with the grossness and licentiousness of the age, both in language and manners of acting, that they were condemned by the Church and all priests were prohibited from attending them. The immorality of these theatrical exhibitions, awoke not only the ire, but the invective powers of the Church, and the clergy endeavoured to supercede the secular by the religious drama; and hence the origin of those productions called Miracles and Mysteries. The actors were the scholars of the clergy; the Church itself was frequently used as a place of exhibition and the rich vestments and sacred furniture employed in the Church service were sometimes permitted to be used by the actors to give superior truth and lustre to their representations." Before the twelfth century we find mention made of miracle plays. Sanderson says, "In the times of Stephen, we have the earliest extant miracle plays—the acting of which was probably begun in this country soon after the Conquest. The authors and the performers were ecclesiastics. They were represented at the Church on occasions of solemn festivals." Hilarius, an Englishman, living in France, wrote two dramas in the time of Stephen. We have one mystery of Hilarius called the "Raising of Lazarus" composed for the enforcement of the doctrine of Resurrection. The "History of Daniel" was his second play. The plays of Hilarius are known as liturgical mysteries.

Prohibition against Secular plays.

Miracles and Mysteries.

Hilarius and his liturgical mysteries.

IN England as elsewhere, had flourished many kinds of entertainments of a dramatical kind. The amusements of the period are given below. These are extracts from the Pictorial History of England. "The jester was now a regular appendage of a princely or noble household; his office was to divert the jaded spirit of his lord by

Amusements of the people.
(a) Jester. (b) Mummings. (c) Pageants. (d) Dramas.

jests either intellectual or practical and to keep the banquet in a roar by his wit as well as by the jingling of his bells and the grotesque display of his cap and bauble." . . . "Mummings also formed a particular amusement of this period. These seem to have been a coarse and primitive kind of Masquerades where the actors more frequently applied themselves to mimic certain of the brute creation than to support fictitious human characters." . . . . "Pageants were sometimes introduced for the amusement of the guests." . . . "Theatrical amusements were frequented."

Geoffrey.

ONE Geoffrey, an eminent scholar and head-master of the school at Dundee, composed a drama on the legend of St. Catherine for being acted by his scholars. This was probably in the year 1110.

Chester mysteries.

There were Chester mysteries in London which were represented on the stage. The author of the Chester mysteries had to go to Rome three times to obtain leave of the Pope to render the Latin mysteries into the English tongue. In the thirteenth and the fourteenth centuries the parish clerks played interludes in many places. King Richard II, his queen and all the court were present when an interlude was played in London in 1390.

Interludes.

Miracle plays.

The miracle plays written in Latin were performed by the ecclesiastics in the fourteenth century. In spite of their protest and prohibition, laymen commenced and continued to imitate them up to the sixteenth century. The manner of their performance is an interesting study to the Indians who have even now preserved the system in their street plays. "Every company had its pageant, which consisted of a high scaffold with two rooms, a higher and a lower, upon four wheels. In the lower they apparelled themselves and in the higher they played, being all open at the top, that all

Pageants described.

beholders might hear and see them. They played in every street. They began first at the Abbey gates and, when the first pageant was over, it was wheeled to the higher cross before the Mayor, and so on to every street; and so every street had a pageant playing before them at one time till all the pageants appointed for the day were played; and when the pageant ended, word was brought from street to street so that they might come in place thereof, exceedingly orderly, and all the streets have their pageants afore them all at one time playing together to see which player was a great resort and also scaffolds and stages made in the streets in those places where they determined to play their pageants." Another description of the pageant vehicle is given in "Hone's Table Book" with an engraving of the vehicle and also of the actors in it. There is a short poem about the attraction of this pageant :—

> "The state and reverence and show
> Were so attractive, folks would go
> From all parts, every year, to see
> These pageants play at Coventry."

No regularly built theatre.

FROM the above extract we can infer that there was no regularly built theatre in England up to the sixteenth century. Whatever may have been the modes of performances in Europe and other parts of Asia in ancient times, we Indians, have a model of them all still preserved in our native land. It may be that other nations took models from India at one time or other, but how and by what means, or through whom, it is not possible at this distant date to say definitely; or it may be that every nation instinctively or independently passed through these stages of natural development.

IN ancient Rome we found the feast of Saturnalia. In England we had the following feasts during which tomfooleries of all sorts were practised by the people who did not care for the authority of the clergy or the king. They were :—

(a) Feast of Fools—

Feast of Fools.

"This was enacted by the populace at large. Its celebration, which took place at the Christmas time, somewhat resembled the Saturnalia of ancient Rome. It was a season of universal license among the commonalty in which all orders and authorities were reversed; the churl became a Pope, the buffoon a Cardinal and the lowest of the mob were converted into priests and right reverend Abbots. In this wild merriment they took possession of the churches and parodied every part of the sacred service, singing Masses consisting of obscene songs and preaching sermons full of all sorts of lewdness and buffoonery."

(b) Dance of Fools—

Dance of Fools.

"This exhibition which was also held during Christmas consisted of a set of drolleries sufficiently profane, the actor who figured in the pageant, being dressed in all respects like the court-fool a personage who as he occupied the highest place of his order became naturally the model to all the fools of England."

(c) The Boy Bishop—

The Boy Bishop.

"In this ridiculous farce, the boys belonging to the choirs of the Collegiate churches, on the arrival of the feast ot St. Nicholas or of the Holy Innocents (and often on both occasions) dressed themselves in full pontificals and obtained possession of the sacred building, while one of their number for the time became the prelate and was adorned with *mitre aud Crozier*. The urchins then proceeded to mimic the devotional services of their clerical superiors; they prayed, chanted and performed mass, and the Boy-Bishop from the altar or the pulpit delivered a sermon to the crowd that assembled to witness the sport and received from them contributions of money at the conclusion of the service. After this profane parody, the whole choir sallied into the streets headed by their juvenile prelate, dancing and singing from house to house, scattering clerical benedictions among the people and receiving offerings in their progress." To know the details of the origin of the mysteries and also that of the feasts known as the "Feast of Fools," "The Feast of the Ass" "The December Liberties," "The Feast of Calends," and the "Boy Bishop," I would refer my Indian readers to the book "Ancient Mysteries Described" by W. Hone and also to the "History of English Poetry" by Warton.

State of the clergy.

WE see the clergy of the twelfth century already growing rich and consequently indolent. In learning the laymen mostly took their place. The necessary consequence was that regard for the clergy lost ground and occasionally satires against them were performed publicly. The poet Walter-de-Map, a court poet, wrote in the twelfth century a sharp satire called "The Confessions of the Bishop of Goliath" and it is a pointed attack on the evil livers among the clergy. This poet was a favourite of the king, a royal chaplain, justiciary and an ambassador. He tried his best to reform the church. The church was corrupt, indolent, avaricious and immoral. The hero of this powerful satire was an imaginary priest by name Goliath representing the class of the clergy of the time. In the satire he is made to hold the wine cup, but his hands shake and he is powerless having been already quite drunk. He sings a drunkard's song. I give below four lines from it :—

Walter-de-Map & his "Confessions of the Bishop of Goliath."

"Die I must, but let me die in an inn
Hold the wine cup to my lips sparkling from the bin
So when angels flutter down to take me from my sin
Ah, God, have mercy on this sot, the cherubs will begin."

Gerald.

AT about this time we also read of a clergyman of immense intellectual powers by name *Gerald* writing satires attacking the system of Civil Government. His appointment as a Bishop was not approved by Henry the Second. He lived in the latter part of the twelfth century and the commencement of the thirteenth. The fourteenth century is not very conspicuous in the matter of dramatical literature and representation. Between the fifteenth and the sixteenth centuries, ancient classical dramas were introduced into England and some of the classical dramas were translated.

Masquerades or Ludi.

During the reign of Henry IV many masqueradings under the classical name of *Ludi* were frequently performed at Court. These formed a part of the national festivities at Christmas. The theatre had a hold on the national life of the people. There were companies of players in the establishment of Richard III, Henry VII and Henry VIII. The actors' position was considerably raised by Henry VIII who employed them at court. His liberality made many actors rich. The local Earls of Leicester, Warwick and Worcester had dramatical companies of their own, and the leading members like the elder Burbage were actors. Much satire was freely made use of in the moralities. From the thirteenth to the fifteenth centuries and even in the middle of the sixteenth century people found pleasure in miracle plays with farces and moralities which contained sharp satires. An eccentric English scholar of high attainments and poet of the fifteenth century is John Skelton. This eminent scholar and churchman is the author of satires against the clergy of his time and also against the great Cardinal who almost ruled England. "Colin Clout" and "Why Come Ye Not To Court" are masterpieces of satire and merciless ridicule composed by this poet. A. W. Ward,

Theatrical companies

John Skelton.

Colin Clout. Why Come Ye Not To Court.

the author of the "English Dramatic Literature," observes that "Skelton by his fearless writings brought down upon himself the ill-will of literary as well as political contemporaries; he was sneered at by Barclay and persecuted by Wolsey. Skelton is extremely and ostentatiously coarse, but it cannot be said of him that he panders to vice or prostitutes himself to the service of immorality. The ends of his satire were in the main moral; and its tendency was in full sympathy with the great movement of his age. His political note is the hatred of the ecclesiastical domination which was one of the motive forces of the Reformation; his literary note is the return to natural sense and vivacity which was one of the main springs of the Reneisance."

Stage-an instrument to reform religion.

DURING the Tudor period people began to discuss upon the questions relating the ecclesiastical affairs. There were many changes brought about as the result of their discussion. Though there were many prohibitions against the popular stage enacting any play touching on religious questions, the people encouraged the stage. They could not dispense with "so convenient an organ of public opinion or sentiment in connection with topics occupying them above all others."

Interludes.

Many interludes were also performed bearing on religious questions of the day. King Edward VI is said to have himself composed an elegant comedy which was designated as 'The Whore of Babylon.' During Queen Mary's reign, "a morality called 'Republica' was represented at the court which was bitterly anti-Protestant in sentiment and introduced Queen Mary herself in the character of Nemesis." By the side of morality plays bearing upon religious controversy, England had also political morality. A play called "The Sackful of News" is stated to have been prohibited by the order of the Privy Council. England

The Whore of Babylon.

Republica Morality play.

Sackful of News.

had also festival plays such as "Hox Tuesday" play. The nature of the morality play is explained in the following, by the author of "The English Dramatical Literature," Vol. I, page 121.

Festival plays.

"IN our English morality, after a brief prologue spoken by a messenger, the action opens with a scene in heaven, where God looking down upon the sinful earth perceives how every man lives after his pleasure as if ignoring the utter uncertainty of tenure of human life. He therefore calls upon death, His mighty Messenger, to proceed to every man and summon him to undertake a pilgrimage which he in no wise may escape and bid him bring without delay a sure reckoning. Death delivers his message to every man who at once appears on the scene and who tries in vain by pleas and bribes to turn away the summons. Then having received a hint that he should "prove his friends if he can" to see whether any of them is so hardy as to accompany him on the journey which he must take. Every man left alone in his terror bethinks him of appealing to his old friend "Fellowship"—his comrade in many a day of sport and play—to go with him. Fellowship accosted as he passes over the stage, is full of assurances for which he will not be thanked. But a mention of the service required soon brings a change over his professions, though he is quite at every man's service for a dinner or a murder or anything of that sort. When he has departed and every man has made a similarly futile appeal to two associates called kindred and cousin he calls to mind one other friend whom he has loved all his life, in his distress. 'Goods' as this abstraction is called—Property would be the modern equivalent—was doubtless represented on the stage by some grotesque allegorical figure. He also disappoints every man and so also "Good-deeds." Then every man appeals to knowledge and with her help addressed

Morality play explained.

himself to 'Confession' who bestows upon him a precious jewel called 'Penance.' With his help every-man appears before the judgment seat. This is the sample of the morality play of the time and in this, various characters, *viz.*, Beauty, Strength, Discretion, Vice, etc., appear.

N. Udal.

NICHOLAS Udal, an eminent scholar and head-master of Eton school, established a theatre at Eton and wrote several plays in Latin to be acted in the long wintry nights by his boys. This renowned head-master is styled the father of English comedy, for he wrote many English comedies for being represented by his scholars. These plays were written at about 1540. His comedy "Ralph Roister Doister" ridiculing conceit and swagger, describes the London manners of the time vividly. This was the first regular English comedy. It is divided into acts and scenes and takes two hours and a half for its performance. Roister Doister is a vain-glorious cowardly blockhead who in his courtship of Dame Custame, a gay widow, falls a victim to the wiles of a servant and sadly discomfited, at last joins in with the humour of others and consents to the union of the Dame with a merchant. At or about the year 1565, John Still, Bishop of Bath, wrote a comedy called "Gammer Gurton's Needle." This was represented in Christ's College at Cambridge. This comedy is based upon a very simple incident of a foolish woman losing her needle and throwing the village into a confusion. A famous scholar by name Thomas Sackville, who subsequently became High Treasurer of England, helped the progress of English dramatical literature assisted by one Thomas Norton. His tragedy of "Gorboduc" was acted in Christmas 1561 at the Inner Temple and was also represented at Whitehall in 1562 before Elizabeth. This is the first regular English tragedy written in blank verse.

Regular English comedy. Roister Doister.

John Still. Gammer Gurton's Needle.

Thomas Sackville.

Gorboduc tragedy.

The plot of Gorboduc is thus stated in the argument of the Tragedy :—"Gorboduc, King of Britain, divided his realm in his life-time to his two sons Ferrax and Porrex. The sons fell to dissension. The younger killed the elder. The mother that loved more dearly the elder, for revenge killed the younger. The people moved with the cruelty of the fact rose in rebellion and slew the father and mother. The nobility assembled and most terribly destroyed the rebels; and afterwards for want of issue of the prince whereby the succession to the crown became uncertain they fell to Civil war in which both they and many of their issue were slain and the land for a long time was desolate and miserably wasted." The above argument goes much against the dramatic attainments of the author. As it is, the audience is expected, throughout the drama, to prepare themselves to hear the death news of the members connected with the Royalty and the country.

Apius & Virginia Tragedy. The second tragedy is "Apius and Virginia" by an unknown author. It was acted in 1563 by the Westminister scholars. The epilogue to this play sings "God save the Queen."

Preston. Cambises. The third tragedy is "Cambises" by Preston. It was written or exhibited in 1569–70. Preston was a Fellow of the King's College at Cambridge. He was a good actor. He is said to have "performed so well in the tragedy of Dido before Queen Elizabeth that, on account of this excellence and his prowess in disputation, she with unusual generosity granted him an annual allowance of £20. He afterwards became the master of "Trinity Hall."

Gascoignes' Jocasta. "Jocasta" by Gascoignes who was assisted by two other eminent men of the day is a tragedy represented at Grays Inn in 1566. This tragedy also is composed in blank verse.

Tancred and Segismonda. "Tancred and Segismonda" is a tragedy composed by five members of the Inner Temple and presented there before Queen Elizabeth in 1568. It is the first English play founded on the plot of an Italian novel. Here, Tancred the father, surprising his daughter Segismonda when with her lover, causes him to be put to death and his heart placed in a golden cup to be presented to his daughter. She fills the cup with poison and drinks her death from it; and her dying wish to be reunited with her lover in the tomb is carried out by the broken hearted father who slays himself with his own hands. In this tragedy both Segismonda and her father die on the stage. Whetstones' "Promos and Cassandra" is another tragedy whose incidents were taken from an Italian novel of Cinthio. In the dedication of this play the author exhibits a highly critical spirit, condemning the dramatic tastes of the principal literary men of Europe. The passage is worth being quoted. "At this day the Italian is so lascivious in his comedies that honest hearers are grieved at his actions; the Frenchman and the Spaniard follows the Italian humour; The German is too holy; for he presents on every common stage what preachers should pronounce in pulpits. The Englishman in this quality is most vain, indiscreet and out of order: he first grounds his works on impossibilities; then in three hours runs he through the world, marries, gets children, makes children men, men to conquer kingdoms, murder masters, and bringeth Gods from the Heaven and fetcheth devils from Hell. . . . ." If objections were taken on this score, there would be no dramatical literature and there would be no dramatical performance. The author should credit the audience with imaginative faculty to some extent. Imagination is capable of constructing for itself the bridges necessary to preserve an action and its continuity. One other tragedy chiefly noticed by the author of the English Dramatical Literature is the tragedy entitled "Misfortunes of Arthur." This was acted before Queen Elizabeth at Greenwich in 1588. Eight members of the Society of Grays Inn co-operated in its

Whetstones' Promos & Cassandra.

Thomas Huges The Misfortunes of Arthur.

composition. Thomas Huges was the author of the whole body of the play. Francis Bacon, who was at that time already a Bencher of Grays Inn and had sat in Parliament, had also helped towards its completion. It is a pure English tragedy. Historical dramas were also written during the sixteenth century. The famous "Victories of Henry V" was performed in 1588. It is this historical drama whence Shakespeare collected materials for his Henry V. Richard Tarleton performed the part of Derrick, the clown. He was the manager of the company of twelve members appointed by Queen Elizabeth for dramatical performances. For the clown's part Tarleton never had his equal. Even Ben-Jonson applauded him. "His humour was of an irresistible kind." We are told that "the self same words spoken by another would hardly move a merry man to smile, which uttered by him would force a sad soul to laughter." He was also an author of a dramatic performance called "The Seven Deadly Sins." "The Troublesome Reign of King John" was another historical drama that was performed in 1591. In 1593 "The True Chronicle History of King Lear and His Three Daughters" was acted. The Inns of Court had often theatrical amusements. A play was a constant part of the entertainment. Queen Elizabeth often honoured the theatres with her presence. It is said that Queen Elizabeth could not do without plays when in town or the country. "The Queen's fondness for dramatic exhibitions or for the pageantry which contained dramatic elements, asserted itself both at her own expense and at that of her subjects from the early years of her reign." In 1577 a company of Italian players performed before the Queen at Windsor. These Italian players, a certain historian observes, "were not tied to any written

Historical dramas.

Richard Tarleton.

The Seven Deadly Sins.

Queen Elizabeth and dramas.

device but who had certain grounds or principles of their own."

> "The Italian Tragedians were so sharp of wit,
> That in one hour's meditation
> They would perform anything in action."

THE age of the Reformation gave a fertile field for satirists to write and act plays of all sorts. In 1529 Luther and his wife were satirized in a Latin morality which was represented at Grays Inn. John Heywood, a strict Roman Catholic, wrote in 1556 a satire called "The Spider and the Fly" in which "the flies are the Roman Catholics and the spiders the Protestants, while Queen Mary is represented by the house maid with her broom (the sword) executing the commands of her master (Christ) and her mistress (the Church)." He also wrote many interludes which, it is said, serve as connecting links between the old moralities and the modern drama. These interludes were introduced into England in the reign of Henry VIII. "They were dramatic dialogues of a satirical nature acted at dinner time between meat and dessert whence the name they bore." These interludes of John Heywood, Mr. Collier observes, "form almost a class by themselves. They are neither miracle plays nor moral plays; but what may be properly and strictly called Interludes, a species of writing of which he has a claim to be considered the inventor, although the term interlude is applied generally to the theatrical productions in the reign of Edward IV." Heywood's interludes however "are all only single acts or more properly scenes and exhibit therefore nothing more than the mere rudiments or embryo of the regular comedy." John Heywood's interludes are many. "A merry play between the Pardoner and the Friar, the Curate and the neighbour Pratte" is a mere fight in the Church. "A merry play between John the Husband, Tyb

John Heywood.

The Spider & the Fly.

Interludes explained.

the wife and Sir John the Priest" is also a farcical domestic quarrel. "The four P's" is an entertaining farce. The humour of the piece is inimitable.

Thomas Heywood.

Thomas Heywood was a good classical scholar, a great author and a dramatic poet. He was also a celebrated actor during the reigns of Elizabeth, James I and Charles I. He is said to have written two hundred and twenty plays. It is also said that several modern authors have borrowed from this dramatist.

Woman Killed by Kindness.

The play "Woman Killed by Kindness" is composed by the author. It is a pathetic tragedy of domestic life. This drama is characterized by Campbell as the author's best performance. "In this play" he says, "the repentance of Mrs. Frankford who dies of a broken heart for her infidelity to a generous husband would present a situation consummately moving if we were left to conceive her death to be produced simply by grief. But the poet most unskilfully prepares us for her death by her declaring her intentions to starve herself and Mars by the weakness, sin and horror of suicide, an example of penitence that would otherwise be sublimely and tenderly edifying." He is styled as the model of light and rapid talent. His distinctive literary gift consists in interfusing homely pathos in the plays. He was endowed with this pathetic power. He thoroughly understood what effective dramatic situations were. Charles Lamb calls him "a prose Shakespeare." His moral purity and natural repose are certainly commendable.

Sir David Lindsay. The Three Estates.

IN 1535, Sir David Lyndsay wrote a satire of the "Three Estates" which is a direct attack against the vices of the clergy in Scotland. This satire was performed before James V and his Queen at Linlithgow. The poems of this dramatist though "often coarse are full of humour, good sense and knowledge of the world and were said to have done more for the Reformation in Scotland than all the sermons of

Knox; for Lindsay shot some of his sharpest shafts at the clergy." He was also unsparing in his exposure of the abuses which had crept into the Government of the Scottish kingdom in the time of James I. In 1543 all plays and interludes which meddled with the interpretation of Scripture were legally prohibited. In 1546 the office of the Master of Revels was established and subsequently in 1549 all kinds of stage plays were stopped. Latin plays were however being acted in the Universities.

Master of Revels appointed.

HALLAM, in his History of Literature, says that the statutes of Trinity College, Cambridge, established in the year 1546 contain a clause to the effect that Latin comedies and tragedies are to be exhibited in its hall in Christmas. Many comedies and tragedies were written for academical representation. Even at this period the writing of miracle plays did not stop. Between 1550 and 1563 John Bale, Bishop of Ossory in Ireland, wrote about twenty miracle plays. They are, it is said, remarkable for having introduced and inculcated the doctrine of the reformed religion. He has also written historical plays; the best of them being "Kynge Johan." The miracle play entitled "The Contention between Liberality and Prodigality" was performed in 1601 before Queen Elizabeth. The authorship of the play was attributed to Robert Green. Mr. Collier observes that "the moral plays were enabled to keep possesion of the stage so long as they did, partly by means of the approaches they had for sometime been making to a more improved species of composition and partly because under the form of allegorical fiction and abstract character the writers introduced matter which covertly touched upon events

John Bale.

Robert Green.

Collier on Moral and other plays of the period.

popular prejudices and temporary opinions." It is said that one Rightwise wrote the tragedy of "Dido" and acted it before Wolsey. Between 1568 and 1580, not less than fifty-two dramas were acted at Court. In 1576 the first public theatre was erected at Blackfriars by the Earl of Leicester's company to whom a license was granted to act plays in any part of England. Several poets wrote dramas and acted them on the stage.

Rightwise. Dido.

Erection of Theatre.

Dramatists before Shakespeare.

Out of the numerous authors of the period, Lyly, Kyd, Greene, Marlow. Peele, John Heywood and Thomas Heywood only are praised as dramatists of merit before the immortal Shakespeare entered upon the stage both as an actor and as an author. Lyly wrote many prose comedies; and his play "The Woman in the Moon" is written in blank verse. In this play the woman is Pandora who creates much mischief among the Utopian shepherds. Thomas Kyd is a dramatist of great fame. His "Spanish Tragedy" is exceptionally popular. This author had been credited with having written the tragedy "Hamlet" and some go to the length of asserting that Shakespeare's Hamlet is only a slight improvement on this. Kyd is a dramatic poet of high and original capacity for dealing with both the matter and the form of the branch of literature tc which he devoted his labours. He proved himself "capable of presenting extraordinary things in original forms and he was at the same time able to exhibit with natural force the operation of incidents upon character and to make a direct and irresistible appeal to the passions that move all men and are felt by generation after generation." Greene was considered the creator of modern English comedy. Though

Lyly. The Woman in the Moon.

Kyd. Spanish tragedy.

Greene.

he was a profligate his writings are pure. He died in 1592.

Marlowe and his Tambourlaine the Great.

Marlowe was a riotous sceptic and he called Moses a Juggler. He said that he would by his plays establish a better religion than Christianity. His "Tambourlaine the Great" in spite of its bombast and violence was considered to be infinitely superior to any tragedy that had yet appeared on the English stage. He was the first to find out the strength of blank verse for the purpose of tragedy.

Edward the Second.

Doctor Foster.

His "Edward the Second" is preferred to Richard II of Shakespeare. His "Doctor Foster" was extraordinarily successful. It is said that this dramatist prepared the way for Shakespearean tragedy. Like Greene, this poet also led a very irregular life and met a violent death in 1593 in a quarrel for a courtesan, when he had not even reached his thirtieth year. In the higher qualities of imagination and in majesty and sweetness of verse he is considered to be inferior only to Shakespeare.

Hazlette's opinion of Marlowe.

Marlowe, says Hazlette, "is a man that stands high and almost first in the list of dramatic worthies. He was a little before Shakespeare's time and has a marked character both from him and from the rest. There is a lust of power in his writings, a hunger and thirst after unrighteousness, a glow of the imagination unhallowed by anything but its own energies. His thoughts burn with him like a furnace with blickering flames or throwing out black smoke and mists that hide the dawn of genius, or like a poisonous mineral that corrodes the heart."

Drayton's opinion of Marlowe.

Drayton, the greatest scholar and poet, speaks of him in the following lines of singular beauty :—

"Next Marlowe, bathed in the Thespian springs
Had in him those brave translunary things
That the first poets had; his raptures were
All air and fire, which made his verses clear
For that fine madness still he did retain
Which rightly should possess a poet's brain."

Ben Jonson refers to "*Marlowe's mighty line*" and some other author describes Marlowe as "Happy in his buskined Muse"—

"Although unhappy in his life and end
Pity it is that wit so ill should dwell
Wit lent from Heaven but vices sent from Hell."

Marlowe is a great dramatist and second only to Shakespeare. I should recommend all to read "The English Dramatic Literature" by A. W. Ward. The author has taken pains to compare the lines of Marlowe's "Jew of Malta" with those of Shakespeare's "Merchant of Venice." All the historians and dramatists are unanimous in the statement, that both in action, characterization and diction Marlowe's Edward II is superior to George Peele's Edward I and Shakespeare's Richard II. In the "Massacre at Paris" and "Dido Queen of Carthage" the author is said to have attained no success. This author is justly styled the earliest of the English dramatists of fame. George Peele was an actor and a dramatist who wrote many plays and died in 1598.

Jew of Malta.

Massacre at Paris. Dido Queen of Carthage.

George Peele.

MOST of the plays of the abovementioned authors were acted by one of the two companies licensed to play dramas in England. In one of these two famous companies the Immortal Shakespeare was an actor. His London life commenced in 1587. It is said that he was decried as an actor before he was known as an author. This I very much doubt. An inspired hero will fail in nothing. It might be a complete want of appreciative attainment in the audience. As an author and an actor he "intensified the national character." It is a pure unalloyed pleasure to read his works; one forgets one's self when reading them. To expatiate on the merits of his works is to fill up volumes, which indeed has been done by some.

Shakespeare.

To render them into other languages is to weaken the force of his language and take away his charming beauties. Edgar Sanderson, M.A., a historian, is justified in his remark that the works of Shakespeare are the second Bible of the English race. This immortal dramatist, himself an actor, found in Richard Burbage, the greatest actor to interpret his greatest dramatic creations. Burbage was known to be the best tragic actor of the time. The poet Flecknoe describes him in the following terms :—" He was a delightful Proteus so wholly transforming himself into his part and putting off himself with his clothes as he never (not so much as in the tiring house) assumed himself again until the play was done. He had all the parts of an excellent orator, animating his words with speaking and speech with acting, his auditors being never more delighted than when he spoke, nor more sorry than when he held his peace. Yet even then, he was an excellent actor still, never failing in his part when he had done speaking but with his looks and gestures maintaining still to the height."

Richard Burbage. Opinions about this actor.

" He was the admired example of the age
And so observed all your dramatic laws
He never went off the stage but with applause
Who, his spectators and his auditors
Led in such silent chains of eyes and ears
As none whilst he on the stage his part did play
Had power to speak or look another way."

Baker's Chronicle contains the following :—

" Richard Burbage and Edward Allen two such actors as no age must ever look to see the like." Canden in his annals of James I, calls him a second Roscius. Such a great actor must have been of immense value to Shakespeare in the interpretation of his ideas. Shakespeare is unrivalled in his historical dramas as Ben Jonson in his comedies.

Ben-Jonson.
Every Man in His Humour
The Case is Altered
The Devil Is An Ass.

BEN JONSON's comedy "Every Man in His Humour" is unalloyedly beautiful. Mr. Collier calls Ben Jonson "the Mirror of manners." In his comedy "The Case Is Altered." he vividly describes how the spectators of the period comported themselves in the theatre. It is a comedy of intrigue. In the comedy "The Devil Is An Ass" he describes the demeanour of a gallant occupying a seat upon the stage as follows :—

"To day I go to the Blackfriars play house
Sit in the view, salute all my acquaintance
Rise up between the acts, let fall my cloak
Publish a handsome man and a rich suit
And that is a special end why we go thither."

"Every Man In His Humour" is justly recognised as a comedy of character proper produced on the English stage. A large proportion of this comedy is in prose. In the prologue to this play, Ben Jonson points out his intention and says that he will not try to delight the audience by mechanical means but only point out human follies. The personages in the play are all real. Captain Bobadil, a Military braggart, is brought to a fall. Charles Dickens was very fond of taking this character for his part.

Every Man Out Of His Humour.

"Every Man Out Of His Humour" is another comedy of his where it is pointed out that every humour is curable by its own excess. In this play two characters are introduced, one to expound the poet's reasons for his dramatic procedure, while the other to urge objections. This is also a comedy of character. "An envious man, a brutal cynic, a pseudo-romantic knight, an empty fool of fashion, a silly city lady, an usurious corn merchant and his rustic brother, all these characters are drawn to the life." This comedy has a moral aim.

Cynthia's Revels.

His "Cynthia's Revels or the Fountains of Self love" is rather a satire than a comedy. The object of the play was most probably to contrast the aim of a true poet with the imbecile follies of those who write for the demands of a depraved and absurd fashion.

Poetastes.

Ben Jonson's comedy "Poetastes" is also a satire. Its object was "to frighten off his adversaries from executing their schemes of avenging upon him the real or supposed wrongs they had suffered at his hands." The comedy of "Volpone" has a moral aim.

Volpone.

The avarice of a villainous Venetian Magnifico is punished in the end. It points out the moral depravity of the age and the author indignantly satirizes upon it. "The Silent Woman" is another comedy.

The Silent Woman.

Dryden in his "Essays of Dramatic Poesy" observes that the intrigue of this play is the "greatest and most noble of any pure unmixed comedy in any language." Coleridge calls it "the most entertaining of Jonson's comedies." The plot is based upon a trick very ordinary among the Hindus. "An old misanthrope to whom all noise is odious marries what he believes to be a silent woman but what proves a talkative body and is ultimately discovered to be a boy." Here the silent woman in the end has to metamorphose herself to a boy. Ben Jonson's comedy "The Alchemist" is esteemed as one of the most notable works.

The Alchemist.

It is a direct satire against the Puritans and the impostors. "Bartholomew Fair" is another comedy of the author which acquired immense success and became very popular.

Bartholomew Fair.

It strongly attacks the Puritans as the natural enemies of playhouses.

GEORGE Chapman is also a great dramatist. He is the translator of many works. His tragedies are good, some of them having attained popularity; but I pass over his tragedies. His comedies are many.

G. Chapman.

The Blind Beggar of Alexandria.

"The Blind Beggar of Alexandria" (1598) is based upon an improbable romance. "An Humourous Day's Mirth" contains an original plot consisting of a series of tricks played for the sake of sport by a mischievous courtier upon a doting old husband and a doting old wife. The comedy of "All Fools" is admirably worked out though the plot is intricate. "The pair of fathers of whom one is deceived by means of a trick, which he helps to play on his friend and neighbour and against the jealous husband and the frivolous gallant are effectively played off against one another; and with a poetic justice not always observable in the comic drama, the disreputable Rivaldo who sets them all by the ears is himself "galled" by his own cupidity." The writing of the play is said to be excellent both in matter and form. The other comedies of the author are (1) The Gentleman Usher (2) Monsiur d'Olive (3) May-day (4) The Widow's Tears. These require no notice. The author is reputed to have helped his contemporary poets in their attempts to write dramas. Thomas Dekker was another dramatist of the period. His comedy "The Shoe-maker's Holiday" wherein the poet says that he purposes nothing but mirth is full of abundant mirth. In this play, the manners and customs of the gentle craft are depicted. The other comedies are (1) Old Fortunatus (2) Satiro Mastix (3) The Honest Whore, Parts I and II (4) The Whore of Babylon (5) If it be not good the Devil is in it (6) Match me in London (7) The Wonderful Kingdom. His "*Satiro Mastix*" is an attack upon Ben Jonson. This comedy is known by the name of "The Untrussing of the Humourous Poet." In "The Honest Whore" the realities of London life are depicted and the terrible sins of London are strongly described. "The Whore of Babylon" is a comedy of no merit. The overthrow of the Spanish Armada and of the plots against the life of Elizabeth are the main springs of

An Humaurous Day's Mirth.

All Fools.

T. Dekker.

The Shoe-maker's Holiday.

the play. It shows the political feeling of England against Rome and Spain. Thomas Middleton was also a dramatist of the Elizabethan period. It was he that gave a real start to Romantic dramas. "The Old Law," "Blurt, Master-Constable," "The Phoenix," "The Witch" and "More Dissemblers besides Women". are his comedies. The story in the "Old Law" is that a certain Duke with a desire to test the virtue of his subjects proclaimed a law that all old men living to the age of eighty years and all women of more than sixty should be cut off as useless members of the Commonwealth. Except by one dutiful son and wife, the law was obeyed by all. The dutiful son hid his father. The Duke after enquiry promulgated another law ordaining that no son or heir shall be held capable of inheritance at the age of twenty-one, unless he be at the time as mature in obedience, manners and goodness, and that no wife who has designed her husband's death shall be allowed to marry for ten years after it has taken place. The comedy of "The Phoenix" is a social satire. Prince Phoenix who was asked by his father to travel abroad to gain experience of the world, travels in his own city in disguise and finds out the vagaries of men of different professions and brings them before the Duke for trial. Middleton's comedies of manners are also many. His "Michlemas Term" is a satire against the every day follies and vices of the age. Usurer's deceptions are well described. His comedy. "A Trick to catch the Old One" describes with spirit the character of a lawyer of the most disreputable kind. The author's play "No Wit, No Help—like a Woman's" is a comedy of intrigue. The comedy called "A Game at Chess" by the same author is a strong satire against the highest personages of the

T. Middleton.

The Old Law.
The Blurt Master-Constable.
The Phoenix
The Witch.

Michlemas Term.

A Trick to catch the Old One.

No Wit, No Help—like a Woman's.

kingdom as well as a foreign sovereign and a displomatist.

S. Daniel.

PASSING by some authors of note, we come to Samuel Daniel who wrote many comedies of an ordinary kind which do not require any special mention here, but who is being remembered as a dramatist who helped the growth of pastoral dramas in England. "The Queen's Arcadia" is a pastoral drama that was presented in 1605 at Christ Church, Oxford, before Queen Anne. The false and perverted civilization which worked immense mischief in Arcadia is vividly described. A physician, a lawyer and a religious charlatan are introduced in the play as agents of corruption. His second pastoral drama "Hyman's Triumph" was played in 1614 before Queen Anne. This play is extolled by Coleridge and other writers.

Pastoral dramas. The Queen's Arcadia. Hyman's Triumph.

Beaumont and Fletcher.

BEAUMONT and Fletcher wrote many tragedies and comedies jointly and severally. Great sweetness of pathos and unbounded vivacity of humour are the peculiar characteristics of Fletcher. "The Woman Hater" is an independant work of Beaumont. It is a sort of burlesque. The plot is not a natural one. "The Faithful Shepherdess" is a pastoral drama composed by Fletcher. It is extolled as a work of true poetic merit. A. W. Ward observes that "The Faithful Shepherdess" remains, in even excellence of execution, without a rival among the examples preserved to us of the pastoral drama of the Elizabethan age." "The Scornful Lady" is a composition of both authors. The lady is a "shrewish coquette brought to compliance at last by a trick; her lovers are uninteresting." "The Maids Tragedy" is also a joint composition of these authors. This tragedy enjoyed a high popularity till the time of the closing of the

The Woman Hater.

The Faithful Shepherdess.

The Scornful Lady.

The Maid's Tragedy.

theatres. Under Charles II its performance was prohibited as it contained the killing of the king by the heroine Evadne and such exhibitions would serve as examples to other Evadnes. "Evadne the heroine scorns to be loved by any but a king and in her sinful ambition she consents to screen her guilt by a marriage shamefully contrived by her paramour. She heartlessly constrains her husband to second that vile scheme but she is cast in too grand a mould to carry out her part in the arrangement. When at last a spirit as fearless as her own is brought face to face with her shame, her brothers' unflinching determination moves her guilty soul to the resolution of taking vengeance on her seducer." She takes vengeance by killing him and herself.

"A King or no King." The theme is in itself immoral. "A King or no King" is another play of the joint authors. In the treating of this play I intend quoting a portion of the criticism on the play by A. W. Ward in his "English Dramatic Literature." He observes "No blame need be visited on a later generation for having refused to applaud so unhealthy, though in many respects brilliant, a production. The motive of the plot remains monstrous under the most poetic treatment—such as has been more than once applied to it—and in the present instance is not redeemed by the anticlimax which is supposed to put things right. Arbaces, King of Iberia, entertains a seemingly incestuous love for his supposed sister *Panthea* which she, though less ardently, returns. In the end it is discovered that they are not brother and sister (and he no king), so that their union not only becomes possible but furnishes the solution of the knot. The immorality of the idea of such a plot lies elsewhere than in the circumstances of the passion to which the hero of the play for a long time guiltily gives way. Revolting as these may be, they are not dramatically unwarrantable, provided that the wrong brings its punishment with it, and "Phedre" and other plays of the same description, though hovering on a dangerous brink, have been saved by virtue of the moral balance preserved in them by the author. But no moral recovery takes place where a consciously intended wrong becomes an actual right; nor is the morally guilty passion of Arabaces and Panthea purified *ex-post-facto* by the discovery that they might have entertained without offending against divine or human law."

Cupid's Revenge.

"*Cupid's Revenge*,"—the theme of this play is also immoral. "A certain king advised by his daughter Hidaspes and his son Leucippus stops the customary rites of the God Cupid who in return takes revenge by making Hidaspes love a dwarf, and Leucippus fall in unworthy passion for the widow Bacha. The dwarf was killed by the king and Hidaspes kills herself. Leucippus when his guilt was discovered makes an honest confession. The aged king himself becomes enamoured of her fading charms and marries her. The Queen Bacha desires her *now step-son* to continue her paramour as usual which he refuses. In vengeance Bacha slays him with her own hand." In this story, the social and moral responsibility of man is set at naught. The tragedy "Thierry and Theodoret" is certainly a horrible play with all the redeeming features it has in it. That a mother with the aid of her paramour, her pander and her physician, should contrive to murder her sons is loathsome and ferocious.

Thierry and Theodoret.

Love's Cure.

"Love's Cure" is a sort of comedy written by these authors. In this a young woman is brought up as a man and a young man is brought up as a woman. They both require love's sharp cure.—

The following plays are written by Fletcher alone :—

(1) Wit without Money (2) Bondeua (3) Valentinian (4) The Loyal Subject (5) The Mad Lover (6) The Humourous Lieutenant (7) Woman Pleased (8) The Island Princes (9) The Piligrim (10) The Wild Goose (11) Monsieur Thomas

(12) The Woman's Prize (13) A Wife for a Month (14) Rule a Wife and have a Wife (15) The Chances.

Valentinian.

"*Valentinian*" is a tragedy where a tyrant Valentinian falls in illicit love with Leucina—the wife of Maximus. Her honour is ruined and she dies. The husband takes revenge by killing the tyrant and taking his widow for his wife. The new queen murders Maximus. Such a theme for a tragedy is not desirable.

The Loyal Subject.

"*The Loyal Subject*" is a comedy highly praised for the choice of subject, vividness of characterization and excellence of style.

The Humourous Lieutenant.

"The Humourous Lieutenant" is a romantic comedy full of indecorous passages leading to grossness and immorality. It however has the redeeming feature of the fidelity of Celia Enanthe to her absent husband Demetrius in spite of the advances of the king. Celia's reply to the king is shortly given by the poet in the following lines :—

> Celia (rising) "I cannot love you
> Without the breach of faith I cannot trust you
> You hang upon my love like frosts on lilies
> I cannot die, but I cannot love. You are answered." (Exit).

The Woman's Prize.

"The Woman's Prize" is a comedy where a wife with her cunning tricks tames her husband who was proud of having tamed to gentleness his previous wife. Fletcher has written many comedies with the poet Massinger. They are no more than mere farces.

The Custom of the Country.

One of them "The Custom of the Country" is said to contain unpardonable licentiousness. Though historians place Beaumont and Fletcher by the side of Shakespeare, the works of these joint authors show that they did not rise above the spirit of the age with reference to the social relationship between man and woman. The authors seem devoid of conception of female purity.

State of England.

THE court of James I was very licentious, and the manners of the people of England during the early part of the seventeenth century grew more and more unrestrained. This tendency to indecent realism tempted even Shakespeare but he triumphed over it by his great genius. Most of the dramatists that lived in the reigns of James I and Charles I were not free from this blemish. The Puritans who were gaining ground during this period remarked that the theatres were so many schools of sedition and chapels of the Devil. The dramatists and the actors with a purpose to taunt them did more mischief than what the Puritans remarked on.

Philip Massinger.

PHILIP Massinger has written many kinds of dramas. "His style and sentiments," it is said, "are altogether those of a man polished by intercourse of good society." The beauty of his language is also much praised. He is ranked as a tragic writer, second to Shakespeare. He is an exception to the dramatists of his age. His strength lies largely in his perception of moral forces and in his regard for them. "Massinger as a tragic poet appears to me," says Hallam, "second only to Shakespeare; in the higher comedy I can hardly think him inferior to Jonson. In wit and sprightly dialogue as well as in knowledge of dramatic effect he falls very much below Fletcher." Massinger was a man of steady religious piety. His play "New Way to pay old Debts" obtained extraordinary popularity. The chief person in the comedy is Sir Giles Over-reach whose vicious character is described in the following lines of the author :—

New Way to pay old Debts.

"To have a usurer that starves himself
And wears a cloak of one and twenty years
On a suit of fourteen groats, bought of the hangman,
To grow rich, and then purchase, is too common;
But this Sir Giles feeds high, keeps many servants
Who must at his command do any outrage :

Rich in his habit, vast in his expenses,
Yet he to admiration still increases
In wealth, and lordship.
He frights men out of their estates
And breaks through all law nets, made to curb ill men,
And they were cobwebs. *No* man dares reprove him.
Such a spirit to dare, and power to do, were never
Lodged so unluckily."

This wicked man cunningly encouraged the prodigality of his nephew, obtained mortgage bonds from him and thus ruined him and others. He hated all wisdom except that of a worldly kind. He involved his neighbours in law suits keeping the judge in his pay. To obtain wealth and to reduce the nobility, is the aim of this character. This wicked man even persuades his daughter "to make light of her virgin purity in order to gain the end which he has in view." In the end he is overthrown and his daughter marries the husband of her own choice. His nephew recovers his bonds. Over-reach goes mad.

The Roman Actor.

"*The Roman Actor*" is a tragedy of a very extraordinary kind. In this tragedy the author defends the profession of an actor. Aesop and Paris are introduced and made to speak as follows :—

AESOP ... "For the profit, Paris
And mercenary gain, they are things beneath us.
PARIS ... Our aim is glory and to leave our names
To after time."

This play is the more charming as in it is introduced a play within the play thrice. The story is about the tragic death of the actor Paris whom Domitian's Mistress seduced.

The Picture.

"*The Picture*" is a comedy containing a beautiful fable worked out with great vigour. The plot runs as follows :—

"Mathias, a poor knight of Bohemia, on sallying forth to relieve his poverty by the need of warlike achievements, obtains from his friend Julio Baptista, a great scholar, a picture of his wife Sophia, which possesses the magic property of changing its hues according to the variations of sentiment and conduct in the conjugal fidelity of its original. Husband and wife are at heart true to one another; but their fidelity is in either case exposed to sore temptations. Mathias' heroic exploits in the service of the King of Hungary bring him to the notice of the imperious Queen Honoria whose haughty temper brooks no rivalry and—to tempt him in person to infidelity, while at the same time seeking to seduce Sophia from the path of virtue by means of two lying courtiers, sent to her with false reports of her husband's conduct. Sophia is thus made to waver in her constancy; and on the picture revealing to Mathias the condition of her mind, he is likewise about to give way to the supposed passion of the queen. But Sophia's virtue is proof against the dangers by which it is beset; and the two courtiers are deservedly caught in their own toils. The Queen sees the error of her ways, and becomes the submissive wife of her uxorious husband; while Sophia after reading Mathias a severe lesson on the wrongfulness of his jealous fears which caused him to provide himself with the test of the picture, is restored to happiness."

The Bashful Lover.

"*The Bashful Lover*" is an interesting romantic drama that was acted in 1636 for the first time. Massinger has written other dramas, some independently and some conjointly with Fletcher, Field Middleton and Rowley. A. W. Ward observes that "the moral dignity of his sentiment is at once the basis and the source of much of his highest dramatic effectiveness."

N. Field.

NATHANIAL Field was an author and actor of great fame as the following lines will show:—

"Field is in sooth an actor, all men know it
And is the true Othello of the poet."

His comedy "A Woman is a Weathercock" is the story of Cressida. Woman's fickleness is well depicted in the play. In order to make amends for females whom he insulted by the above play he wrote another drama called "Amends for Ladies."

A Woman is a Weathercock.

Amends for Ladies.

John Ford.—This author produced many tragedies and comedies. The "Lover's Melancholy," "It is a pity she is a whore," "The Broken Heart," "Love's Sacrifice" "Francis chaste and noble," "The Lady's trial," "Perkin Warbeck" are the plays of this author. "The Broken Heart" has an extraordinary plot, the details of which are written below as taken from a foot-note of the play from the English Dramatical Literature by A. W. Ward. "A youthful pair of lovers, Orgilus and Panthea, have been separated by the ambition of the lady's valerous brother, the Spartan general Ithocles. He has caused Panthea to marry Bassanes, a jealous dotard whose insane suspiciousness of itself suffices to drive the suffering Panthea to distraction. Ithocles bitterly repents his act; Orgilus, in order to gain access to Panthea, has pretended a journey to Athens, while in reality remaining at Sparta in the disguise of a pupil of philosophy in the school of the wise Tecnicus. In an interview with Panthea, however, he learns that no hope is left for him—she loves him still but will not stain her honour by breaking the loathsome bond to which she is condemned. To take vengeance upon Ithocles, the original author of his and Panthea's misery, now becomes the object of the life of Orgilus. Ithocles is enamoured of the Princess Calantha, whose hand her royal father wishes to bestow upon the Prince of Argos; and in order to further his revenge, Orgilus urges on this desperate suit. Calantha returns the affections of Ithocles; having been sweetly moved thereto by Panthea; and Orgilus resolves to prepare for them a misery like that to which he has been doomed himself. Thus the situation is wrought

The Broken Heart.

up towards the climax. The death of the gentle Panthea who has lost her reason, but with her dying breath bewails her lover's wretchedness and her brother's cruelty, determines Orgilus to accomplish his purpose. This he effects by a strangely realistic device. In the presence of the wronged Panthea's corpse, Ithocles is inveigled into a chair so contrived as to hold fast the sitter in an inextricable grasp; and then Orgilus stabs his victim, who dies without a groan. Meanwhile a festival is in progress at court over which the king being mortally sick has asked his daughter Calantha to preside. While she is leading the measure, the tidings are brought to her, first of her father's death, then of Panthea's, then of that of her beloved Ithocles—the last message being whispered to her by the murderer himself. But in each case she orders the dance to proceed; and then calmly causing the intelligence to be repeated to her, bids the self confessed assassin make himself ready for death and orders her coronation, for she is now queen to be proceeded with. In the last act all are assembled for the solemnity, when Calantha, clad in her royal robes, proclaims her last will making over her kingdom to the Argive Prince and disposing of the great offices of the state. She then declares that the oracle sent from Delphos by Tecnicus, which had darkly foretold all the incidents of the catastrophy is fulfilled down to its last clause,—that 'the lifeless trunk shall wed the broken heart';—and, placing a ring on the finger of the corpse of Ithocles she sinks dead by his side."

Love's Sacrifice.

"Love's Sacrifice" is an admirable tragedy though Bianca's love for Fernando when she has a legally married husband is not excusable. How she was tormented by love, how she was sometimes inclined to submit and how her better nature counselled her not to yield—these feelings are well depicted. The crowning virtue of *Bianca* with all her faults consists in her bold conduct in pleading the innocence of her lover and in admitting her own guilt. "Perkin Warbeck" is a historical drama of great merit. Swinburne in his "Essays and Studies" speaks very highly of Ford and states that his name "is one of the loftiest landmarks of English poetry."

Perkin Warbeck.

"WEBSTER," says a writer in the Edinburgh Review, "was an unequal writer of gloomy power but with touches of profound sentiment and deepest pathos." "The White Devil," a tragedy by this author is said to be a masterpiece. "The Duchess of Malfy" is another tragedy of a horrible nature wherein the brother of the Duchess murdered her for the sin of her having loved and married her steward. Intensity of imagination and elaborateness of workmanship for producing horrible spectacles, are the characteristics of this author. His comedy "The Devil's Law Case" is romantic in its nature and complicated in its plot.

Webster. The White Devil. The Duchess of Malfy. The Devil's Law Case.

James Shirley is a great dramatist who has written many tragedies and comedies. His comedy "The Wedding" is considered to be one of high merit. "The Example" is a comedy of high merit, where a woman brings her wicked seducer to the right path. The story is as follows :—"The chief personages of the action are Sir Walter Perigrine, who being involved in debt, quits his country for a time in order to seek his fortune in the low country wars; a wild gallant Lord Fitzavarice falls in love with his wife. The current of Lord Fitzavarice's guilty passion for Lady Perigrine is broken by her fainting away, when in a pretended excess of rage he has drawn his dagger upon her and is changed to repentance when, on recovering from

James Shirley. The Wedding. The Example.

her swoon, she tells the trembling man how she has had a short but pleasing vision.—

> "Methought, from a steep precipice as you were falling
> Into the sea, an arm chained to a cloud
> Caught hold, and drew you up to heaven."

His thoughts are now entirely directed to proving his penitence and his reverence for the woman who has awakened his conscience ; and he sends her as a gift, together with a rich neck-lace a mortgage into which her husband had entered with him. At this point—an admirable contrivance—the husband returns on a sudden visit to his wife and rashly construes the gifts of gratitude into a proof of guilt. A duel is about to be fought between Perigrine and Fitzavarice when a foolish gentleman who is anxious to escape from the office of *second*, procures the serving of a writ upon Perigrine for another debt owing to Fitzavarice and it is not till the latter has himself caused Perigrine's release that the truth begins to dawn upon the husband's mind. The duel is however fought, Lord Fitzavarice who has revealed the story of his own wickedness and its overthrow, seeking death ; but both the combatants are wounded and honour being thus satisfied, all ends happily. Fitzavarice marries Lady Perigrine's sister Jacinta whose treatment of a brace of foolish lovers has furnished the comic under-plot of the play." "*The Royal Master*" is a comedy of intrigue and was considered the best comedy of the period. A beautiful girl of 15 years of age "mistaking the king's promise to provide her with a husband for a proof of personal affection, fixes her love upon him." She rejects the courtesies of Octavio. The king tests her purity by feigning to make her a dishonourable offer which she rejects. In the further course of the play she is married to Octavio. There are several other comedies of very interesting character written by this author. He is mostly original in his plots. Though some of the passages in his

The Royal Master.

plays tend towards immorality he is careful to see that virtue gains a victory over vice. Lamb observes that this author "claims a place amongst the worthies of the period not so much for any transcendant genius in himself as that he was the last of the great race, all of whom spoke nearly the same language and had a set of moral feelings and motives in common."

Thomas Randolph.

THOMAS Randolph is a dramatist of great fame. His comedies "Muses' Looking-glass" and "Amyntas" are greatly praised.

John Milton.

MILTON, the greatest poet of the seventeenth century, was also a dramatist. His "Arcades" was acted probably in 1633. His "Comus" was acted in 1634. These two plays are masques.

BESIDES the dramatists who are specially named above, there were many who wrote dramas and enriched dramatic literature during the period between the writings of Shakespeare and of Milton.

William Prynne.

AN event occurred in 1632 which, though unfortunate in itself, resulted in producing a healthy tone subsequently for some time. William Prynne, an eminent and very independent author, wrote the "Histrio Mastix" containing many invectives against the virtue of ladies. He was prosecuted and was sentenced to perpetual imprisonment and a fine of £ 5,000. He was released some time after. In 1636 he attacked Laud, Archbishop of Canterbury, and he was again fined £ 5,000 and was pilloried. This author was dead against stage-plays as the following sketch would show. The following is the course of argument of this work. "Stage plays had their original from the devil, were invented and practised by his instruments, and are therefore necessarily sinful and unlawful unto Christians; they are the pomps and vanities of this

Histrio-Mastix or Players Scourge.

wicked world which Christians renounce in baptism. They are unlawful because their style and subject matter are scurrilous, obscene, bloody and tyrannical, heathenish and profane, false and fabulous, often impious, sacrilegious and blasphemous, most satirically invective against persons and offices, especially against religion and religious Christians, idle, frothy, superfluous and unprofitable."

Prosperity of the Stage.

AT the beginning of the seventeenth century, eleven regular play-houses were seen in London. The increasing popularity of dramatical performances was wonderful although there was opposition here and there. The progress of the stage, commencing with the reign of Elizabeth continued with glory in the reigns of James I and Charles I. Before 1631, seventeen play-houses were built in London. Public applause and favour of the princes were abundant. During the time of Shakespeare and subsequently for some years, woman's parts were acted by boys, many of whom obtained considerable celebrity. The dramas enjoyed the favour and good will of the courts under a condition that no modern Christian king should be represented on the stage. The sympathies of the court were always with the stage.

Sir W. D'Avenant.

Sir William D'Avenant wrote many comedies and tragedies which were performed on the stage with much scenic effect. It is said that in 1634 he wrote the play called "The Temple of Love" which was performed by the queen and her ladies at Whitehall on Shrove Tuesday.

The Temple of Love.

He was made poet-laureate in 1637. In 1642 all theatres were closed on account of the Civil War and therefore of public calamity.

Theatres closed in 1642 for Civil War.

An ordinance was published to the effect "that while these sad causes, and set times of humiliation continue, public stage plays shall cease and be forborne."

Stage suppressed by Puritans.

The Restoration lifted up the Stage.

Unfortunate Lovers.

THE Puritans during the Commonwealth were in power and checked dramatical growth with all their fanatical zeal. Real hostility commenced between the theatre and Puritanism. The theatre bitterly felt the oppression and waited for an opportunity for revenge. When the Restoration gave it help and relieved it, it rose with all its vengeance. It heaped its bitterest and often coarsest attacks upon the Puritans and the Puritan spirit. Even when the Puritan power was at its height during the Commonwealth, Sir William D'Avenant "by the help of some influential friends, obtained permission to open a sort of theatre at Rutland House in Charter-house yard where he began a series of representations which he called *operas* as an inoffensive term." This dramatist was a great friend of Milton. They mutually saved each other's lives when in danger. It was during the management ot this dramatist that simplicity was exchanged for outward decoration and splendid scenery. In the prologue to his comedy "Unfortunate Lovers" he complains of the growing fastidiousness of his audience :—

"............to the theatre would come
Ere they had dined to take up the best room
There sit on the benches not adorned with mats
And graciously did veil this high crowned hats
To every half dressed player as he still
Through the hangings peeped to see how the moon did fill
Good easy judging souls! with what delight
They would expect a jig or target fight
A furious talo of Troy which they ne'er thought
Was weakly written so 'twere strongly fought."

Cowley.
Pyramus and Thisbe.
Love's Riddle.
The Guardian.

THE famous poet Cowley who in his tenth year composed the "Tragical History of Pyramus and Thisbe," wrote a pastoral comedy called "Love's Riddle." Besides other comedies written both in English and Latin, Cowley wrote a play called the "Guardian" which was acted before Charles I, with great success. "In Cowley," says Hazlitt, "there is an inexhaustible fund of sense and ingenuity, buried in unextricable conceits and entangled in the cobwebs of the schools. He was a great man, not a great poet." During the Civil War, the plays were performed in Dublin privately.

Licenses granted to only two Companies.

THESE dark days for dramas continued almost up to 1660 when licenses were granted for only two companies with a stringent condition that neither of the rival companies should ever attempt a play produced by the other. This, it is said, "operated beneficially both upon the activity of the dramatic authorship and upon the progress of the art of acting." When the oppressors of the actors were suppressed, a certain poet wrote in a moralising tone the following lines :—

"See the strange twirl of times ! when such poor things
Outlive the dates of parliaments or kings
This revolution makes the exploded wit
Now see the fall of those that received it
And the condemned stage hath now obtained
To see her executioners arraigned
There is nothing permanent ; those high great men
That rose from dust to dust may fall again
And fate so orders things that the same hour
Sees the same man both in contempt and in power."

Betterton—the actor.

IT is from this time that the actors' art commenced to flourish. It is at this time that the actor Betterton highly praised by Addison lived. Thomas Betterton, the greatest English actor whom the stage produced, was the leading spirit at the Duke's house.

He flourished from 1660 to 1710. Betterton was not only an actor but also a dramatist. It was he that introduced scenery on the English stage. He was a friend of Pope, Dryden, Addison and Archbishop Tillotson. A short conversation between the Prelate and the actor is well worth noting. Tillotson one day asked the actor "how it came about, that after he had made the most moving discourse that he could, was touched deeply with it himself, and spoke it as feelingly as he was able, yet he could never move people in the Church near so much as the other (actor) did on the stage"? "That," says Betterton, "I think is easy to be accounted for; it is because you are only telling them a story and I am showing them facts". The historian Hallam states that Betterton was styled the English Roscius. He "was sent to Paris by Charles II, that, taking a view of the French stage he might better judge of what would contribute to the improvement. Charles II not only countenanced the theatre by his patronage but by so much personal notice of the chief actors and so much interest in all the affairs of the theatre and their condition". He was a friend as it were of Betterton. In Sir William D'Avenant's play of "Love and Honour" produced in 1662, the king gave Betterton his coronation suit in which he acted the part of Prince Alvaro. It is said that by the extraordinary powers of this actor, the tragedy of Hamlet held its own in popularity. When Betterton died he was interred with something like royal honours in Westminister Abbey. Isac D'Israeli in his "Curiosities of Literature" observes about this actor as follows:—

Isac D'Israeli's opinion.

"Betterton although his countenance was ruddy and sanguine when he performed Hamlet, through the sudden and violent emotion of amazement and horror at the presence of his father's spectre, instantly turned as white as his neck cloth while his whole body seemed to be affected with a strong tremor; had his father's apparition actually risen before him he could not have been seized with more real agonies. This struck the spectators so forcibly that they felt a shuddering in their veins and participated in the astonishment and the horror so apparent in the actor." Davies, in his 'Dramatic Miscellanies' records this fact; "we find that the first time Booth attempted the ghost when Betterton acted Hamlet, that actor's look at times struck him with such horror that he became disconcerted to such a degree that he could not speak his part. Here seems no want of evidence of the force of the ideal presence in this marvellous acting. These facts might deserve a philosophical investigation. Addison records this fact. "Such an actor as Mr. Betterton ought to be recorded with the same respect as Roscius among the Romans. I have hardly a notion that any performer of antiquity could surpass the action of Mr. Betterton in any of the occasions in which he has appeared upon our stage. The wonderful agony which he appeared in when he examined the circumstances of the handkerchief in the part of Othello, the mixture of love that intruded upon his mind upon the innocent answers Desdimona makes, betrayed in his gesture such a variety and vicissitude of passions as would admonish a man to be afraid of his own heart, and perfectly convince him that it is to stab it to admit that worst of daggers—jealousy. Whoever reads in his closet this admirable scene will find that he cannot (except he has as warm an imagination as Shakespeare himself) find any but dry incoherent and broken sentences. But a reader that has seen Betterton act it observes there could not be a word added, that longer speeches had been unnatural, nay, impossible, in Othello's circumstances. This is such a triumph over difficulties that we feel almost persuaded that the deficiencies themselves contributed to the success." Blackwood's Magazine published in 1861 observes "Betterton was the greatest actor the English stage ever produced, with the exception perhaps of the more versatile Garrick. Almost incredible accounts remain to us of the effects produced by his performances. The magnetic influence of tone and expression seemed to mesmerize an audience and make them the followers of his slightest intonation. Almost without speaking he could let them into the workings of his mind and anticipate his next motion, as if it arose from their own volition."

Barton Booth.

AFTER the death of this great actor of the age came Barton Booth, James Quin and David Garrick. Barton Booth had great advantages from birth and education. He was a scholar and a poet. He was a relation of the Earl of Warrington. "His professional merit recommended him to Lord Bolingbroke who was so pleased with his company and conversation that he sent his chariot to the door of the theatre every night to convey Booth after the play was finished, to his country seat. There was in his look an apparent goodness of mind which struck everybody that saw him. He was an actor of genius and amiable man." "The whole nation," says Johnson, "was at that time on fire with faction. The wigs applauded every line (in the play) in which liberty was mentioned, as a satire on the Tories, and the Tories echoed every clap to show that the satire was unfelt. The story of Bolingbroke is well known. He called Booth to his box and gave him fifty guineas for defending the cause of liberty so well against a perpetual dictator." "In connection with Barton Booth as Cato of which he was the original representative, there is a story told, the application of which tended to place the stage on a level with the pulpit. Booth and his gifted fellows went down to Oxford to play Addison's famous tragedy before the most learned audience in the world. After the third and the last performances was concluded Dr. Sandrige, Dean of Carlyle, addressed a letter to Barton, in which the writer remarked 'I heartily wish all discourses from the pulpit were as instructive and edifying,' as pathetic and affecting as that which the audience were then entertained with from the stage.'" Chetwood in his "General History of the Stage" says of this actor "he had a vast fund of understanding as well as good nature and a persuasive elocution even in common discourse, that would compel you to believe him against your judgment of things. Notwithstanding his exuberance of fancy, he was untainted in his morals. His profound learning was extraordinary." Aaron Hill says "his (Bartons) secret for attaining the great lesson for the theatre was an adaptation of his looks to his voice by which artful imitation of nature the variation in the sounds of his words gave propriety to every change in his countenance."

Woman on the stage.

IT is recorded that woman appeared on the stage as an actress on the 8th December 1660 for the first time and played the part of Desdemona. She was Mrs. Hughes. Some assert that a Mrs. Coleman performed the part of Ianthe which stamps her as the first female who appeared on the public stage in England. Long before this event the French ladies in 1629 met on the Engliah stage with a very unfavourable reception. Prynne speaks of the women actors as monsters and applies most severe epithets to their histrionic efforts ;—"Impudent, shameful, unwomanish, graceless and such like." Even subsequent to 1660 woman's parts were personated for some time by boys. We read that in 1661 a man by name Kynaston performed the heroine's part in "The Silent woman." Pepys, the diary writer of the day, pronounced the young actor the prettiest woman in the whole house. In the following epilogue an appeal is made to the ladies :—

> "But, ladies, what think you? for if you tax
> Her freedom with dishonour to your sex
> She means to act no more and this shall be
> No other play but her own tragedy
> She will submit to none but your commands;
> And take commission only from your hands."

A certain prologue describes the appearance of woman on the stage and defends her act as follows :—

"I come unknown to any of the rest
To tell the news: I saw the lady dressed
The woman plays to-day, mistake me not
No man in gown, or page in petti-coat

....

"Tis possible a virtuous woman may
Abhor all sorts of looseness and yet play
Play on the stage—where all eyes are upon her
Shall we count that a crime, France counts an honour ?
In other kingdoms husbands safely trust 'em
The difference lies only in custom."

WHEN women were introduced on the stage, many appreciated the innovation, but some strongly criticised and condemned it as being most immoral. Boys wearing the dress and affecting the airs of women was considered deplorable by some ; and women mingling on the stage with all sorts of men was deemed horrible by others. In this contest woman came out successful. Before women were introduced on the stage, Hart, Mohun, Clun, Shatteral and Burt had been boy actresses. Mohun was a major in the Military Department. Though he was not less than thirty-five years of age he appeared as Bellamante, one of the heroines of Shirley's tragedy of "Loves Cruelty." "All accounts exhibit Kynaston as the most celebrated actor of woman's parts of his day. Some assert that it was not until after the Restoration that women performed on the stage and that they were introduced by Sir William D'Avenant into his theatre in Lincoln's Inn Fields in 1662. The play was the "Seige of Rhodes" in which Mrs. Sanderson the first female actress that ever played for hire before the public in England, took the part of the heroine. In 1593 one Doctor Reynolds had published a foaming invective against stage plays in which he vigorously attacked the sin of boys wearing the dress and affecting the airs of women ;

yet Tom Nash in his "Piere Pennilesse" applauds the English stage for not having courtezans or woman actors (the definition is his), as they have abroad. D'Israeli attributes the change less to an improved taste than to necessity; for he says "the boys who had been trained to act female characters before the Rebellion during the suspension of the theatre (by the Puritans) had grown too masculine to resume their tender office at the Restoration." "This innovation of actresses pronounced an indecorum, though copiously apologised for, grew speedily popular, so much so indeed, that before long, plays were represented of which the cast consisted wholly of women." Evelyn's diary, dated 18th October 1686 shows the repugnance which continued to be felt against the practice after the Restoration. He records that he "now (and never till now) found indecent women acting and descanted on the evil results of such practice." A historian records that the expediency of the change was considered open to grave doubts even by the warm friends of the theatre. In the book known as "Stage Whispers" I read that in the mystery plays, half the town including men and women were generally engaged for "the well-being of their souls." At the Coventry and Chester mystery plays, Warton writes, that "Adam and Eve" appeared naked on the stage. He observes "that this extraordinary spectacle was beheld by a numerous company of both sexes with great composure." In "The Harrowing of Hell," the condemned souls of both sexes, were supposed to wear no clothes, this being indicated by close fitting shirts, whilst children might wear their "birthday garments." Such things, if true, must have been tolerated by the society on account of their religious character.

THE English stage would have flourished more splendidly even without this change. It is a mistaken idea entertained by some English authors that on the Indian stage women appeared when the classical dramas (Sanscrit) were played. I for one could not find any authority in the

Sanscrit literature. On the other hand we have names in Sanscrit *viz.*, Bhrakoomsa, Bhrukoomsa and Bhrookoomsa which denote a male pantomimist in female dress. I do not think that the introduction of females on the stage was ever intended by the Sanscrit dramatists. Female (I mean the courtezans, dancing-girls and other whores who set the Indian social rules at naught) appeared on the stage here and there only in the fifteenth and the sixteenth centuries. I earnestly hope for the sake of Indian dramatic literature that Indian females will not appear on the stage till India and Indian female education reach the height to which England has at present risen, and also till Indian manners and customs become as refined as the English. In this connection only I venture to point out what I have found by a close study of English dramatic literature about the sort of women that were first introduced on the stage immediately after the Restoration. Let us take for granted that Mrs. Hughes was the woman that was introduced on stage for the first time. Who was this Mrs. Hughes? She was the mistress of Prince Rupert (*Vide* foot-note 2 in page 253 Vol. III of English Dramatic Literature by A. W. Ward). Then comes Mrs. Annebracegirdle. She was the mistress of Congreve. (*Vide* foot-note in page 30 of Representative Actors by Clarke Russel). Mrs. Barry was another actress of fame. She was the mistress of the notorious Earl of Rochester (*Vide* page 57 of the above). She was the coquette who was the cause of the early death of the famous English poet Otway. Then comes Mrs. Oldfield. She was under the protection of General Charles Churchill. Sir C. Hanbury Williams describes Churchill in the following lines :—

> "None led through youth a gayer life than he
> Cheerful in converse, smart in repartee
> Sweet was his night and joyful was his day
> He dines with Walpole and with Oldfield lay."

There may be many other actresses of the above description

during that period, and it is on account of this element that the Restoration dramas were impeached for immorality. Perhaps the three or four names I selected from the list of actresses may be exceptions, and it is only these exceptions when too many that become rules for criticism. I see the morality of the stage of the nineteenth century in England was improved to an extent far above adverse criticism. The close of the seventeenth and the beginning of the eighteenth centuries gave cause for people to find fault with the stage on the ground of immorality, both behind and before the curtains. Leaving that period aside, the history of the stage has been always bright. On certain occasions the action of the drama requires an actor to become an actress for a certain time, and immediately to resume his former impersonation of an actor. We have an example of this in "The Silent Woman." In such cases it is necessary that the actor should wear a female dress and affect the airs of woman. In India, women of respectable family do not generally go out and the gallant in love cannot get access to them unless he passes off as a female. The interview ends sometimes with success and sometimes with disappointment. There are many Indian stories where beautiful girls were passed off as boys and many boys passed off as girls. In such cases one sex should wear necessarily the dress of the other. In India men can pass off as women and defy almost a close search. I plead therefore for India's sake that the system of introducing females on the stage on the basis of English stage may not be, for a century or two to come, adopted. To allow courtezans and whores to tread upon the stage, which we Indians consider as a temple where the noble art of drama is to receive adoration from the learned, the moral, and the honest men, is to cut it at the very root.

I know that there is a Sanscrit stanza which condemns a man taking a female character which is certainly degrading. I know also that there is a religious saying that "the woman shall not wear that which pertaineth unto man, neither shall a man put on a woman's garment." But it would be removing dramatic representation altogether from the face of the earth, which is not possible till the time of deluge. I know also there is much obscenity in the very idea of a man becoming a woman, though temporarily. I am not unaware of the fact that the spontaneous grace, the melting voice and soothing looks of a female, greatly add to the beauty of dramatic representation. With all this I plead against the appearance of Indian women on the stage for the reason that the national moral stamina of the Indians is, at present, rotten at the root by adverse circumstances, and the ancient golden rule that man should treat a woman other than his wife as is mother or sister has been respected only in its breach. Moreover to make an Indian woman, uneducated as she is, appear on the stage will be not only rude but also upsetting all Indian manners and customs. It is also repulsive to a civilized educated Indian to see whores and dancing girls come on the stage and degrade the height of dramatic dignity.

There were no females on the Grecian stage. Plutarch mentions that a certain tragedy was not played as one of the actors refused to impersonate the queen unless he had a mask and suitable dress. It is stated by Demosthenes that Theodorus appeared as "Antigone." The following anecdote shows the probable age of an actor when he impersonated woman's part. "An actor named Polus having been cast for the female character of Electra is, during the progress of the play, supposed to enter with an urn containing the ashes of Orestes. Polus having sometimes previously been deprived by the death of a beloved son, in order to heighten the effect of grief the more, brought in an urn from the child's tomb the real ashes, which so affected him that he embraced it with genuine sorrow as to burst into tears." I have

Polus.

seen grown up men impersonating female parts beautifully well. Nothing is impossible for art. It can even represent nature as art is nothing but a rectified nature. When reading the book "Stage Whispers" by R. J. Broadbent I came across the following story and wondered at the height of foolishness and iniquity to which the Roman Emperor Nero (37-68 A.D.) reached. I quote the para in full.

"Nero appeared on the public stage both as an actor and a pantomimist—actors acted female parts. This Monarch, who carried everything to the height of foolishness, in a public play had, with an actor named Sporus, who performed female parts, been espoused, and these two worthies, must needs, we are told (Sporus dressed in the imperial robes and decorated with the jewels of the Roman Empress) drive through the streets of Rome. Sporus, strange to relate however, sometime after, being appointed to impersonate a nymph to be exhibited before Vettellins, rather than endure the "indignity" of wearing a female dress he committed suicide."

If a male heroine by his charms captivated the Emperor (foolish he may be) so much in dramatic representation, the female heroine must necessarily captivate the stoic hearts of even great philosophers. There are also other considerations which urge me to say that the Indian stage is not yet fit for women to enter. Plutarch in his "Life of Sylla" writes:—"Notwithstanding he (Sylla) had married so extraordinary a woman, he continued his commerce with actresses and female musicians."

It is true that great inconvenience is caused by a male taking a female part especially if he happens to be a grown up boy. Such inconveniences are to be put up with by the audience. Charles II visited a theatre. The performance was not commenced at the usual time. The Monarch wanted to know the reason, when the manager wittily replied "that the queen was not yet shaved." The merry

Monarch waited calmly. It is this king that gave sanction for women to appear on the stage in the following royal rescript. "Whereas the women's parts in plays have, hitherto, been acted by men in habits of women, at which some have taken offence, We do permit and give leave from this time to come that women's parts be acted by women."

About women appearing on the stage, Miss Cayvan's opinion recorded by P. G. Hubert in his book "The Stage as a Career" may be read with profit. Dr. Johnson once said to David Garrick :—

> "I'll come no more behind your scenes, David; for the
> Silk stockings and white bosoms of your actresses excite
> My amorous propensities."

Thomas B. Shaw, M.A., in his "History of English Literature," observes as follows :" It is true that this custom of the female parts being acted by boys may have in some degree exaggerated that tendency to double enterdre and indecent equivoque which was unfortunately but too universally the vice of the stage; but even this objection will lose some of its weight when we reflect that the habitual appearance of women on the stage seems, so far from checking, absolutely to have aggravated the frightful profligacy and immorality which defiled the society and the literature of the country at the epoch of the Restoration, and which reached its highest intensity in compositions destined for the stage."

Dumb-show commencement.

The established custom of the theatre almost up to the Restoration period was to commence the action of the play with dumb-shows. Before each act was actually performed, a certain actor would come forward and inform the audience of the events of the ensuing act, by gestures, postures and glances. Sometimes these dumb-shows served "as a compendious introduction of such circumstances as could not commodiously be comprehended within the bounds of representation." They "supplied deficiencies and covered the want of business." "And occasionally they were employed to stop the breaches of the strict laws of dramatical composition, to remedy neglect of the unities of time and place." A certain author wrote the following prologue telling the audience to know the action of the play by the show :—

"The actors are at hand, and by their show
You shall know all that you are like to know."

WHEN the power of the Puritans was destroyed, political and religious partizans generally in accordance with the dominant reaction against Puritanism, were allowed to give expression in the directest and coarsest form upon the stage. The introduction of female performers acted as a charm, as it were, to attract the people who were naturally fond of theatrical representations. I think that the introduction of females on the stage is mainly due to the anti-Puritan reaction. The stage and the dramatists had their own rich patrons who always indulged in unblushing indecency and coarse manners. The character of the dramas became consonant with the character of its patrons. Tragedies became scarce as the state of the mind of the people was not inclined for noble and serious things. Shakespeare's plays were out of fashion. "There was a demand for the plays of the French-school—with rhyming lines and artificial sentiment—for comedies of intrigue and equivoque, after a foreign pattern in lieu of English plays of art, humour and character". These are known as "Comedies of the Restoration". The author whose living depended upon pleasing his patron and the people had to take his moral tone from them. W. C. Sydney writes "with the return of the Stuarts, the English stage was deluged with a flood of licentiousness so widespread that posterity fairly

Restoration Dramas.

W. C. Sydney-on the Restoration Stage.

stands aghast at the height that it reached and at the more extraordinary openness with which it was displayed. Mischief when once promulgated on the stage is irremediable. The plays were generally bad, poorly contrived and abominably immoral, coarse and indecent. The sense of shame seems then to have been utterly unknown". Though the issue of the main plot was on the side of virtue, licentiousness corrupted the spirit of the comic art. Lord Macaulay in his essay on comic dramatists of the Restoration, criticises the authors of that age as being sensual and immoral.

Macaulay on the Restoration Stage.

He says that a systematic attempt on the part of the dramatists of the age of the Restoration "to associate vice with those things which men value most, and virtue with every thing ridiculous and degrading" is traceable in the literature of the age. He also gives cogent reasons for the society of that age growing recklessly immoral—a feature that was not so before that period and which the subsequent two centuries did not imitate. Savage intemperance of party spirit ruled the age. Even the great poet Dryden was not an exception to this general rule. Most of the dramatists had a fiendish spirit of annoying the whigs by their satires. These satires and taunts were recited by women who have long been taught to discard all compassion." The above remark is made by Lord Macaulay in his "History of England" and he refers to Dryden's epilogue to the "Duke of Guise" for verification.

THE most important dramatists of the Restoration period were Wycherley, Congreve, Dryden, Vanbrugh, Farquhar, Sir George Etherage and Sir Charles Sedley. The last two were men whose moral character was said to be questionable. Of Sir Charles Sedley, Macaulay says, that

Dramatists of the period.

he is "one of the most brilliant and profligate wits of the Restoration." Rochester wrote of him as follows :—

"Sedley has that prevailing gentle art,
That can with a restless charm impart
The loosest wishes to the chastest heart."

The account given by Lord Macaulay of the life of Wycherley would lead any reader to infer that this poet was a profligate and also a man of no deep learning. It is no wonder, though not a necessary consequence, that his comedies are immoral. His comedies are :—(1) *Love in a Wood* (2) *Gentleman Dancing Master* (3) *Country Wife* (4) *Plain Doctor.*

Wycherley.

Congreve.

Congreve was a man of real learning and of very superior wit. His early life was not free from blame. His comedies though of superior merit, are not beyond the criticism of moralists. He was very much respected by the literary men of the day. Macaulay contrasting Congreve with his fellow dramatist Wycherley says, "Wycherley had wit; but the wit of Congreve far out-shines that of every comic writer, except Sheridan who has arisen within the last two centuries. Congreve had not, in a large measure, the poetical faculty but compared with Wycherley he might be called a great poet. Wycherley had some knowledge of books; but Congreve was a man of real learning. Congreve's offences against decorum though highly culpable were not so gross as those of Wycherley." His plays are :—(1) *The Old Bachelor* (2) *The Double Dealer* (3) *Love for Love* (4) *The Mourning Bride.*

Vanbrugh.

Vanbrugh is a dramatist of much humour combined with wit. He led no bad life in his youth. He wrote on morals. He built a theatre of his own to play his own dramas in; he was an architect himself. There is no reason why he should have written immoral comedies unless it was to please his patrons and the people in general.

In 1714 he was knighted. His comedies are :—(1) *The Relapse* (2) *The Provoked Wife* (3) *Aesop* (4) *The Confideracy* 5 *The Provoked Husband* 6 *The Mistake.*

Farquhar. Farquhar was the son of a clergyman and was brought up by a Bishop; he was a married man and father of two children. There is nothing to show that he led a wicked life in his youth; he was poor; such a man could not have written immoral plays unless it were to pander to the taste of the audience. His comedies are :—(1) *Love and a Bottle* (2) *The Constant Couple* (3) *The Inconstant* (4) *The Stage Coach* (5) *The Twin Rivals* (6) *The Recruiting Officer* (7) *The Beaux' Stratagene.* Lastly we come to the famous

Dryden. Dryden. He was also accused of having written immoral plays and he was put on his defence. He excused himself by pleading the example of earlier and contemporary English dramatists. This defence was not admitted by the critics. Dutton Cook in his "Book of the Plays" says, "Dryden was no reformer, in truth to suit his own purposes he pandered laboriously to the follies and caprices of his patrons, nevertheless, he was fully sensible of the errors of the time and often chronicled these in his prologues and epilogues." He writes :—

"True wit has run its best days long ago
It ne'er looked up since we are lost in show
When sense in doggeral rhymes and clouds was lost
And dullness flourished at the actor's cost
Nor stopped it here, when tragedy was done
Comedies sunk to trick and pun
Let them who the rebellion first began
To wit restore the monarch if they can
Our author dares not be the first bold man."

....

"But when all fail to strike the stage quite dumb
Those wicked engines called machines are come
Thunders and lightning now for wit are played
And shortly scenes in Lapland will be laid

Fletcher's is despised, your Jonson out of fashion
And wit the only drug in all the nation."

Dryden was not an ordinary poet; he was the cleverest satirist. He was a man of principles. In 1668 he was made poet-laureate. There was nothing to show that he was immoral. His life written by G. Saintsbury proves that he was free from all blame. There must have been strong reasons for such a great man to write gross plays. He wrote altogether twenty-eight dramas. He made many enemies among the nobles by his satires. A few of the nobles who suffered from the satirical invectives of the poet tried by all means to annoy him. An inferior poet by name Settle was raised to a high position by a vain admiration of him by Dryden's enemies, and his drama, "Empress of Morocco" was played not only on the public stage but also at Whitehall by the court-lords and ladies. Dryden was waylaid and beaten at the instigation of the Earl of Rochester and the Duchess of Portsmouth and others on a suspicion of his having been the author of an Essay on Satire, while the real author of it was the Duke of Buckingham. Dr. Johnson takes a very favourable view of the conduct of Dryden and says "his tendency to profaneness is the effect of levity, negligence and venturing to be wicked as far as he durst. His works afford too many examples of dissolute licentiousness and an abject adulation but they were probably, like his merriment, artificial and constrained; the effect of study and meditation and his trade, rather than his pleasure." Dryden himself in one of his prologues complains of the bad taste of the audience and the authors in the following words:—

Settle.

Empress of Morocco.

"You now have habits, dances, scenes and rhymes,
High language often, aye, and sense sometimes."

Dryden when accused by the critics of the day of having borrowed from the French drama the plot of his play called

"An Evening Love or the Mock Astrologer" his explanation was—

> "He still must write and banquier-like each day
> Accept new bills and he must break or pay
> When through his hands such sums must yearly run
> You cannot think that the stock is all his own."

In some of his prologues and epilogues Dryden describes some of the prevailing follies of the times in regard to dress and manners—

> "But only fools and they of vast estate
> The extremity of moods will imitate
> The dingling knee-fringe and the bib-cravat
> Fop comer now is free from civil war
> White wig and wizard mass no longer jar
> France and the fleet have swept the town so clear."

When Dryden was accused of terrible grossness in one of his plays he could not disown it and he could not justify it. He said that he knew not any law that prescribed morality to a comic poet. The soundness of this argument is questionable. That a man of genius like Dryden should allow his mind to trade in corruption and write indecent and immoral comedies and thereby spread contagion in society is extremely regrettable. What defence Dryden could have put forward if a charge of immorality had been framed against him for having translated "Ovid's Art of Love" is not known. This is a book which ought to have been suppressed by the civilised world. The publication of a Sanscrit book less indecent and gross are suppressed by the British Government of India, and it is a wonder that Dryden's translation of "Ovid's Art of Love" is passing like a current British gold sovereign and is published and read by the public. Thousands of immoral and grossly indecent comedies are nothing in comparison and would not corrupt society so much; but a book of this kind boasting of ancient origin and coming from a poet of high standing reputation would,

Ovid's Art of Love.

I dare say, irrecoverably corrupt all English-knowing society on the face of the earth. Dr. J. Warton makes the following remarks about this book.—"We cannot see, without real regret and mortification, such a waste of time and talent as what our author has flung away in translating so loose and flagitious as well as trifling work of his favourite Ovid, full of some of the most exceptionable and nauseous circumstances of ancient mythology. I most undoubtedly shall make no comment on the two succeeding translations." We are glad however that Dryden admits in a straightforward manner his guilt in the following lines :—

"O gracious God! how far have we
Profaned thy heavenly gift of poesy!
Made prostitute and profligate the muse
Debased to each obscene and impious use
Whose harmony was first orduined above
For tongues of angels and for hymns of love!
O wretched we! why were we hurried down
This lubric and adulterate age
Nay, added fat pollutions of our own
To increase the steaming ordures of the stage?
What can we say to excuse our second fall?"

Charles Knight on dramas.

CHARLES Knight, in his "Popular History of England" Vol. IV, describes the state of drama in the following words :—"The drama had come back after an exile of twenty years. When the drama was banished Tragedy was still a queen wearing her purple and her pall; and the "Woodnotes wild" of comedy were as fresh and joyous as those of the lark in spring. The drama came back in the shameless garb and with brazen look and the drunken voice of the lowest strumpet." The same author in Vol. V of his History observes that "in the period from the Restoration to the middle of the eighteenth century there was unquestionably a very low estimate of the female character. In theatrical representation of life there was scarcely an attempt to exhibit a woman of sense and modesty. The high ideal of female excellence which we find in Shakespeare and which to a certain extent he must have derived from the realities of the age of Elizabeth, could scarcely be expected from the Drydens and Faquhars and Wycherleys and Congreves of the age of Revolution." If from the middle of the eighteenth century a sense of decency denoting something more of respect for the female character was found in the dramas, it was in some degree an evidence that the female character was itself improving. "The great ladies ceased to be painted as profligate intriguers in their masks."

BEFORE we close our remarks upon the Restoration dramas and Restoration dramatists the name of one other dramatist is worth mention here. He is Thomas Otway. His figures of speech mostly resemble those of Indian dramatists. The scenes in his tragedies are gross and repulsive. His "Don Carlos" though a well written tragedy is, in my opinion, one not to be exhibited to the public. Illegal love between a son and his step-mother is repugnant to Indian taste. Such love is made much of in the tragedy. Carlos' speech to his father is highly objectionable, granting the conduct of the father was reprehensible. Schiller also has written a drama on this subject. Indian dramatists would admire Otway's tragedy of "Orphan" if the incestuous connection there were stopped by some mysterious impediment and the mistake found out by the brothers. The "Venice Preserved," deducting the comical scenes, is a noble piece. The "Soldier's Fortune" is so immoral that in my opinion it should not have seen the light of day at all.

Thomas Otway.

Don Carlos.

The Orphan.

The Venice Preserved.

Soldier's Fortune.

IF these Restoration dramas were immoral and the actors of the period were impudent and devoid of sense of shame it was the audience that was to blame. The audience made it so; the stage reflected only the sentiments and opinions of the audience. The stage pandered to the moods and humours of the audience. The stage was the creation of the audience.

Grounds for indecent dramas.

DRAMA was fairly supported in Queen Anne's reign (1701 to 1714). For restraining the play-houses from immorality, Queen Anne issued the following proclamation on the 17th January 1704. "Whereas We have already given orders to the Master of Our revels and also to both the companies of comedians acting in Drury Lane and Lincoln's Inn Fields, to take special care, that nothing be acted in either of the theatres contrary to religion or good manners, upon pain of Our high displeasure and of being silenced from further acting and being further desirous to reform all other indecencies and abuses of the stage, which have occasioned great disorders and justly given offences, Our will and pleasure therefore is and We do hereby strictly command that no person of what quality soever, presume to go behind the scenes or come upon the stage, either before or during the acting of any play. That no woman be allowed or presume to wear a vizard mask in either of the theatres. And that no person come into either house without paying the prices established for their respective places."

Queen Anne—to reform the stage.

THE actors of the reign of Queen Anne with a few exceptions were not men of genius. The following short history of the actors of the period is extracted from the "Social Life in the Reign of Queen Anne" by John Ashton. "The 'Phoenix of the

Actors.

Stage'—Betterton—stands pre-eminent among the actors.

Colley Cibber. Colley Cibber is known more as a play-wright or poet than as an actor. He was poet-laureate of George II in 1730. Booth was an Ariosto of the profession. He was not only nearly related to the Earl of Warrington but in 1704 he married a daughter of Sir William Barkham, Bart., of Norfolk. He shone in acting the Latin plays at Westminister. He was a pupil of Betterton.

Kynastin. Kynastin, the boy actor, had the good turn to appear in three shapes; first as a poor woman in ordinary clothes to please the morose; then in fine clothes and in them was the prettiest woman in the whole house; and lastly as a man, and then likewise did he appear the handsomest man in the house. Of him Betterton writes "that it has been disputed among the judicious, whether any woman could have more sensibly touched the passions." He seems to have been the last of the male actors who took female parts.

IT is about the stage of this period that the famous Jeremy Collier wrote. The actors of the period with very few exceptions became impertinently independent. The dramatists of the period systematically tried to put all their loosest verses into the mouths of woman.

Sir Robert Walpole. THE stage continued in this state till Sir Robert Walpole in 1737 perceiving that it would be inexpedient to allow it to become a vehicle of anti-ministerial abuse, brought the Licensing Act strictly into force.

His attempts to abridge the liberty of the Press and Stage. The minister wished to abridge the liberty of the Press and the Stage. These institutions exposed and ridiculed the errors of his conduct, his systematic corruption and all the blemishes of his administration.

Henry Fielding. Henry Fielding, the "Homer of English Prose" and the "Father of English Novels," was also a dramatist. In 1736 he took the management of a theatre in the Hay-market where he brought out his two burlesques, "Pasquin" and the "Historical Register," containing a strong satire against the ministry. This was also one of the causes for the Licensing Act coming into force. The ministry waited for the best opportunity to suppress, if possible, these institutions. The stage too was uncontrollable and sometimes transgressed the highest limits of liberty. Political allusions were strong and often spiced with personalities that would not be tolerated even in this age of complete liberty. The "Pasquin' of Henry Fielding is a dramatic satire on the times, being the rehearsal of two plays, *viz.*, a comedy called "The Election" and a tragedy called "The Life and Death of Common Sense." The satire was chiefly aimed at the electoral corruptions of the age, the abuses prevailing in the learned professions, and the servility of placemen who derided public virtue and denied the existence of political honesty. His "Historical Register" contains allusions of more pointed and personal kind. Walpole himself was brought upon the stage and under the name of Quidan, violently caricatured. He was exhibited as silencing noisy patriots with bribes and then joining with them in a dance. . . . . Besides these satires the press also exposed the minister's corruption. Smollet in the "History of England" writes as follows :—

Pasquin. The Historical Register.

Smollet on the state of the Stage.

"The next effort of the minister was obliquely levelled at the liberty of the press which it was much for his interest to abridge. The errors of his conduct, the mystery of that corruption which he had so successfully reduced to a system and all the blemishes of his administration had been exposed and ridiculed not only in the political periodical writings produced by the most eminent hands but likewise in a succession of theatrical pieces which met with uncommon success among the people. He either wanted judgment to distinguish men of genius or could find none that would engage in his service; he therefore employed a set of authors void of understandiug and ingenuity. They undertook the defence of the ministry and answered the animadversions of his antagonists. The match was so extremely unequal that instead of justifying his conduct, they exposed it to additional ridicule and contempt and he found himself in danger of being despised, by the whole nation. He resolved to seize the first opportunity to choke the torrent censure had flowed upon his character." An unknown author wrote a farce by name "Golden Rump" containing treason and abuse heaped upon Parliament, the Privy Council and even the King and gave it to one Gifford, the manager of Goodman's Fields Theatre and of a booth in Bartholomew fair, for performance. The manager impelled by loyalty went to Walpole and laid it before him. The minister praised Gifford for his loyalty and purchased the manuscript.

Golden Rump.

A bill to curtail the liberty of the Stage.

After possessing it, the minister introduced a bill to curtail the liberty of the stage by enforcing each play to the severe scrutiny of the Lord Chamberlain. There was much opposition in the House of Commons. The minister made such an effective use of his dreadful manuscript that the bill became a law.

The speech of Earl of Chesterfield in defence of dramas.

In the debate, the Earl of Chesterfield made an excellent speech, which is given below to show to readers the good and rational nature of gentlemen of high position in England. In the House of Lords, Chesterfield had stigmatised the measure both as an encroachment on liberty and an attack on property. "Wit, my Lords," he said, "is a sort of property. It is the property of those that have it and too often the only property they have to depend on. It is, indeed, but a precious dependence. Thank God, we, my Lords, have a dependence of another kind. We have much less precarious support and therefore, cannot feel the inconvenience of the bill now before us: but it is our duty to encourage and protect wit, whosesoever's property it may be. . . . I must own, I cannot easily agree to the laying of a tax upon wit but by this bill it is to be heavily taxed—it is to be excised; for if this bill passes it cannot be retailed in a proper way without permit and the Lord Chamberlain is to have the honour of being chief gauger, superviser, commissioner, judge and jury." He argued further "that our stage ought certainly to be kept within due bounds; for this purpose, our laws, as they stand at present, are sufficient. If our stage players at any time exceed these bounds, they are to be prosecuted; they may be punished. We have precedents, we have examples of persons punished for things less criminal than some pieces which have been lately represented; a new law must therefore be unnecessary and in the present case it cannot be unnecessary without being dangerous. Every unnecessary restraint is a fetter upon the legs, it is a shackle upon the hands of liberty. One of the greatest blessings we enjoy, one of the greatest blessings a people can enjoy is liberty. But every good in this life has its alloy of evil. Licentiousness is the alloy of liberty. It is an ebullition, an excrescence; it is a speck upon the eye of the political body which I can never touch but with a gentle, with a trembling hand; lest I destroy the body, lest I injure the eye upon which it is apt to appear. If the stage becomes at any time licentious. if a play appears to be a libel upon the Government or upon any particular person, the king's courts are open; the law is sufficient to punish the offender. If poets and players are to be restrained, let them be restrained as other subjects are, by the known laws of their country and if they offend, do not let us subject them to the arbitrary will and pleasure of any one man. A power lodged in the hands of a single man to judge and determine without limitation, control or appeal, is a sort of power unknown to our laws, inconsistent with our constitution. It is a higher or a more absolute power than we trust even to the king himself and therefore I must think we ought not to vest any such power in His Majesty's Lord Chamberlain."

Garrick.

IN the year 1741 Garrick opened a new era for the stage. "His incomparable natural gifts enhanced by a careful and continued literary training, enabled by a purpose which prompted him to essay the noblest" reformed not only the actors but English society in general. It is he that pointed out the way to establish the principle that in a free country, the vigilence of public opinion and the criticisms of the press are the only ways to prevent the abuse not only of the stage but also a society. Before Garrick, James Quin was the greatest actor in England. Garrick and Quin both played together in the Fair Penitant in 1746 and the best judges pronounced Garrick superior to Quin. He was a student and a friend of Dr. Johnson. Both went to London from Lichfield. By his acting, this greatest actor pleased alike the intelligent and the ignorant. He was praised by statesmen, poet and the masses. It is envy that railed against him. This actor was accused by Dr. Hill of bad pronunciation. Garrick, it appears, pronounced I's as if they were U's. This was found fault with. In reply Garrick wrote the following in verse :—

The Fair Penitant.

"If 'tis true, as you say, that I've injured a letter
I'll change my note soon and I hope for the better,
May the just right of letters as well as of men
Hereafter be fixed by the tongue and the pen,
Most devoutly I wish that they both have their due
And that 'I' may be never mistaken for 'you.'"

It is recorded that Garrick had an extraordinary command of facial expression. "At moment's notice he completely varied his aspect conveying into his face every possible kind of passion, blending one into another and as it were shadowing them with infinite number of gradations." In short, his face was what he obliged you to fancy it;—age, youth, plenty, poverty, everything it assumed. When Garrick (incognito) appeared for the first time on the London stage in the character of Richard III, Pope said "that young man never had his equal and never will have a rival."

Sheridan describes him in the following lines:—

"The grace of action, the adopted mien
Faithful as nature to the varied scene
The expressive glance—whose subtle comment draws
Entranced attention and a mute applause;
Gesture that marks with force and feeling fraught
A sense in silence and a will in thought
Harmonious speech whose pure and liquid tone
Gives verse a music scarce confessed its own."

The style of acting before Garrick may be gathered from the following opinion quoted by Fitz Gerald in his life of Garrick. "Garrick's voice," it says, "was neither whining, bellowing, nor grumbling, but perfectly easy in its transitions, natural in its cadence and beautiful in its elocution. He never drops his character when he has a speech, by either looking contemptuously on an inferior performer, unnecessary spitting or suffering his eye to wander through the whole circle of spectators." "By what he did not do, we are made to see what the others did."

Quin.

QUIN, was also a great actor. He taught Piozzi as to how to repeat with effect Satan's speech to the Sun in the Paradise Lost. Horace Walpole said that "Quin in Falstaff was as excellent as Garrick in Lear." Davies gives an illustration of Quin's acting. "When Lothario gave Horatio the challenge, instead of accepting it instantly, with the determination and unembarrassed bow of superior bravery, Quin made a long pause and dragged out the words 'I will meet thee there.' He paused so long before he spoke, that somebody, it was said, called out from the gallery 'Why don't you tell the gentleman whether you will meet him or not.'" Garrick wrote the following lines about this great actor :—

"That tongue which set the table in roar
And charmed the public ear is heard no more;
Close are those eyes, the harbinger of wit
Which spake before the tongue what Shakespeare writ;
Cold is that hand which, living, was stretched forth
At friendship's call to succour modest worth;
Here lies James Quin."

Quin was known to be a very charitable man. Thomson in his "*Castle of Indolence*" writes of this actor thus :—

"With double force the enlivened scene he makes,
Yet quits not nature's bounds. He knew to keep
Each due decorum. Now the heart he shakes,
And now with well urged sense th' enlightened judgment takes."

This actor was very particular with pronunciation of words. One William, fellow actor of Quin in the tragedy of Cato, was slain by him in a quarrel caused by the mis-pronunciation of a vowel in the word Cato. William pronounced it as "Keeto."

JOHNSON said that Garrick's death "had eclipsed the gaiety of nations." In speaking with Mrs. Siddons, Dr. Johnson said of Garrick, "Garrick, madam, was no declaimer. There was not one of his own scene shifters who could not have spoken 'To be or not to be' better than he did, yet he was the only actor I ever saw whom I could call a master both in tragedy and in comedy, though I liked him best in comedy. A true conception of his character and natural expression of it were his distinguished excellences." Before we leave Garrick to lie in rest we will mention a sad incident in his life as manager of Drury Lane Theatre taken from "A Book of the Play" by Dutton Cook. "There was a great trouble, for instance at Drury Lane Theatre in 1755 when Mr. Garrick's 'Chinese Festival' with its French dancers was sternly, even savagely, condemned by the audience. The manager was overfond

The Chinese Festival.

of spangles and spectacles or inclined to over-estimate his public regard for such matters and a sharp but necessary lesson was read to him upon that occasion. Then he was very obstinate, and in such wise roused the British lion inordinately. He would not withdraw the play from his stage; promptly the audience determined that no stage should be left him upon which to represent either the 'Chinese Festival' or anything else. Of course he had to yield at last as managers must, when play-goers are resolute; he had to live by pleasing and not displeasing. But he did not give way until there had been some six nights of uproar and riot. In vain did various noble lords and gentlemen, friends of the management and supporters of spectacle and the ballet, draw their swords endeavouring to awe malcontents, to restore order and to defend the theatre from the outrage. The mob would have its way. The benches were torn up, the decorations torn down, chandeliers smashed, even scenes and properties were ruthlessly destroyed. There was indeed a wild proposition rife at one time to fire the house and burn it to the ground. Garrick could not strike his flag and yield up his 'Chinese Festival.' Still it was agreed that he had hesitated too long. The mob therefore repaired to Southampton street and smashed his window panes doing other mischief to his property there. He began even to tremble for his life and from his friends in power, obtained a guard of soldiery to protect him. Strange to say, on two of the nights of riot, the king was present—a fact that did not in the least hinder or mitigate the violent demonstrations of the audience. But it was not so much the ballet that gave offence as the ballet dancers whom Garrick had brought from Paris. Peace was at length restored in Drury lane and the dancers sent back. The management lost £4,000 ;—Garrick purchasing knowledge of his public at rather a high rate." The public of that time had a hatred for these ballet-dancers for their gross impropriety and unseemliness. The art of a ballet-dancer is of a shocking kind. Scantier style of dress worn by dancers was considered indecent. The movements of the dancers of necessity involve a greater display of human form than is required by the simpler acts of riding, walking and sitting.

Ballet-dancers.

THE tone of the stage did not completely improve subsequently. Authors of no great merit commenced to write plays. Their language was vulgar and gross. Ballad operas reigned on the stage. Horace Walpole in his letter to George Montague, dated 16th October 1769, writes, "I am sorry those boys got at my tragedy. I beg you would keep it under lock and key. . . . It is not an age to encourage anybody. There is a total extinction of all taste. Our authors are vulgar, gross and illiterate. The theatre swarms with wretched translations and ballad operas and we have nothing new but improving abuse." This rigid author did not approve even of Garrick. The tragedies of the eighteenth century were not so good as those of the seventeenth. "Cato" by Addison was much praised as also the "Seige of Damascus" by Hughes, and some other tragedies. Edward Young whose tragedies and satires were much praised lived and wrote in this century. After writing the tragedy known as "The Revenge" he went to the length of challenging comparison as regards the treatment of the subject with the best tragedies of the time.

Addison—His Cato.

Hughes—Seige of Damascus.

Edward Young.

The Revenge.

FROM 1725 Pastoral dramas, operas and Burlesques, became the fashion of the stage. Burlesque was the cause of the

Pastoral dramas. Operas. Burlesques.

decline of the comedy. Satires also ruled the stage.

Samuel Foote.

Samuel Foote, who won renown by his wit, wrote many comedies and farces. He was a tolerable actor. He introduced the abuse of personal mimicry on the comic stage. He made his first appearance on the stage in 1744, and subsequently he "ventured to give upon the stage of the Hay-market a monologue entertainment called "Diversions of a Morning." In this a certain manager of a rival theatre was satirized and the performance was therefore prohibited. The author was not discouraged by this prohibition and by dint of wit and impudence for some time baffled the authorities. He invited his friends to attend the theatre at noon and drink the dish of chocolate with him." He promised that he would endeavour to make the morning as diverting as possible; and notified that Sir Dilbury Diddle would be there and Lady Betty Frisk had absolutely promised. He went on drawing friends by this stratagem and treated them with a dramatical representation. Of this great comic actor, Churchill said as follows :—

"By turns transform'd into all kinds of shapes
Constant to none Foote laughs, cries, struts and scrapes,
Now in the centre, now in van or rear,
The Proteus' shifts, bawd, parson, auctioneer,
His strokes of humour and his bursts of sport
Are all contained in this one word, distort.
Doth a man stutter, look as quaint or halt
Mimics draw humour out of nature's fault;
With personal defects their mirth adorn
And hang misfortunes out to public scorn."

Cooke speaks highly of this actor. He says that "Foote was only by far a better scholar than Garrick; and to this superiority he added also a good taste, a warm imagination, a strong turn for mimicry, and a constant fresh supply of extensive occasional reading from the best authors of all descriptions. He could likewise supply all these advantages with great readiness; so that either with his pen or in conversation he was never at a loss." Sentimental comedies also came into vogue during this period. Oliver Goldsmith wrote some comedies for the stage. His "Good Natured Man," a character comedy, was admired by all. The "Jealous Wife" and the "Clandestine Marriage" of G. Colman were comedies of genuine merit produced at the latter part of the seventeenth century. Sheridan's "Rivals" and the "School for Scandal" were admired for their uniform brilliancy of dialogue, for their tact and for their pungency of social satire. It is not out of place here to say that Sheridan when he was the manager of Drury Lane Theatre introduced on the stage Mrs. Siddons, the Queen of tragedy, and Mrs. Jordon, the most surprising comic actress. Sheridan had under him three of the greatest performers of that age, Mrs. Siddons, Mrs. Jordon and John Kemble.

Oliver Goldsmith.

Good Natured Man.

Jealous Wife.
G. Colman.
Clandestine Marriage.

Sheridan
The Rivals.
School for Scandal.

OF the histrionic development in England during the reign of George II, (1727–1760) Smollet, in his "History of England," observes that "the public acknowledged a considerable share of dramatic merit in the tragedies of Young, Mallet, Home and some other less distinguished authors. Very few regular comedies during this period were exhibited in the English theatre; which however produced many less favoured pieces abounding in satire, wit and humour. The 'Careless Husband' by Cibber and 'Suspicious Husband' of Hoadley are the only comedies of this age that bid fair for reaching posterity. The exhibitions of the stage were improved to the utmost exquisite entertainments by the talents and management of Garrick, who greatly surpassed all his predecessors of this and perhaps every other nation in his genius for acting, in

Smollet's opinion about the stage and the actors of the nineteenth century.

sweetness and variety of his tones, the irresistable magic of his eye, the fire and vivacity of his action, the elegance of attitude and the whole pathos of expression. Quin excelled in dignity and declamation as well as in exhibiting some characters of humour equally exquisite and peculiar. Mrs. Cibber breathed the whole soul of female tenderness and passion; and Mrs. Pritchard displayed all the dignity of distress." . . . . "Music became a fashionable study and its professors were generally caressed by the public. An Italian opera was maintained at a great expense and well supplied with foreign performers. Private concerts were instituted in every corner of the Metropolis." Dryden characterises an opera "as a poetical tale or fiction represented by vocal and instrumental music adorned with scenes, machines, and dances and adds that the persons of this musical drama are generally supernatural." The tendencies encouraged by operas were pernicious to the progress of dramatic literature. Scenes, machinery and costume helped to its decline.

Girald Griffin on the stage in the beginning of the nineteenth century.

GIRALD Griffin, during his sojourn in London between 1823 and 1830 saw the decline of legitimate drama in England and wrote as follows:—"I perceived the public taste was vitiated and that the managers so far from taking any steps to improve it, lent themselves to the child's fancies of the multitude with all the zeal that a love of full house and of money could inspire. The theatre indeed had become the scenes of many exhibitions of an amphitheatrical kind tending merely to attract the admiration of the senses and of such gorgeous and imposing a character that many persons of good taste who longed for a better state of things were for a time dazzled by their brilliancy, while the literary portion of the pieces represented had become quite subordinate and wanting in every quality that could give it the best claim to public attention. The scenery of decorations, field of battle, burning forest, and cataract of real water afforded a succession of splendours I had no conception of, but I was heartily tired of eternal gallopping, burning, marching and counter-marching and dull speechifying with which it abounds. A lady on horseback riding up a cataract is rather a bold stroke but these things are quite a rage now." All enjoyment that depends upon scenic effect, dresses, and grouping of figures, though quite legitimate in its place, is of itself of an inferior temporary and comparatively unintellectual kind.

Legitimate dramas lost in outward shows.

Dramatists of the nineteenth century.

SIR HENRY TAYLOR (1800–1886) wrote four tragedies and a comedy. His style was much admired. Lord Lytton, Lord Tennyson, and many other gentlemen of high position wrote for the stage in the nineteenth century. Robertson, Gilbert, Boucicault, Byron, Bernard Albery and Wills were also poets who did their best to write for the stage. Pinero, Grundy, Jones, Swinburne and Austin are dramatists of reputation who wrote romantic and realistic plays which are now frequently represented on the stage.

Lord Tennyson.

LORD TENNYSON commenced his dramatic career in his old age and his plays except "Becket" were not therefore successful.

Robertson.

ROBERTSON (1829-1871) was an actor and a famous dramatist. His plays of monosyllabic titles such as "Ours," "Caste," "Plays," "School," "Home," and "Dream" made him a celebrated dramatist.

Gilbert.

GILBERT wrote many burlesques, dramas, comedies and operas both independently and also jointly with Sir Arthur Sullivan.

A. W. Pinero.

A. W. PINERO is an original fertile dramatic humourist. He was also an actor. His plays (1) *£ 200 a Year* (2) *The Squire* (3) *The Rocket* (4) *Sweet Lavender* (5) *The Profligate* (6) *The Second Mrs. Tanqueray* (7) *The notorious Mrs. Ebbsmith* (8) *The Princess and the Butterfly*," place him almost the first among the modern dramatists. "The Second Mrs. Tanqueray" is reported to be an admirable comedy.

Sydney Grundy.

SYDNEY GRUNDY is also a famous dramatist. His dramas (1) *The Glass of Fashion* (2) *A Fool's Paradise* (3) *A White Lie* (4) *Sowing the Wind* (5) *The New Woman* and (6) *The Greatest of These*, are popular.

H. A. Jones.

HENRY ARTHUR JONES is a well known dramatist of great originality. His plays (1) *Only Round the Corner* (2) *The Silver King* (3) *Saints and Sinners* (4) *The Middleman* (5) *The Dancing Girl* (6) *The Case of Rebellious Susan* (7) *Michael and His Lost Angel* (8) *The Liars* and (9) *The Manoeuvres of Jane*, are favourably noticed.

A. C. Swinburne.

A. C. SWINBURNE is not only a great dramatist but also the greatest metrical inventor in English Literature.

Alfred Austin.

ALFRED AUSTIN, the present poet-laureate, is a great dramatist.

Actors of the period.

IN treating of the English Stage, I cannot but say a few words about its actors. Of Shakespeare, Betterton and Garrick I have already said what is sufficient for my purpose. Many actors of the nineteenth century deserve unreserved praise and admiration from the people, for it is to them and to their merit that the dramatic public is indebted for the reformation of the stage. The English actors of this century did to the stage more good than the actors of the Elizabethan age. The stage before the Elizabethan age was rude and the actors of that period had to try their best to remove its rudeness; but the actors of this century had to contend against public opinion with regard to their personal character. The mischievous effects of the stage after the Restoration continued till the beginning of the last century. Public opinion was against the stage.

Miss O'Neill. (Lady Beecher).

IN the beginning of the nineteenth century an actress by name O'Neill appeared on the stage and took London by surprise. A certain author says of her "this charming and youthful actress has rejected all pomp, pride and circumstance of the studied drilled and mechanical heroine of the stage; discarding the trammels of custom, precedent and conventional rules, handed down from one actress to another—preferring her own judgment and the pure effusions of nature working direct from the heart. On the first night of her appearance at Covent Garden she established a fame by far exceeding that of any actress before her—although possessing the advantages of high provincial celebrity, years of experience and family interest. Miss O'Neill is truly original; and previous to her entry on the London boards she never witnessed any of the great people. Her figure is of the finest model—displaying at once purity of mind and loveliness of countenance. Her demeanour is graceful and modest, her voice, melody itself in all her tones; and with the exception of the greatest actress of her day, the celebrated and original Lady Randolph, Miss O'Neill is the only actress with that genuine feeling that is capable of melting the audience to tears. In her hand the handkerchief is not hoisted as the only signal of distress. Her pauses are always judicious and impressive; her attitudes appropriate and effective either in regard to ease or dignity. She indulges in no sudden starts: no straining after effect; no wringing of hands or screaming at the top of the voice; no casting her eyes round the boxes, searching for applause, or addressing her discourse to the lustre or the Gods in the upper regions;

no whining or pining, moaning or groaning, roaring or bellowing out-heroding Herod. No, the great beauty of Miss O'Neill is that she never o'ersteps the modesty of nature ; thus casting to the winds all the little tricks which secondary actresses resort to." This famous actress in the full splendour of her triumphant career left the stage and became the wife of Sir W. M. Beecher, M.P., for Mallow, county of Cork.

The family of Kemble.

THE family of Kemble (three brothers, a sister and a daughter) distinguished itself during the latter part of the eighteenth and the beginning of the nineteenth centuries. It is said that Kemble had no superior on the stage as a tragedian. Of J. P. Kemble, Byron said that he was the most supernatural of actors. Thomas Campbell writes the following lines in his praise :—

"Fair as some classic dome
Robust and richly graced
Your Kemble's spirit was the home
Of Genius and of Taste
Taste like the silent dial's power
That when supernatural light is given
Can measure inspiration's hour
And tell its height in heaven.
At once ennobled and correct
His mind surveyed the tragic page,
And what the actor could effect
The scholar could presage."

Sir Walter Scott in speaking of this actor said "we lose in him an excellent critic an accomplished scholar and one who graced our forlorn drama with what little it has left of good sense and gentleman-like feeling. Stephen Kemble and Charles Kemble were also said to be equally good actors.

Sarah Siddons.

HIS sister Sarah Siddons reached the highest perfection as a tragic actress. It is said that she was unsurpassed by any player of any age or any country. She is known as "The Tragic Queen of the British Stage." Of Mrs. Siddons, Byron says, "of actors, Cooke was the most natural, Kemble the most supernatural, Kean the medium between the two, but Mrs. Siddons was worth them all put together." If you ask me what is a Queen I should say, Mrs. Siddons. Henderson said "she was an actress who never had had an equal nor would ever have a superior." Lord Erskine said "her performance was a school of oratory; I had studied her cadences and intonation and to the harmony of her periods and pronunciation I am indebted for my displays." Hazlitt observes "The Enthusiasm she excited had something idolatrous about it; we can conceive nothing grander. She embodied to our imaginations the fables of mythology of heroic and deified mortals of elder time. She was not less than a Goddess or a Prophetess inspired by the Gods. Power was seated on her brow; passion radiated from her breast as from a shrine; she was tragedy personified." Burke, Wyndham and Sir Joshua Reynolds—all testified to her commanding talents.

Helen Faucit.

HELEN FAUCIT (Mrs. Theodore Martin) was also a celebrated actress of the period. De Quincey in his usual rhetorical style describes her thus. "Then, suddenly—oh heavens! what a revelation of beauty! —forth stepped, walking in brightness, the most faultless of Grecian marbles, Mis Helen Faucit, as Antigone. What perfection of Athenian sculpture!—the noble figure, the lovely arms, the fluent drapery! What an unveiling of the ideal statuesque! Is it Hebe? Is it Aurora? Is it a Goddess that moves before us? Perfect she is in form; perfect in attitude:—

"Beautiful exceedingly
Like a ladye from a far countrie!"

It flattered one's patriotic feelings to see this noble young country-woman realising so exquisitely, and restoring to our imagination the noblest of Grecian girls! Sir Arthur

Allison praised this actress very highly. He said "if powers of the very highest order united to fascinating beauty, and the most lofty conceptions of the dignity and moral objects of her art could have arrested the degradation of the stage, Miss Helen Faucit would have done so. But this highly gifted actress arose in the decline of the drama, and even her genius was unequal to the task of supporting it in the days of corrupted taste. She is a combination of Mrs. Siddons and Miss O'Neill; with the majestic air and lofty thoughts of the former and as great pathetic power, not less winning grace, but far greater variety than the latter. Flexibility of power is her great characteristic, versatility her distinguishing feature. Like Garrick, she excels equally in tragedy or elegant comedy: it is hard to say whether her Rosalind is the more charming or her Lady Teazle the more fascinating, her Belvidera the more moving or her Juliet the more heart-rending. Dark raven locks, a fine figure, and singularly expressive countenance, bestow on her all the advantages which in addition to the highest mental gifts beauty never ceases to confer on women; and a disposition marked by deep feeling alternately lively and serious, sportive and mournful, playful and contemplating, gives her that command of the expression of different emotions and that versatility of power which constitute her great and unequalled charm. She has the highest conception of the dignity and moral capabilities of her art, and by the uniform chasteness and delicacy of her performances does the utmost to uphold it in its native purity; but it is all in vain. Her lot was cast in the days of the decline of taste, and notwithstanding her great genius and celebrity, she is unable to arrest it. She has risen to the very highest rank in her profession, but that profession in Great Britain is on the verge of extinction."

Edmund Kean.

EDMUND KEAN was the greatest of all actors. He had a natural gift for dramatical art. He was a rival of Kemble. Lord Byron who was one of the managing members of a dramatic committee called him a genius. Sir Henry Irving describes him as the greatest genius that the English stage has ever seen. Coleridge is reported to have said that to see Kean act was, "like reading Shakespeare by flashes of lightning." It is said that this famous actor blended the realistic with the ideal in acting. He is followed closely by William Charles Macready in this art. J. P. Cooke quotes in his lecture on dramas, the opinion of Count de Soligny about this famous actor. "His eyes glare, his teeth grind against each other, his voice hoarse and broken, his hands clenched and open alternately as if they were revelling in the blood of his enemy and his whole frame seems to have imbibed the will and the powers of a demon." This is how the famous actor acted the part of the *Moor* in Shakespeare's *Othello*. "The ghastly convulsion of his rage and the mighty power of his glare were such that he frightened once a fellow actress by name Mrs. Glover into fits." Mr. Kean was also noted for his proficiency in fencing. He pleased his audience with it also. He was a low comedian under Mr. Moss. In the seventeenth year of his age he saw Moss representing *Shylock* and he was so pleased with it that he exclaimed "if ever I should play *Shylock* it shall be after the style of Mr. Moss." The actors laughed at him but in nine years afterwards this actor did play *Shylock* and he got the applauses of the people. Byron, Hazlitt and Sheridan pronounced Kean to be the best *Shylock* since the days of Macklin. Many rival actors of fame were brought into the field to annihilate him, "but as fast as they came he sent them withering into obscurity or what was almost as contemptible into a melo-dramatic position." Kean was also considered the best harlequin. Hazlitt, the greatest critic of his age, speaks of Kean's superiority in the characters of *Richard* and *Shylock*. He said "it is impossible to form a higher conception of *Richard the Third* than that given by Kean; never was character represented with greater distinctness and precision and perfectly articulated in every part. If Kean did not succeed in concentrating all the lines of the character, he gave a vigor and relief to the part which we have never seen surpassed. He was more refined than Cooke; bolder and more original than Kemble. The scene with Lady Anne was an admirable specimen of smooth and smiling duplicity. Wily adulation was firmly marked by his eye, and he appeared like the first tempter in the garden of Eden. Kean's attitude in leaning against a pillar was one of the most graceful and striking positions ever witnessed. It would have served a Titian, Raphael or Salvator Rosa as a model. The transitions from the fiercest passion to the most familiar tone was a quality which Kean possessed over every other actor that ever appeared. Many have attempted this style but all have most egregiously failed." Donaldson in his "Reflections of an Actor" says "Kean took the town by surprise. No paragraphs from the provinces heralded his coming; no puffing; no friends. His look, his manner, his walk, the brilliancy of his searching eye, his expressive face, his pathos all combined to direct the attention of his audience; such was his masterly skill in the scene with Tubal that all judges pronounced him the first actor of the age. As a swordsman he stood quite alone. He was a musician, a dancer, a pantomimist and a dramatic scholar; in fact he was everything that constituted a powerful and finished actor; and as a proof of genius he was no copyist but perfectly original." In his entirety none but himself could be his parallel. "He was alone in force, energy, power, originality and conception. Every impersonation was instinct with truth and bore evidence of highest genius. What was perhaps his most remarkable distinctiveness was perhaps his perfect transfusion, as it were, of himself into the lifelike embodiment of the character he represented. For the time being he was wholly and absolutely the person he enacted." Gerald Griffin once said "what would I give to see Edmund Kean act Hardress Cregan—just to witness him at the party before his arrest where he is endeavouring to do the polite to the ladies while the horrid voice of guilt is in his ear. The very movement of Kean's countenance in such a scene as that would make one's flesh creep. Every motion and attitude of his ghastly efforts at complaisance and his subdued sense of impending ruin—would be all sufficient to keep an audience in a thrill of horror and without a word spoken would indicate the whole agony of his mind." Another historian writes of Edmund Kean that he was study as interesting to the mental philosopher as to the play-goer, so extraordinary was his possession of this single gift. He died in 1868.

W. C. Macready.

WILLIAM CHARLES MACREADY was also a celebrated actor of the nineteenth century. He studied for his profession and considered that "to be a great actor it was advisable for him to become a good scholar, an accomplished gentleman, a well ordered man with a well regulated mind and finely cultivated taste." Alfred Tennyson wrote the following lines in his praise :—

"Farewell, Macready, since to night we part :
Full-handed thunders often have confest
Thy power well-used to move the public breast.
We thank thee with one voice, and from the heart.
Farewell' Macready, since this night we part.
Go' take thine honours home ; rank with the best ;
Garrick and statelier Kemble, and the rest,
Who made a nation purer thro' their art.
Thine is it that the drama did not die,
Nor flicker down to the brainless pantomime,
And those gilt gauds men-children swarm to see.
Farewell, Macready ; moral, grave, sublime,
Our Shakespeare's bland and universal eye
Dwells pleased, thro' twice hundred years on thee."

Sir Bancroft.

MR. and MRS. BANCROFT are actors of very wide reputation. Bancroft commenced his career as an actor in 1861 and he has been an important character in most of the modern plays. In 189 he was knighted by the Gracious Queen Empress Victoria.

Kendal and other actors.

Mr. and Mrs. Kendal are also well known as actors of the first rank and so also are Arthur Cecil and Forbes Robertson. Mr. Hare is a well known comedian and a very popular actor; so also is Charles Wyndham who by his French farces and musical comedies is pleasing the English audience. Stanley Jones in his book "The Actor and His Art" says, "Inconsistently the most fascinating actor on the English stage is Charles Wyndham, once the first of our light comedians, now our best actor on high comedy."

C. Windham.

Mr. Beerbohm Tree is an actor and a manager of indefatigable energy. Of Mr. Irving and Miss Ellen Terry I need not say anything as their fame is already well known throughout the world. Ellen Terry is the leading English actress of the day, as Sir Henry Irving is the leading English actor. They both give their performance in the Lyceum Theatre. The brilliant successes of these two actors are unrivalled in European dramatic history. The prosperity of the English stage reached its zenith under Sir Henry Irving—the king of actors. The following extract from the "England, its People, Polity and Pursuits" by T. H. S. Escott will show to the reader what Sir Henry Irving has done towards reforming the stage. "At the close of these observations on the contemporary English stage there may be briefly noticed a question which used often to be heard among the play goers. Is a revival of Shakespearean dramas in England more probable than a revival of the classic drama in France? Four or five years ago the answer would have been in the negative. All those existing conditions of the stage and of society to which reference has been made in this chapter pointed to one conclusion which a flash of fashionable enthusiasm for single actor of originality and distinction,

Sir H. Irving and Miss Ellen Terry.

whose principle and most popular successes have been won in modern realistic drama and in modern comedy confirmed rather than contradicted. The more Shakespeare's plays are read the less perhaps would they be represented. An audience sufficiently cultivated to enjoy the plays as literature to take the quality of the poet's language and the subtlety of his imagery was supposed to be proportionately less disposed to tolerate the personation of all but one or two characters in the piece by actors such as Hamlet describes in his advice to the players. This anticipation however has been completely falsified by events and at no time has the Shakespearean drama been in greatest favour with the English public than at present. This fact is the result chiefly of the genius of Mr. Henry Irving who has done more than any one else to popularise the plays of Shakespeare." A few extracts in praise of him by Englishmen of letters and the clergy will not be out of place here. In Dublin the Lord Mayor presented him with an address written by Professor Dowden, the Lord Lieutenant being present on the occasion. "Your fame and the common delight which you have given on each side of the Atlantic have linked the lovers of art in the two hemispheres. You have proved your power to interpret not alone the extremes of human passions but also the depth and subtleties of thought. You have given an example of what is the finest moral distinction of art." In Edinburgh and Glassgow Sir Henry Irving gave a performance of "Becket." All ministers of the Church of Scotland, nay the very moderator of the church sat on front seats in the theatre. The state officially recognised the actor in 1895, when our beloved Queen Empress conferred the title of Knighthood on Mr. Irving. The Revd. Cannon Thompson on proposing a toast in honour of Sir Henry Irving said "the Drama was the greatest of all works of creative literature. Socrates was glad to sit at the foot of Euripedes and to acknowledge the sovereignty of dramatic representation. . . The actor is a real and living force in the community." The church now acknowledges the influence of the drama and many of the clergy are to be found among the audience at the theatres. The crowning success of the stage was at the end of May 1895 when Sir Henry Irving recited Tennyson's "Becket" in the form of a drama in the "Chapter House of Canterbury Cathedral almost at the very spot where according to tradition the Archbishop met his death." It is certainly a memorable fact that an actor, however gifted and scholarly, should be asked by the Dean of Canterbury, Dr. Farrar, to act "Becket" within the precincts of a Cathedral which has been the ecclesiastic centre of England. Dr. Sinclair said "he believed the mission of the stage to be a high one." Mr. Gladstone at a dinner in honour of Charles Kean of *Princes Theatre* said that "drama is a handmaid to Christianity." "Mr. Gladstone, meeting Mr. Irving twenty years ago in Bond Street stopped, introduced himself to him, and spoke of the keen intellectual pleasure he had derived from his performance. Now and then Mr. Gladstone might be seen behind the scenes of the *Lyceum*, where owing to his deafness, a sort of box was fitted up for him in the wings during the performance. It is at present the sincere opinion of English society that the man who does not care for the play is not so good a citizen as the good play-goer. To be born without the dramatic instinct is regarded by the European society as a calamity like colour-blindness. They say that the most broadly humanising influence in the world is the stage. On 6th March 1895 our beloved and bemoaned Queen Empress gave a reception at Buckingham Palace to Mrs. Keely, the famous actress. Our noble Queen sent for her, spoke to her kindly and gave her a photograph which contained on its top right hand corner an autograph "Victoria R.I. 1895." The famous Mrs. Keely was then eighty-nine years old and had put in a service of seventy years on the stage. There are many others of reputation both in England and on the

Mrs. Keely.

continent who are striving their best to improve the art. The book *On Actors and the Art of Acting* written by George Henry Lewes is well worth perusal.

BEFORE finishing the history of histrionic development of Great Britain during the nineteenth century I would desire to add something to show how the Britons have been aspiring to improve their national dramas. The following is an extract from Cabinet Annual Register, dated 31st May 1832. "In the House of Commons, this day, Mr. E. L. Bulwer moved for a select committee to inquire into the state of laws affecting dramatic literature and the performance of the drama. In the licentious period in which the first patents were granted, the reign of Charles II, the minor theatres were the scene of very disorderly and improper exhibitions and it was therefore desirable to suppress them; that was no longer the case. The patents were granted to two theatres for the preservation of the dignity of the national drama. They had not produced that object. No sooner were the patents obtained than the national drama began to deteriorate and a love of scenic effect *superseded* it. This reproach to the Patentees had constantly existed, and existed with peculiar justice at the present time. We were tempted to ask with the Lord Chancellor, not how many plays had been produced of our literature, but rather how many plays had been produced fit for grown up men and women to go and see? They might be assumed there would be no more theatres than they could find audiences to fill them; and he thought there ought to be as many theatres as the public were willing to support. He wished all restrictions on the legitimate drama to be removed. He required no novel experiment, he only asked them to leave it as it was in the days of Massinger and Beaumont and Fletcher and Johnson and Shakespeare, when seventeen theatres were constantly open to a metropolis, a tenth part of the size of London at present, and a population by a hundred degrees less wealthy and intellectual. The honourable member then adverted to the laws regarding literary property and dramatic copy-right in particular and remarked upon the injustice done to literary men who were the only portion of the community to whom was denied that necessary blessing pledged by every free state to its subjects, the protection of property. Sir Charles Wetherill opposed the motion. The abrogation of the patents, he argued, would tend to multiply theatres, but not to improve them. At Paris there are thirteen or fourteen theatres but he had not heard of any modern Corneille or Racine. Besides, there were reforms enough on hand already and enquiry on such a subject must certainly be useless and might be mischievous.

MR. LAMB thought the time had arrived when some enquiry into the anomolous state of privilege and law respecting theatres and dramatic copy-right was requisite. He trusted it would lead to improvement.

MR. W. BROUGHAM, MR. HUME and other gentlemen supported the motion.

MR. SHIEL said 'experience had shown that a dramatic censorship was neither necessary nor desirable. The spirit of true decorum and refinement would, he believed, always forbid the performances of irreligious or immoral compositions.'

THE appointment of a select committee were agreed to"

CHAPTER VI.

GERMANY.

EDUCATION in Germany before the nineth century was confined mostly to the Church. So long ago as 883 A.D. the Gospel was turned into verse in the vernacular tongue. An historian remarks "we here find rhyme instead of alliteration." From this it may be inferred that before rhyme was chosen for verse, alliteration was in vogue in poetical works. The Germans had, even before this period, the old Teutonic and other pastoral ballads peculiar to every country in its barbarous condition. The existence of ballads, even of superior merit, is no indication of learning and literature, for, we see in India, a villager who cannot even sign his name, composing ballads on various themes full of rhyme and containing sometimes noble ideas couched in figurative language. This may be considered a natural gift to a selected few. Even a learned author of many poems cannot produce a thing of this kind. In the tenth and the eleventh centuries we find the prevalence of Latin poetry. Vernacular poetry again came into vogue in the beginning of the twelfth century. A. M. Selss in his *Outline of the Literature of Germany* names the period between 350 and 1150 as monastic age and mentions the existence, during that period, of alliterative popular ballads narrating the legends of Beowulf, Hildebrandslied and also the religious poems of Muspilli and Heliand. During the latter part of the twelfth century, The Germans commenced to write epic poems. Then came the love-songs of Minne-singers. These songs contain dialogues between lovers. The poets of Provence called Troubadours were the first composers of them. From France they spread to Flanders and thence to

Education.

Minne-Singers.

Germany. The German Knights who returned from the first crusade composed these songs and were known as Minne-singers. Several mighty princes composed the songs, and considered it an honour to do so. During the thirteenth century the German nobility were engaged in wars and became independent. They then thought it not honourable to write poems. During the subsequent period, literature took care of itself, caring not for the protection of princes and nobles. In the beginning of the fourteenth century many burghers of towns became poets, and they were known as Meister-singers.

Hrotsvitha.

TILL the tenth century Germany had no dramas. In this century, an abbess by name Hrotsvitha wrote many comedies, the themes for them being the legends of the saints. She introduced love and laughter into her religious plays. She was said to be a nun of noble birth. She lived between 935 and 1000 A.D. She sang the praises of Otto the Great and commemorated the origin of his house. She wrote dramas in Latin. Her object was to give a fresh vigour to the traditions of the Christian church.

Musical schools.

THE favourite recreation of the Germans during the twelfth century was music. There were singing schools established during this period. The minne-songs and Meister-singers could be traced to these institutions. The clergy wrote dramas on Scriptural subjects representing Pagan festivals. They were acted as usual in the churches at first, then in open courts and subsequently in market places. Day after day, for many hours, they were represented in the presence of large audiences. Along with these ecclesiastical plays, there were also farces known as *Shrove Tuesday plays*. These were acted in the public rooms of an inn or before the door of a prominent citizen without much dramatic ceremony. Such sort of *Shrove Tuesday Plays* are common in India especially in Tirupathi where recently I saw a farce of this kind.

Shrove Tuesday Plays.

A religious man, rather elderly, had two young wives. The husband and wives were at logger-heads with each other. There was much fun and laughter in the old husband requesting the wives not to lead a bad life because religious books prohibit such a course in women and the wives replying haughtily that they were not taught by him to learn morals from religious books, and so on. This farce was carried on in the form of a dialogue in speech and comic songs. The players wander through towns performing the farces in front of big men's houses for half an hour or so and receive whatever paid to them as remuneration.

In Germany there were many famous writers of dramas and farces of the above kind in the fourteenth century. In the fifteenth century the *Shrove Tuesday Plays* and *Miracle Plays* became popular but they assumed questionable form. The farces contained invectives against the clergy—nay—even the miracle plays became satires more or less against religious men. It is said that "in a certain miracle play the leading character of which was Joanna (a mythical female pope) a clerical author did not hesitate to pour contempt on the Roman See itself." A famous author by name "Reuchlin" wrote many plays in Latin about 1494 and the students of Heidleberg represented them before German audiences. Conrad Celtes produced many tragedies and comedies in the public halls of German cities. Heidelberg was the chief seat of Rhenish society which established an academy there for the cultivating of ancient learning, music and poetry. Dances also formed an amusement of this society. It had branches all over Germany. It was from the famous Conrad Celtes

Reuchlin.

Conrad Celtes.

abovenamed, that Saxony acquired taste for learning.

Carnival plays.

The Carnival plays which were played during the carnival feasts enjoyed much patronage from the people. Taking advantage of the license of the season many tragedies, comedies and tragi-comic drama by name "*Apotheosis of Pope*" was performed in 1480. It was the age of the great Reformation.

Effect of Renaissance.

THE movement of Renaissance germinating in Italy in or about the fourteenth century grew into a tree in Germany and extending its branches all over Europe, fructified at last in the shape of religious reformation in the sixteenth century. The people enjoying the benefit of learning mostly in the fifteenth century opened their eyes and saw the abuses of all kinds emanating from the very seat which was till then falsely supposed to be the source of the highest ideals. The deplorable state of the church, the appalling degeneracy of the clergy, the pride and rapacity of the cardinals, the immorality of the priests, the overwhelming luxury, licentiousness, and avarice of the Popes raised the honest indignation of the people, amonst whom some conscientious ecclesiastics were also included. They gave vent to their feelings, some in the form of letters, some in the shape of books and others in the form of dramatical satires against the clergy of the day. The latter representations enlightened the masses. They then knew their position with reference to the Roman church and also the deception practised by it on their ignorance. Thus we see the scholars of the Renaissance movement became agents of the Reformation and used the stage as one of the vehicles to carry their work through. They dramatised both in Latin and in the vernacular the narratives of the Bible.

Luther.

Hans-Sacho.

Luther, the author of the Reformation, encouraged these representations. By his encouragement Hans-Sacho wrote many plays and became known as the father of German dramas.

DURING the sixteenth and the seventeenth centuries Germany had, besides the above species of dramatical representations, "School Comedies" written in imitation of Plautus and Terence and acted in the Universities and public schools. An extract from *the History of German Literature* written by James Sime, M.A., will interest the reader and is well worth perusal. "Luther with a large humanity characteristic of him when dogmatic disputes were not in question, encouraged these comedies and was indeed friendly to dramatic effort of all kinds. To persons who complained that modesty was often offended by the actors, he replied that "if they carried out their principle they would have to refrain from reading the Bible." When the Jesuits began to agitate in opposition to Protestantism, they detected at once with their usual tact the importance of this element in popular life and through their influence more attention was paid not only to the plays but to the manner in which they were represented.

School comedies.

TOWARDS the end of the sixteenth century, Germany was visited by a band of English comedians who went about acting in their own language. They appear to have produced a deep impression. In the middle of this century theatres were built in Nuremberg and Augsberg; and other cities soon followed the example. Duke Julius of Brunswick not only built a theatre in his capital but also maintained a permanent company. He wrote many comedies and tragedies for it. From 1618 to 1648 the country was desolated by *the Thirty Years' War*. During this period dramatical literature faded with the prosperity and the population of the country. During the seventeenth century there was no dramatical progress. Italian Operas were being performed in courts. With all the efforts of literary men, the German stage unfortunately could not

Theatres.

Italian Operas.

accommodate itself to the dramatic literature. It is no wonder therefore that the dramatic art did not improve.

Neuber. Leipsic.

AT the commencement of the eighteenth century, Neuber, as directress of a company of actors, assisted by Gottsched, the professor of poetry in Leipsic framed stringent rules for the guidance of the actors. She so managed the company as to maintain a friendly link between the stage and literature. A large number of literary works intended for the stage were brought forward by authors for performance. A. W. Schlegel also wrote a drama by name "Ion." They all formed themselves into a company known as the Leipsic School.

Leipsic School.

This School produced a great effect upon the progress of the art of acting, in which a famous actor by name Eckhof won the highest renown. The Leipsic enterprise was encouraged by the critic Lessing (1729–1781). He established a national theatre at Hamburg. His criticisms subsequently became rules of dramaturgy for the guidance of authors and actors. The character of Harlequin which was hitherto a necessary element on the German stage as 'Vidushaka' was on the Indian stage of ancient days, was dispensed with by the exertions of this critic. The Emperor Joseph II encouraged dramatic performances. Lessing, the great scholar and critic, wrote also many dramas. Wolfgang Menzel in his *History of Germany* writes that "Lessing, by his triumph over the scholastic pedants, completed what Thomasius had begun, by his irresistible criticism, drove French taste from the literary arena, aided by Winckelmann, to promote the study of the ancients and to foster the love of art, and raised the German theatre to an unprecedented height. He was the boldest, freest, finest spirit of the age."

Lessing.

His plays.

HIS tragi-comedy "Minna Von Barnhelm" is based on an incident from military life. It was the first good drama composed in Germany. His tragedy "Emilia Galloti" will not suit the refinement of modern age as it contains an unnatural incident that a father stabbed his lovely daughter to save her from the best of the prince. In his drama "Nathan the Wise" Lessing has preached the moral lesson of religious toleration by relating the famous parable of the three rings.

Schiller and his plays.

SCHILLER (1759–1805) wrote many dramas to improve the German Literature. He wrote the play "Robbers" while he was yet a school boy. His tragedy "Fiesco" contains a plot for the overthrow of the Dorias and is said to be well-written. "The Court's Intrigue and Love" is a domestic tragedy and describes the fatal effects of passion and the cruelty of a sordid parent in crossing his son's affections. "Don Carlos" is another tragedy similar almost to the tragedy of that name by Otway. "Wallenstein" is a historical drama of merit, where the hero meets his tragic end in consequence of his fatal ambition. The tragedy of "Mary Stuart" shows "the unhappy queen suffering for her Catholic faith and doing compulsory penance for the sins of her earlier life." In the drama "Maid of Orleans." the author has vindicated the character of Joan of Arc from the ridicule of other writers. The "Bride of Messina" is a tragedy wherein two Sicilian brothers who hate each other fall in love with a maiden, without knowing that she is their sister. In the duel, one brother is killed and the other runs away. "William Tell" is a drama of high merit containing "the struggle of the Swiss against their Austrian oppressors and their final deliverance from a foreign yoke."

Goethè and his plays.

GOETHE (1749–1832) was a friend of Schiller and wrote many dramas. His "Gotz" is a historic political drama indicating the "evil consequences of feudal turbulence." His "Iphigenia in Tauris" is an imitation of the Greek tragedy of Sophocles. "Egment" is a tragedy whose subject is the martyrdom of a Dutch Count. "Tasso" is a domestic drama where the agony of disappointed love is described. His "Faust" is a drama of high merit. Here Dr. Faust, a scholar, desirous of knowing the mysteries of the supernatural world gave up his soul to the devil. The first part of this tragedy though lengthy is very well written and is worth perusal. The second part is a mere confusion.

Iffland.

A POET by name Iffland composed dramas and acted on the stage. He was considered a distinguished actor. The Romantic school established by Goethe did much towards the progress of German literature, though the country itself was distracted by the French invasions. The most distinguished dramatist of this school was Henirich Von Kleist, (1776–1811). His "Kathehen Von Heilbronn" is a popular Romantic drama wherein the heroine falls blindly in love with a Knight. The Knight is charged with witchcraft as he raises in her an unusual degree of passion. The heroine is thereupon sent to a nunnery. She escapes and saves her lover from flames just before his marriage with another lady by name Kunigunde. The Knight admires her bravery and makes her his wife.

THE "Hermann's Schlacht" is a political drama indirectly showing the impending downfall of Napoleon and his generals.

THE "Broken Pitcher" is a comedy describing a petty Sessions case in a Dutch town, in which the Magistrate of the District turns out to be himself the Chief offender.

Fate tragedies.

AT this period another class of dramas known as "Fate Tragedies" came into existence. The author of these was the poet Werner. He raised the literature of the drama to classic force and dignity.

Young German School. Heinrich Haine.

HEINRICH HAINE (1799–1856) was the most gifted poet of the Young German School. His dramas "Almansor" and "Ratcliff"—though not successful on the stage are admired for the language. A noble Arab chief sought for the hand of a Christian girl who was in love with him. The relatives of the girl promised her to him in case he abjured Mahommedanism and became a Christian. His conscience did not permit him to become a Christian and his love for the girl did not allow him to lose her. He therefore eloped with his mistress. They were pursued and to escape capture they leaped together down a precipice. This was performed on the stage in 1823 but was a failure. "Ratcliff" is a drama where a Scotch rake, "under the influence of supernatural visions first slays his rival and puts an end to his own life."

Karl Gutzkow.

ANOTHER member belonging to the "Young German School" was "Karl Gutzkow (1811-1878) who wrote many dramas for the stage. Most of his dramas related to the political and social questions of the day. His dramas are (1) *Nero*, (2) *Richard Savage*, (3) *Patkul*, (4) *Wullenweber*, (5) *Prototype of Tartuffe*, (6) *Zopt und Schwert*, (7) *Uriel Acosta*. The last play is a tragedy containing a struggle between love and Jewish fanaticism. A scholar by name Acosta was expelled from the Jewish community for publishing a book. He was promised re-admission on the intercession of his betrothed Judith Vanderstraten, on the condition that he should retract his errors and undergo penance in the synagogue. After many mental struggles and for the sake of Judith he passed through the preliminary stages of the punishment imposed. When undergoing this insult, he learnt that after all Judith was to be given in marriage to his rival, rushed into the Church but found that the marriage ceremony had already ended. Judith went to meet him and drank in his presence the poison which she prepared.

Austrian School.

IN the nineteenth century Austria established a school of poetry known as Austrian school. F. Grillparzer (1791-1872) was the author of "Die Ahnfrau," "Sappho," "Hèro."

F. Halm.

F. HALM (1806–1876) was a famous dramatist of Austria. He wrote thirteen dramas of which three have attained considerable fame. "Griseldis" is a drama wherein the husband, a Knight of the "Round Table," by various cruel experiments tries the fidelity and devotion of his wife. "The son of Wilderness" is a drama illustrating the civilizing power of love upon a savage. Here a woman by her charms subdues the tyranny of a savage wildman. The dramas of the author are sensational in language and action.

F. Hebbel.

F. HEBBEL was the author of many tragedies which contain, it appears, poetical beauties of a high order. His dramas "Nibelungeu," "Judith," "Genofeva," "Mary Magadalane," "Gyges and his Ring" contain horrible incidents. His subjects are generally adultery and murder. His language is highly poetic.

IN Germany the best imaginative writers find scope for their energies for the theatre. Germany is really proud of great men like Schlegal, Lessing, Goethe and Schiller and the improvement in dramatical quality is sufficiently satisfactory.

IT is said that Goethe wrote many plays and was in the nabit of often going to the theatres with his friend Schiller. Naturally in these circumstances, one would expect higher merit in the dramatical performances. An article published somewhere, by professor Litzmann says "The actors of late recognised the dramatists as having the first claim upon them, with the result that not only were the master-pieces of dramatical literature interpretted with a beauty and intelligence which had been long foreign to the stage. A new light was thrown of late upon the true principles of acting."

CHAPTER VII.

RUSSIA, DENMARK, SWEDEN, NORWAY AND HOLLAND.

THE earliest written literature in Russia is in the eleventh century. Before that the Russians had oral literature in rude songs in praise of their Gods and heroes. Not to speak of the satires of Kanteurir we hear of dramatical literature in Russia only in the beginning of the eighteenth century. Religious dramas were however in existence. They were imported from Poland in the twelfth century. Puppet shows were the amusement of the people till the seventeenth century. These puppet dramas treated themes both secular and religious and were popular. One Lomonossoff wrote tragedies at first. A poet Sumarokoff wrote also many tragedies, comedies and satires. In 1756 a theatre was first opened in St. Petersburgh. They had their religious plays. A poet by name Visin wrote a comedy called "Nidorosl" in which he satirized the coarse features of Russian society, the ill-treatment of the serfs and other matters. Ozeroff wrote many tragedies. These are works produced in the eighteenth century during the reigns of Catherine II and Alexander. The Empress Catherine II is stated to have written many comedies which are well-hit satirical sketches of the follies and foibles of her subjects. Pushkin was the greatest poet and dramatist of the nineteenth century. Before the nineteenth century and during it also plays of Moliere, Corneille and Racine were translated and performed on the stage. Griboiedoff was an author of many comedies. His comedy "Gore ot Uma", (which means grief out of wit) is said to be a master-piece. The misfortune of being too clever is illustrated in this clever comedy. The nineteenth century produced a few dramatists and the dramatical progress of Russia is not as encouraging as in other countries of Europe. In Russia dramas are freely performed, but the Church is protected against the satire of the stage.

A. B. GRANVILLE in his book "Travels to St. Petersburgh" Vol. II mentions that at St. Petersburgh, the general direction of the theatres vests with the Imperial Government and the Emperor spends large sums of money to encourage poets, dramatists and actors.

DENMARK.

UP to the seventeenth century, there was no dramatical representation–nay–dramatical literature even, in Denmark. Hansan's plays were nothing but the mixture of religious themes and farces. Holberg, the author of the "History of the World" was the first dramatist in Denmark. In 1721 a play house was constructed in Copenhagen and the poet Holberg wrote twenty comedies for it in the course of four years. It is said that "in his thirty-three dramas he has left his most important positive legacy to literature." In his comedies he did not sacrifice decency to a desire for popularity or a false sense of wit. Joannes Ewald wrote many dramas, pure and simple, and revived the taste for Scandinavian History, and Mythology. For some time, afterwards, people finding no new national dramas commenced to perform the tragedies of Voltaire. The poet Wessel wrote a national drama "Love without Stockings" the effect of which was magical. From this time forward, the French tragedies and even Italian operas were ejected and no

Holberg.

Joannes Ewald.

Wessel.

performance that was not national and that was not in the Danish language was ever performed. It was at this time that the Danish school of music was also started. From the history of Denmark, we find that the dramatical element, though long in taking its root in Denmark, has grown with double vigour, and it is a happy feature of Denmark that its poets completely ruled its literature.

SWEDEN.

SWEDEN before the sixteenth century is barren of dramatic element. The kings and the people had enough of war, internal and external, to engage their attention. The first drama that was performed in Sweden was a comedy of "Tesbe" acted by the school-boys in 1610.

Messenius.

A poet, Messenius, intended to write the history of Sweden in fifteen plays. He finished six. They were performed. He wrote some dramas in prison where he was confined for twenty years for treason against the King. Many poets both clergy and laymen wrote comedies, tragedies and tragic-comedies and they were acted by the school-boys and University youths. The new Royal theatre was opened in 1737 and Dalin, the greatest poet of the age, acted his tragedy "Brynhilda." His comedies and satires show his skill if not the strength of his imagination.

NORWAY.

THE antiquity of pastoral and love ballads of this country is great, but its history is merged in that of either Denmark or Sweden. Norwegian dramatists have been coming into prominence of late.

A. Munch.

Andrews Munch was a well known poet of the beginning of the nineteenth century and his historical dramas are very popular. Ibsen and Bjornson are two modern dramatists of very great fame.

Ibsen.

Ibsen's dramas are translated and played in Germany, France and England. Opinion is divided as to the dramatical merit of his plays.

HOLLAND.

HOLLAND commenced its dramatical career with religious dramas. History records that these dramas were played at the different centres of the Empire by the clergy from 1400 to 1500 in their Churches. Semi-religious companies outside the church acted also theological dramas with farces. These ancient theatrical companies gave rise to an element of rhetoric.

Chambers of Rhetoric

"Chambers of Rhetoric" were formed in many places. The poets of Holland saw that in the development of these associations there would be a perfect development of arts, literature and national character. To educate the populace, the poets of these chambers continued to write mysteries and miracle plays. The prominent member of each "Chamber of Rhetoric" wrote plays and performed them. Towards the end of the fifteenth century each small town had its own "Chamber of Rhetoric" and performance. The representatives of noble families became the honorary members of these chambers and assisted them with money to erect pageants. In '561, twenty-eight chambers met in Antwerp to show their skill and the towns-people gave one ton of gold for distribution among the members as prizes. 1583 we see already satires against the clergy. Though for sometime the literary effort of Holland was dull, it soon opened its eyes under the encouragement of the daughters of Roemer Vesscher.

Vondel and Brideroo.

The tragedies of the glorious poet Vondel, the comedies of Brideroo—a literary genius—and the farces of Koster were written at this time.

P. C. Hooft.

In 1598 a youth of eighteen years, by name Pieter Cornelissen Hooft, of a partician family wrote the tragedy of "Achilles and Polyxena", in an admirable manner. He also wrote many other dramas in a pure language. In 1638 a large public theatre was erected in Amsterdam and Vondel opened it. We see even up to date Holland is grateful to this dramatist for its dramatical improvements.

PART II.

INDIA.

CHAPTER VIII.

INDIA.

BEFORE I commence to write about the dramatic development in India I would desire to quote the opinion of A. W. Ward, Professor of English Literature, Owen's College, Manchester. He observes that "The origin of the Indian drama may unhesitatingly be described as purely native. The Mahomedans when they overran India brought no drama with them; the Persians, the Arabs and the Egyptians were without a national theatre. It would be absurd to suppose the Indian drama to have owed anything to the Chinese or its offshoots. On the other hand, there is no real evidence for assuming any influence of Greek example upon the Indian drama at any stage of its progress. Finally it had passed into the decline before the dramatic literature of Modern Europe had sprung into being."

Purely native origin of Indian dramas.

THE antiquity of the Indian dramatic elements may be traced to an age far beyond that of Indian mythology. Religion pervades each and every ancient Indian institution. Music is considered by the Indian's as the principal feature of education. A verse in Sanscrit says of the Goddess of Learning (Saraswati, the wife of the Creator of the world) that music is her one breast and general education the other. The sweets of the latter come only after hard study but the former is always sweet and can be enjoyed easily. The Veda is our religious musical drama. Saraswati, the Hindu Goddess of Learning and Music, and her son Narada—the sage—are always represented as holding the "Veena" and the "Tambouri." It is said in praise of music that it pleases infants, brutes, serpents and inanimate things as well. Pindar, the ancient choral poet of Greece, describes the

Antiquity of the Indian Music.

soothing effect of the harp in a song, the gift of which is that it soothes not only the human passions but also the wrath of the Gods, and it has an influence on brutes and the inanimate nature, the eagle and the lightning. The snake charmers in India even now use a musical instrument known as 'Nagaswara' to tempt the snake to come out of its hole. Sree Krishna used his flute and made not only the nymphs (Gopikas) stand still in admiration of his power but also herds of cows and calves. When the powerful ten headed demon Ravana in his pride lifted the Kilasa mountain, the risidence of Siva, it fell on his hands which he could not extricate, when it is said, he cried in lamentation in so many different tunes in praise of God, that Siva was pleased with his music and relieved him from his agony. That gods are pleased with music is admitted by all nations. In I Samuel Ch. XVI, it is said thus :—"And it came to pass when the evil spirit from God was upon Saul, that David took an harp, and played with his hand. So Saul was refreshed, and was well, and the evil spirit departed from him." Again in Luke Ch. XV it is said "as he came and drew nigh to the house, he heard music and dancing." Isaiah speaks of the tabret or timbrel, as used in their (easterns) feasts. That "music frequently accompanied eastern meals, especially those which were of superior kind" is unquestionable as even now in India a music party is arranged after meals in marriages and other grand occasions. Homer describes the meal of Ulysses as follows :—

SONG AS THE BARD.

"Chanted, he ate ; and when he ceased to eat
Then also ceased the bard divine to sing."

It is also said that this elevated art was gathered from the Vedas by the Creator Brahma, who taught his son Narada, who in his turn taught a learned sage, most probably the sage now known as Bharata. In the Yajurveda, Yagna Valkya is described as the inventor of an instrument like a

Veena having a hundred strings. According to our mythology there is a class of semi-gods or heavenly beings known as Gandharvas who are proficients in music. A skeleton description of Indian music is given by W. H. Beauty-Kingston in his book "Ancient and Medieval India" Vol. II

Indian dance.

THE dance also has its origin in Indian Gods. The Nymphs of heaven are said to dance before the Gods. Siva has a peculiar dance of his own known as Tandava, and his wife, her own, known as "Lasya." She taught it to "Woosha," the daughter of Banasura. Krishna's delightful dance is the *Rasa* or cyclic dance which he taught to his beloved Gopikas. This Rasakreda is described in the epic poem Bhagavata which celebrates the deeds of Krishna. The Rik, Yaju, and Atharvana Vedas repeatedly mention dancing in their songs. There is no religious or historic treatise in India which does not speak of music and dancing in glowing terms of praise. Our native kings in all ages have taught their children music and dancing, employing teachers, and constructing a separate building for their study. The music and dance hall of Uttara, daughter of "Virata," in the epic poem "Bharata" is a striking example. A peculiar kind of dance (to us very rude now) is found in the hill-tribes known as "Tandas." In the Vindhya mountains, the Bhill tribes have a peculiar dance known as the Holee. This dance is practised by professionals amongst them. The women with long poles and the men with short sticks engage in a sham fight. There is always in this entertainment a clown covered with leaves and wearing a mask. They say this amusement is heriditary among them, existing from time out of the living memory of the people. In rural parts the agriculturists after their tiresome day's work dance in the moon-light and this is known as the "Kolatam" dance. Number of men each holding two short sticks one in each hand and either standing in a circular form or one se t opposing the other dance with vocal music. Boys in pial schools during the first half of the seventh month of the year, perform a sort of dance with vocal and instrumental music. Among the Brahmins known as "Dasestas," a kind of dance is used by the votaries of the goddess of Bhavani with songs in praise of that goddess with a sort of musical instrument peculiar to them. This may be compared to the ancient tragedy of the Greeks. In India there has been and is a set of people who make dancing their profession. They are the dancers in all temples in India. They were known as "Devadasis" or 'maid-servants of God'; they once led a respectable life though they are now treated as little more than harlots. This is due to the Mahomaden conquest of India. In Sanscrit a dance without gesticulation and speech is called "Nritta," that with gesticulation but not speech is called "Natya," from which the Nataka or Drama takes its origin. Thus we see that Indian music and Indian dancing take their origin in Divinity.

Gesticulation.

THE art of Minos (gesticulation) had its origin in India. It is known as *Abhinaya* science and is as ancient as our music and dancing are and as complete as one would wish it. The regulation of the movements of the different parts of the body even to the lowest finger and of the wrinkles of the face and eye-brows to denote a given idea, nay, a given word is described in it. The science is so copious and complicated that even an intelligent student takes years to master it. The authorship of this science is attributed to Bharata. In all Sanscrit dramas and dramaturgies and in all books on music, dancing and Abhinaya, we find the name of Bharata as the original author or the original codifier of the science. "Bharata," some say is not the name of the man. What his real name is, is not known for

Bharata explained.

certain. Bharata consists of three syllables. Bha, stands for Bhava which is gesticulation, Ra, stands for Raga which is vocal music and Ta, stands for Tala which is keeping time by means of cymbals. These are known as Bharata. This classification gives prominence to gesticulation or action, and I think the classification is just, for, without action, amusement is dull or parrot-like.

Indian classic literature (Sanscrit).

STATING thus in brief the principal elements of Indian dramatic art I proceed to write concisely about the beauties of the Indian literature and append a few rules of Indian dramaturgy. Commencing with the literature I need not say much about the Sanscrit language which is perfect in itself. Frisdrich-von-Schlegal, the great German scholar, says that of the languages of the world "The Indian is the most ancient and the source from whence others of later origin are derived. It would be difficult to find any so skillfully and exquisitely framed as that of which we have been speaking. . . . All the preceding proofs appear clearly to establish the fact that the Sanscrit is of higher antiquity than the Greek or Latin, not to mention the German or Persian." Max Muller in his book Leiture on science of language" observes "The Hindus are the only nation that cultivated the science of grammar without having received any impulse directly or indirectly from the Greeks.

Other Indian languages.

THE various Indian languages are the off-shoots of the Sanscrit language, as the French and the Italian are of the Latin language. There are some Indian languages which take Sanscrit words, nay Sanscrit sentences, with certain case terminations and verbal changes. The Telugu and the Canarese languages are saturated with Sanscrit words, and their literature is mostly Sanscrit. If an author wishes to write his book in pure Telugu or in pure Canarese he can do so with much exertion, like an English author attempting to write a book in pure Anglo-Sax. The Maharatti and the Bengali languages are mere corruptions of Sanscrit. Though Tamilians say that their language is free from Sanscrit words we hear Tamil verses from epic poems repeated by scholars, containing a few Sanscrit corruptions. When compared with other Indian languages it may be said that the Tamil language had not much help from the Sanscrit.

Indian Dramaturgy.

WE find in India dramas in all the above languages and the Sanscrit rules of dramaturgy guide us. Though the rules are not strictly followed by the present generation we have still so much respect for the ancient rules that whenever rigid critics find fault with us, we excuse ourselves by saying that we have followed the European method and not by professing contempt for Sanscrit rules. They do not much differ from those of European dramaturgy. The Sanscrit dramatists have divided their dramas into acts, but the present Indian dramatists have sub-divided the acts into scenes as being most convenient both for representation and for action.

Unities.

The dramatic unities also are not much violated by this method. In almost all the Indian dramas the unity of action is closely observed. The unity of time is not cared for, though there is a rule that the duration of the act should not exceed one day. The rule about the unity of place is not even noticed. With all the complicated rules and theories, the Indian dramatists are more practical and leave much to the imagination of the audience. Some omit the prologues and epilogues to gain time and some change the religious character of the Indian dramas by not repeating the prayer verse.

Ancient rules of dramaturgy.

FOR a pure drama, dramaturgy requires the hero to be a well-known king or a sage. He must have so many qualifications in him, that to find an exalted personage of that stamp it would take years of vain search. So also for the heroine.

Indian dramaturgy divides dramas into ten knds—*viz*., (1) *Nataka*, (2) *Prakarana*, (3) *Bhana*, (4) *Viayoga*, (5) *Samavakara*, (6) *Dima*, (7) *Ehamruga*, (8) *Anka*, (9) *Veethi* and (10) *Prahasana*. Nataka is a pure and full drama where we see a perfect species of dramatic composition—a celebrated subject—an historical or mythological romantic story. The hero and the heroine should be exalted personages. The action should be one of love or heroism. To be more explicit, the subject of the play should be either a love affair or an heroic deed—other passions acting as only auxiliaries. The duration of one act should not exceed one day. (There is a difference of opinion about this). If to preserve the unity of time, the less important events come in your way, you may, by introducing a character or characters appropriate to the action, give, in the form of a narrative, the portion to be omitted. This seems to be a healthy rule in as much as the audience catch the whole story of the drama; otherwise the connecting link is lost and the action is not complete. Such connecting links may be introduced between the acts. Thus in a limited space and time you give much information about the action and by this means you prepare the minds of the audience to receive what comes next on the stage. If what could thus be represented in five minutes by an actor or two is to be represented regularly in a dramatic form, you take much time and the services of many actors without any corresponding advantage. This device is technically known as Nishkambha. The hero should be an exalted person having the qualification of a "*Dherodatta*," *i.e.*, a man possessing strength, energy and courage, always deserving glory, always ready for heroic deeds and always bent upon protecting the virtues mentioned in the Vedas.

Different kinds of dramas,

Vishkambha explained.

The gualifications of a hero.

He should either be a king of noble birth or a sage or a devine being. The story should be one taken from the well-known authoritative books. If in the story there is anything whose representation demeans the noble charater of the hero, avoid that portion. Avoid exhibiting on the stage the travelling over distant places, death, battle, epidemics, seige of a town, eating bathing, kissing, applying sandal to the body, removing the clothing and many other acts of this nature whose exhibition on the public stage would be repulsive to refined taste. Never exhibit the death of a hero or a heroine. Do not even cause it to be mentioned on the stage. But if the representation of their death is necessary to please the Divine will or to fulfil the will of a dead ancestor, do not omit it. In one act, only one set of acts which make up a part of complete action is to be represented. This set of events should be such as could have happened in one day. At the end of the act, all the actors that appeared on the stage should leave it. This kind of drama should have not less than five acts and not more than ten acts. This kind of drama is known as "*Nataka*," in which prominence is given to the hero. If the heroine is a prominent figure it is called "*Natika*." The latter species of drama should not have more than four acts. There are other differences also but they are not material. The heroine should be a lady of royal descent, of depth of character, *i.e.*, a woman who would not by her appearance make her intentions plain; of somewhat sensitive temper and very loving to her husband. She should be a young lady of vigorous health.

Nature of the story.

What to be avoided on the stage.

Division into acts.

Nataka and Natika explained.

IN the second species of drama called "Prakarana," the story is more or less a fable which is the outcome of the dramatists' imagination. It should deal with the ordinary events of human life. The

Prakarana explained.

hero should be either a minister or a brahmin or a trader. He should be bent upon virtue or love or money. He should be a "Dheerasantà," *i.e.*, beautiful, pure in mind, discreet, fond of self-respect, and mild. The heroine may be a family woman or a courtesan or both. The Nataka rules apply to this also.

Bhana explained.

THE third species of drama is "Bhana." Here the hero is a learned gallant. He is to narrate what happened to himself or to others, or the experiences of gamblers. This hero, without the help of a second actor, should hold a dialogue with questions, such as "what happened next?" or "what is the reply?." He should in this dialogue narrate heroic deeds, love affairs, the beauties of nature and of women. It is to be finished in one act. It is to be written in a high style of diction known as "Bharati."

Viayoga explained.

THE fourth kind is "Viayoga." It is a drama of one act wherein a number of persons act. The theme is mythological. The hero should be "Dheerodatta." Of the nine humours, those of love, merriment and calmness do not enter into this drama. The other six *viz.*, courage, pity, marvel, fright, sarcasm and cruelty, play their part freely. The cause of the battle that is to take place in this drama should not be a woman.

Samavakara explained.

THE fifth is "Samavakara" where the heroes are twelve consisting of angels and demons. The story should be mythological. The heroes should be Dheerodattas. Courage or daring should form the principal passion, the other eight humours acting only as auxiliaries. It should be finished in three acts. Three kinds of cunning, three kinds of flight, and three kinds of love should be exhibited in this drama. The three sorts of cunning are, one caused by himself, one caused by divine beings and the third caused by enemies,

The three sorts of flight are those caused by seige) battle and fire. The three sorts of love are those caused by virtue, money, and passion.

Dima explained.

THE sixth kind of drama is "Dima". The story should be mythological. It should be written in other than the "Kisika" style. (The Kisika style is gentle). The heroes should be sixteen, consisting of Angels, Gandharvas, Yetchas, Ratchasas, Mohoragas, Bhootas and Pisachas. Love and merriment should not enter into this drama. The principal humour should be wrath, and its consequence cruelty. Cunning, juggling, battle, anger, the acts of a madman, the eclipse of the sun or the moon may be representad on the stage in this performances.

Ehamruga explained.

THE seventh species is "Ehamruga." It should be in four acts. The story may be partly from the ancient books and partly a fable invented by the dramatist. The hero may be a man or a divine being or both. At the end of the story, the hero or heroes should be represented as having forcibly seduced a divine lady or ladies against her or their will. Though there may be an attempt at making war, there should actually be no war. A great man who is helpless should not be killed. As the hero here hunts after a lady who does not love him, the drama is known as "Ehamruga", which means search.

Anka explained.

THE eighth kind is "Anka." The word is not to be mistaken for the "Anka" which means an act. The "Anka" under treatment is a species of drama. The story may be taken either from well known books or may be one invented by the dramatist. The heroes are illiterate men and the humour is "pity." Female lamentations with their quarrel with others, their success and defeat are to be exhibited on the stage.

THE ninth species is "Veethi." In this, the story is entirely the dramatist's own. It should be written in an easy style and it should treat of love. In this there are one or two actors only. The heroine should not be a family woman. She must be a loving "Parakeeya," which means a woman who conceals her love of the man whom she loves most probably to enhance the love of her lover.

Veethi explained.

THE tenth is the "Prahasana" which means a farce or a burlesque. This is sub-divided into three kinds (i) "Suddha" or pure, (ii) "Viekruta" or corrupt and (iii) "Sankeerna" or mixed. In the first, Buddhas, atheists, mean Brahmins, male and maid-servants, and gallants crowd on the stage. Jocular characters and language are the important features in it. In the second, gallants, messengers, watchmen gather and speak in their colloquial ungrammatical tongue. Eunuchs, old men and those who watch the harem may also be characters in it. The third is that where thieves and gamblers meet and hold dialogues. The language of the Prahasana drama should be such as to excite the six kinds of laughter, *i.e.*, (i) Smita or smiling (ii) Hasita or laughing (iii) Vihasita, a laugh where the whole set of teeth are exposed (iv) Prahasita, a loud laughter (v) Apahasita, a loud noise with laughter and (vi) Parihasita, a laughter caused by a funny dialogue between a man and a woman.

Prahasana explained.

Six kinds of laughter explained.

THESE are the ten kinds of dramas which are deemed to be the principal types. The eighteen kinds of auxiliary dramas are so confusing that I think it better not to mention them here. (Mr. Wilson's work on Dramas may be read with advantage). In England and other countries of

Europe there are many varieties of dramas brought into existence of late. They are Mysteries, Miracles, Moralities, Interludes, Tragedies, Comedies, Histories, Pastorals, Pastoral-comical dramas, Historical-pastorals, tragical-historicals, tragical-comical-historical-pastorals, Melodramas, Farcical comedies, Burlesques, Pantomimes, Operas and Burlettas. I have touched here only on the most important points and have not descended into details or technicalities. The ancient authors treat of how the dramatic seed is to be sown, how it is to be nourished, whither the branches should extend and where they are to be cropped, how the manager should introduce the story in an ordinary dialogue with a *Nati* or a buffoon, and how the dialogue is to be carried on by the actors, and which portion of the action is to be strengthened, which to be exhibited to the public view, which to be suggested and which to be omitted and various other details. If there is a difficulty or an abstruse problem and man's intelligence is not enough for its solution, some divinity appears and unravels the mystery and the matter is satisfactorily settled. H. H. Wilson in his book called "*Dramas*" gives a summary of the Indian dramaturgy. Though it is not exhaustive it gives sufficient information to the English reader about the construction of Indian classical dramas.

The English varieties.

A FEW words about the beauties of Sanscrit prosody may not be out of place here and may serve to show how our ancient Sanscrit authors spent their mental energies in working out even the minutest details in a satisfactory manner. An English professor says that the "Sanscrit prosody which is probably not surpassed by any other, either in variety of metres or in harmoniousness of rythm, recognises two main classes of metre, *viz.*,—such as consist of a certain number of syllables of fixed quantity and such as are regulated by groups of breves or metrical kinds according as it is, or is not, bound

Prosody.

by a fixed order of feet." To a novice, the above extract is really unintelligible. I have therefore tried to give certain details on the subject. The laws of Sanscrit prosody apply to most of the Indian languages. European poets and dramatists commence and complete their book with one kind of metre with little or no variety. Ten-thousands of lines are written in one metre. The Indian poets would feel it rather irksome to follow the European method. They are glad if they change the metre every fifth or ninth line. If a certain verse extends over four lines in one metre it is styled Malika. Such Malikas are very few and they are specially written. In Sanscrit each letter is a syllable. The long syllable is known as *Guru* and denoted thus U. The short syllable is known as *Laghu* and is denoted thus I. A set of three syllables is called a *Ganam* or class. Three long syllables denoted thus UUU, are known as Magana class. Three short syllables denoted thus III, are known as Nagana class. The following table will show the different variations of syllable groupings with their appropriate names :—

UUU	is Magana	or say 'M'
IUU	is Yagana	or say 'Y'
UIU	is Ragana	or say 'R'
IIU	is Sagana	or say 'S'
UUI	is Tagana	or say 'T'
IUI	is Jagana	or say 'J'
UII	is Bhagana	or say 'B'
III	is Nagana	or say 'N'
UU	is Gaga.	
UI	is Gala.	
II	is Lala.	
IU	is Laga.	
U	is Ga.	
I	is La.	

These fourteen Ganas or classes, appear in regular verses which I describe hereafter. The student before he advances, must be well acquainted with these rudiments.

In Sanscrit, the longest line in a regular verse does not exceed twenty-six letters. There should be four lines to complete a verse. A verse of a single letter in each line is called "Ukta"; of two letters is called "Atiukta" and a verse of twenty-six letters in each line is called "Utkruti." The following table shows the names of the parts of the Prosody. The reader is required to follow it carefully:—

Number of letters in a line.	Name given to the same.	The number of verses that can be formed out of this.
1 letter ...	Ukta	2
2 letters ...	Atiukta	4
3 „ ...	Madhiama	8
4 „ ...	Pratistu	16
5 „ ...	Supratistu	32
6 „ ...	Gayatri	64
7 „ ...	Ooshinth	128
8 „ ...	Anustup	256
9 „ ...	Bruhati	512
10 „ ...	Pankti	1,024
11 „ ..	Tristup	2,048
12 „ ...	Jagati	4,096
13 „ ...	Atijagati	8,192
14 „ ...	Sakwari	16,384
15 „ ...	Atisakwari	32,768
16 „ ...	Yasti	65,536
17 „ ...	Atiyasti	131,072
18 „ ...	Dhruti	262,144
19 „ ...	Atidhruti	524,288
20 „ ..	Kruti	1,048,576
21 „ ...	Prakruti	2,097,152
22 „ ...	Aakruti	4,194,304
23 „ ...	Vikruti	8,388,608
24 „ ...	Sukruti	16,777,216
25 „ ...	Abhikruti	33,554,432
26 „ ...	Utkruti	67,108,864

The total number of different verses that can be thus formed is 1,342,177,726.

I will illustrate here how such a vast number of different metres is possible. From table I we see that eight verses of three letters in each line can be made out of the third classification. I shall take another instance and verify the statement made in this table. Suppose you wish to make a verse which contains four letters in each line :—

UUUU This is the first line in the verse, and all the four lines must be even, *i.e.*, four long letters. Give some technical name to this verse. Now you have a verse of four lines which contains four long syllables in each line.

IUUU Here the first syllable is short, and the other syllables are long. Make all the four lines even, and you have a second verse.

UIUU The second letter is short and the other letters are long. You have got a third verse.

IIUU This is the fourth verse.

UUIU This is the fifth.

IUIU This is the sixth.

UIIU This is the seventh.

IIIU This is the eighth.

UUUI This is the ninth.

IUUI This is the tenth.

UIUI This is the eleventh.

IIUI This is the twelfth.

UUII This is the thirteenth.

IUII This is the fourteenth.

UIII This is the fifteenth.

IIII This is the sixteenth.

Thus from four letters we can form sixteen different verses of different metres. There are rules to show to what number of verse, a particular classification belongs. If a question is put as to which number the following kind of verse denoted as IUII belongs, I shall just write down the denotion as IUII and put the figures 1–2–4–8 and then add up all the figures under short syllables as $1+4+8=13$; again add one to it and give out fourteenth as the answer. Such rules are many. When so many different kinds of metres are readily available, who would not be tempted to make some use of them? Most of the verses thus formed are harmonious and can be sung consistently with the keeping up of time. The actors sing these verses musically as if they were songs. The peculiarity of regular verses is, that all the four lines should contain an equal number of letters in each. There are other verses which are irregular, in which if the first line contains eight letters, the second may contain 12, 13, 14 or 16 or any number of letters—the third may differ from the first two and the fourth may differ from all. These are also subject to certain regulations. In the regular metrical verse if the first line contains "M" + "N" + "S" + "T" + "J," the other three lines should exactly resemble the first.

Regular & irregular verse explained.

Now I say a few words about rhyme. The second letters in all the four lines of the quatrain should rhyme. The rhyming letters should be the same in all the four lines; it is not sufficient if only the second rhymes. If the author pleases he can make other letters also rhyme. In addition to the second letter the last letter or letters also are made to rhyme sometimes to add to the beauty. This is a burden to an author but it is a pleasant burden. Added to this, the Telugu poets have created another difficulty by introducing the system of "Yati or Virama" or resting place. There are rules framed by which if a line contains a certain number of letters, the first letter and a certain other letter in that line should be the same. As for instance, suppose there is a verse whose first line contains nineteen letters. In each of these lines the first and the thirteenth letter should be either the same or some cognate letter. So also are the rules for the vast number of verses we have. In Sanscrit the purpose of Virama or resting place is served by ending the word at the twelfth letter and commencing the thirteenth with a new word.

Rhyme explained.

Yati explained.

I proceed to say what qualifications a poem should contain. It is a rule that every poem should describe (1) *a town*, (2) *a sea*, (3) *a mountain*, (4) *the seasons*, (5) *the rise of the moon and the sun*, (6) *the pleasure garden*, (7) *a pleasant walk in it*, (8) *swimming*, (9) *drinking*, (10) *enjoyment with woman*, (11) *feasting*, (12) *the separation of lovers*, (13) *marriage*, (14) *the birth of a son*, (15) *the council*, (16) *gambling*, (17) *a journey and* (18) *the success of the hero.*

What the poem should contain.

THE style of the verse is divided into four parts, (i) Kisiki, (ii) Arabhati, (iii) Satwati and (iv) Bharati. "Kisiki" flows smoothly with fine and homely words and good ideas. This style is to be used where you wish to raise the feeling of "love" or "pity." "Arabhati" flows like a torrent with words of learned length and is to be used to express anger and sarcasm. "Satwati" is akin to "Kisiki" but is more classical. This is to be used to express courage or fright. "Bharati" is akin to "Arabhati" and "Kisiki," *i.e.*, not so bombastic as Arabhati and not so smooth as Kisiki. It is used to denote merriment, calmness and wonder. The ideas in the verse come under the three following classifications known as "Pakams." The first "Dratcha" which means grape. The second kind is "Kadali" which means plantain, and the third is "Narikala" which means cocoanut. The verse written in the first form is very plain and no effort of the reader is required to understand it. The verse written in the second form is not very plain but requires a slight exertion on the part of the reader to know its meaning. The idea in the verse written in the third form is very deep and is not understood by the reader till he exerts himself much. The grape is eaten

Styles explained. Kisiki style explained.

Arbhati style explained.

Satwati style explained.

Bharati style explained.

Pakams or ideas explained. Dratcha pakam explained. Kadali explained.. Narikala explained readily; the plantain requires a little trouble in removing the rind and the cocoanut cannot be eaten without much ado. A poet comically describes how a verse should be. "The idea in a verse should not be so deeply hidden as the breast of a Gujarati woman nor should it be seen as plainly as that of a Dravida lady. It should be like the breast of an Andhra lady neither deeply hidden nor open to the public gaze. If the verse is not like this, it will be ridiculed." The idea conveyed by this verse is better than the simile.

A few figures of speech explained.

As for figures of speech, Sanscrit writers have exhausted the subject. They have divided them into two classes—those of words and those of ideas. In the first classification come the different species of rhyme. They are of four sorts—

Four kinds of beauties in rhyme or prasa explained.

(1) "*Chekanu prasa*," (2) "*Vritianu prasa*," (3) "*Latanu prasa*" & (4) "*Yamaka prasa*." The word *prasa* means rhyme.

Chekanu prasa.

(1) "*Chekanu prasa*" means a set of words immediately followed by another set of the very same words, *e.g.*, "*Raja Raja*,"

Vritianu prasa.

(2) "*Vritianu prasa*," means rhyming at every second or third letter, *e.g.*, "*Sura-pura-vara-kara*,"

Latanu prasa.

(3) "*Latanu prasa*" means the use of the very same words without any difference of meaning, *e.g.*, "*That hand is the hand which protects the poor*." In the meaning of the word "*hand*" twice used here, there is no difference of meaning. The idea may be quite different. Here in this example it shows no other hand can be called by that name than the one which protects the poor.

Yamaka prasa.

(4) "*Yamaka prasa*" The beauty of this rhyming can be realized by those who know the language. Here the very same words are used either in all the four lines or in some of the lines following each other with a difference of meaning, *e.g.*, "Ma-ra-ma-nu."

This word may be used twice in a verse with a different meaning, *i.e.*, "O, Cupid, live." It may also mean "Our lady." This is a Telugu compound word. This example may not be sufficient for the English readers. In Antony and Cleopatra, Act I, Scene v, Cleopatra questions Mardian as follows :—

Cleo : Hast thou affections ?
Mar : Yes ; gracious madam.
Cleo : *Indeed* ?
Mar : Not *in deed* madam ; for I can do nothing.

Here a pun is played on the word "*indeed*." In Sanscrit there are words which would convey about ten meanings if properly divided. Although foreigners to the language not being able to appreciate the beauties of this kind of rhyme call it a childish play upon letters or words, the Indians think there is much beauty in this and therefore follow it carefully. The rhyming verses in Indian languages are always full of good thoughts. Rhyme without reason is ridiculed by the Indians who agree with Dryden's lines :—

"Whatever you write of pleasant or sublime
Always let sense accompany your rhyme
Falsely they seem each other to oppose
Rhyme must be made with reason's laws to close.
And when to conquer her you bend your force
The mind will triumph in the noble course
To reason's yoke she quickly will incline
Which far from hurting renders her divine.
But if neglected will as easily stray
And master reason which she should obey
Love reason then ; and let whatever you write
Borrow from her its beauty, force and light."

Indian writers care for reason, the rhyme following as a matter of course. The Sanscrit language itself is full of rhyme.

THERE is in Telugu, one of the Indian languages, a kind of poem known as "Dwipada" or couplet. These couplets may extend over any number of lines like English poems. They are divided into eight classes with rhyme and resting places. In regulated songs also rhyme is considered a necessity and a beauty.

Figures of Speech based on ideas.

THE figures of speech based on ideas are very numerous. I shall name here a few of the most important. i. Oopama. (Simile). This is sub-divided into many parts. For example, your face is like the moon in brightness. Here the thing compared is the face and the thing to which the face is compared is the moon. The comparing word is "*like.*" The quality common to the face and the moon is "*brightness.*" This is a perfect simile. Sometimes the comparing particle and sometimes the quality and sometimes both are omitted, *e.g.*, (*a*) your face is the moon in brightness—"like" is omitted. (*b*) "Your face is like the moon"—"brightness" is omitted. (*c*) "Your face is the moon—"both the words "like" and "brightness" are omitted.

Oopama.

Ananwaya.

ii. "Ananwaya" or a thing that cannot be compared. O, moon, you are comparable to yourself and none else in brightness.

Upamayopama.

iii. "Upamayopama." The thing compared and the thing to which it is compared change places. *e.g.*, In Autumn, the water is as sky and the sky is as water, in clearness. Here the sky is compared to water and *vice-versa*.

Prateepa.

iv. "Prateepa." Here the objects to which the things are generally compared stand for things themselves. *eg.*, O, woman, the lotus is like your eye and the moon is like your face. (Generally we say the eye is like the lotus and the face is like the moon). Here the order is changed though the meaning is the same.

Roopaka. v. "Roopaka." Metaphor.

vi. "Parinama." The object to which things are compared are made to act the part of the things themselves. *e.g.*, A lady saw her lover with her "eye-lotus." Here lotus taking the functions of the eye is made to see the lover. It is the eye that sees, but the lotus stands for the eye.

Parinama.

vii. "Oollakha." A single object appearing in different lights to different persons. *e.g.*, O, King! in you the ladies see the form of Cupid and your enemies see that of Pluto; or we may say "he is a Burke in oratory, a Wellington in war and a Gladstone in council."

Oollakha.

viii. "Smruti." Here, by the sight of the object one recollects the thing to which that object is generally compared. Thus by the sight of the lotus or by the sight of the moon, one recollects the eyes or the face of the lady in love.

Smruti.

ix. "Bhranti Mada." Here by the sight of a thing, one mistakes the object to which it is compared. *e.g.*, O, lady, this bee hovers round your face (mistaking it for a lotus).

Bhranti Mada.

x. "Sandeha" or doubt. Here when a thing is seen, one is in doubt to say exactly what it is. Thus when the eyes of a fair lady are seen, one says "I do not know what they are? they may either be bright and moving fish or full blossomed lotuses or the eyes."

Sandeha.

xi. "Apanhava." Here the real quality of a thing is negatived and other attributes are given to it, either to praise or to blame that thing. Thus a lady separated from her lover at night, sees the moon and says the following:—"you are not a moon as your rays are not cool. You cannot be a sun as the sun

Apanhava.

is not visible at night; therefore you must really be a mass of fire called "Badabagni" born in the sea." This figure of speech is divided into six classes.

Ootpratcha.

xii. "Ootpratcha." To attribute some cause to the real quality of a thing. *e.g.*, O lady! the moon wishing to be friendly with your face became an enemy of the lotus. The moon is always described by the poets as an enemy of the lotus. In the above example some cause is attributed for the enmity. The cause is not real but only serves to show that the face is so beautiful, bright and pleasing that even the moon courts its friendship. This figure of speech is divided into many classes and the dramatists make a free and excessive use of it.

Atisayokti.

xiii. "Atisayokti." Exaggeration or hyperbole. This also is divided into many classes. Two examples are shown here. This is the figure of speech in which the Indian poets indulge excessively. (i) O, lady: Look at this wonder: from the two black lilies shoot out many fiery arrows. Here black lilies are the eyes and the arrows are the side-long glances of the lady. (ii) The turrets of this town give shelter to the horses of the sun. This is to say that the turrets are very high.

Tuliayogita

xiv. "Tuliayogita." By the occurrence of a certain thing, two or more consequences follow: (i) By the rise of the moon, the lotuses are dejected as also the faces of wanton women. (ii) By the rays of the summer sun, the day-time as also the lotuses are increased. (iii) O, lady! at the sight of your face the brightness of the moon and also that of the lotus disappear.

Prativastupama.

xv. "Prativastupama." Where qualities are separately mentioned in the two objects to be compared. *e.g.*, the sun is shining on the eastern mountain and the king is shining on the throne. Here the king is compared to the sun; his throne to the eastern mountain: and shining is the quality common to both.

Drushtanta.

xvi. "Drushtanta." In the two sentences that stand for comparison, the common qualities should reflect on each other. *e.g.*, O, king, you are the glorious personage in this terrestrial world; and the moon is all shining in the celestial world. The king is compared to the moon, his world to the heaven and his glory to the moonlight. In this and in many others the peculiarity of the Sanscrit words acts charmingly.

Nidarsana.

xvii. "Nidarsana" or example. To the two sentences that stand for comparison, one quality is attributed. *e.g.*, (i) If harshness is found in a charitably disposed man, it will be like a stain in the moon. The black spot in the moon is natural as also *harshness in a charitable man*. The stain is the same as harshness. (ii) To serve a fool is to sow seeds in a barren soil. Here the result is the same.

Vyatireka.

xviii. "Vyatireka." Here two things stand for contrast; and something is shown to denote the thing to which the object is compared is devoid of some qualification, good or bad. *e.g.*, Good men like mountains are high but the former are soft and gentle, meaning thereby that the latter are hard. Good men are compared to mountains not in size but being as steady and noble as the latter; but in good men we find qualities which are not found in the mountains.

Sahokti.

xix. "Sahokti." In this a beautiful idea is hidden in the sentence. *e.g.*, (i) O, hero! your glory has spread over all the corners of the world with your enemies. Here the glory of the hero is wide spread and the consequence of that is that his enemies have left their homes and hidden themselves in the corners of the world. (ii) In the hot summer, during mid-day, the shadows of trees being afraid of the rays of the sun as it were take shelter under the trees as travellers do.

Samasokti.

xx. "Samasokti." Here by the description of one thing some other description is intended. *e.g.*, O, Lady, look at this morning moon. He is kissing his lady "*Indri*" (eastern side). Here the idea is the wish of a lover to kiss a lady. (The moon here is masculine). In this figure of speech, much depends upon the pun on the words.

Slesha.

xxi. "Slesha." Use of a word in different ideas. There are many books written in this style. There is a book known as "Yadava-Raghava-Pandaviam," wherein each verse conveys three different meanings—one to narrate the story of Krishna, one that of Rama, and the third to narrate the Bharata—the battle between the Pandus and the Kurus.

Prastutankura.

xxii. "Prastutankura." Describes one subject to denote another. *e.g.*, A wife seeing a bee playing about a '*Kataki*' flower leaving its nest in the '*Malati*' flower, addresses it in the following words in the presence of her husband who is not constant:— "O, bee, why do you leave your '*Malati*' which is fond of pleasing you with her scent and juice and fly about '*Kataki*' which is surrounded by thorns of all sorts." The wife by this description of a subject which is before her, advises her husband indirectly.

Pariyayokti.

xxiii. "Pariyayokti." Here by the description of a certain idea you denote another idea or by the description of an act, you denote the man who did the act. *e.g.*, (1) O, husband, to what further pains is your hard heart determined to put my soft legs? Here the wife says that her legs are tired of walking and asks her husband "how far she has to walk more." (2) I prostrate before him who deprived the female demons of enjoyment with their husbands. Here Krishna who killed all the demons is described not by name but by his action.

Vyajastuti.

xxiv. "Vyajastuti." Here you praise by blame and blame by praise. (1) O, Lord, where is wisdom in you? You protect even the sinner. (By blame you praise). (2) O, maid, you suffered much from my lover on my account. (By praise the lady blames her maid).

Vyajaninda.

xxv. "Vyajaninda." Here by blaming one, you blame another also. A man tired of life addresses the four-headed creator Brahma as follows:—" O, Creator! Eswara who beheaded one of your five heads is to blame." If Eswara had beheaded Brahma of all his heads, the latter would not have been in existence and therefore could not have created the world and could not have left the speaker in tire-some life. Here to blame Brahma you blame Eswara.

Atchapa.

xxvi. "Atchapa." It means mere dispute or questioning. Much meaning is hidden in this figure of speech. It is divided into three classes. I think it may further be sub-divided into many classes. I give below two examples:—(1) O, friend, shew me your moon; otherwise I have my lady. (Here he means to say that the moon is not seen but I have a more brilliant moon in the face of my lady and your moon is therefore useless). (2) A wife unwilling to send her husband to a foreign country and unwilling also to say that he should not go, addresses him in the following words to show the intensity of her affection towards him: "O, husband: you may go to that country. My next birth also will be there." In this example so much meaning is hidden that the reader is really charmed. The wife could not hinder her husband's journey by plainly asking him not to go, for that will be considered by an Indian as an ill-omen. She could not say that she would die from being separated from him for that also is an ill-omen. She makes her husband know also that she believes in re-births. She therefore conveys the idea that he should not go and if he goes against her wishes, her affection towards him is so intense that she would die immediately after separation and her second birth will be in a place where he goes to, so that she may be reunited to him. It also means when dying she would think of him, and by that process reunite herself with him by law of affections. Here though she seems to consent to his going, she wishes him not to go.

Vibhavana.

xxvii. "Vibhavana." Producing effect without cause or with defective cause or a different cause, etc. *e.g.*, (1) O, king! your glory shines like moonlight without the moon. (2) O, Cupid, you conquer the world with your soft flowery arrows. (3) O, woman: I hear the melodious sounds of a lute issuing out of a conch. (Here the conch is her neck and the sounds of a lute, her voice). (4) The rays of the moon burn her. (The quality of the rays is refreshing and cool but here they burn).

Vishama.

xxviii. "Vishama." Here two things quite contrary to each other are described, sometimes one as arising from the other. *e.g.*, (1) "She is as soft as Sireesha flower and the Cupid's fever she has, is as high and unbearable as fire." (2) O, hero! from your black sword, arises a white and brilliant glory.

Chitra.

xxviv. "Chitra." Doing a certain act in order to obtain a result quite different from what one would expect from the action. *e.g.*, Virtuous men bend down to rise high.

xxx. "Karanamala." The effect produced from a cause, becoming a cause in its turn to produce another effect and so on. *e.g.*, Right conduct gives wealth; wealth gives you a desire to be charitable; charity brings on fame.

Karanamala.

xxxi. "Arthantharanyasa." To mention a certain occurrence and deduce from it a general truism. *e.g.*, (1) The monkey-God jumped over the ocean. What is impossible for great men? (2) O, king, the Goddesses of riches, education and the world smile on you. Is there any want for fortunate men?

Arthantharanyasa.

xxxii. "Samanya." Here no difference is discernable in the two things that generally stand for comparison. *e.g.*, We cannot see the faces of women that are swimming in the lake full of lotuses.

Samanya.

xxxiii. "Uttara." This figure of speech is divided into many parts. (*a*) Gudhottara—which means a reply containing a deep meaning. (*b*) Chittrottara—which means a reply containing a skilful meaning in the very same words of the question.

Uttara.

xxxiv. "Soochana." Here the idea is made out, not from words but from a hint which can be understood only by very intelligent men. "When a lover saw a lady she covered her red mark on the forehead with her black hair." Here her red mark on the forehead is to be understood as the sun and the hair as darkness. It means therefore a reply that the lover should visit her after sunset when there is darkness.

Soochana.

xxxv. "Swabhavokti." Describing things, as they naturally are. *e.g.*, He saw antelopes with erect ears and bright, broad, roving eyes.

Swabhavokti.

THE above figures of speech are only a few out of many which the ancient Sanscrit writers have taken enormous pains to use. These figures of speech came under the art called "Rhetoric" and every author is supposed to know them fully. There are many commentaries written upon this science. Unless one has well read the commentaries, it is very difficult sometimes to differentiate one figure of speech from another. A few of the figures of speech above described are classed under Wit and Humour in the English language (*vide* "the Science of Wit and Humour" by Yorick).

Elastic character of Verbs.

THE elasticity of Sanscrit verbs is such that they can be turned to any form with facility. The ancient classical authors who made a life-long study of Grammar were able to compress any idea in a short verse.

Antiquity of dramas.

THOUGH there is no reliable evidence that the ancient epic poems were played as they are, still there are in them all the elements necessary for dramatic performances. The sages were never fond of speeches. The antiquity of our dramas is older than our Mythology. In our Mythological books, a reference will be found to dramatic companies. In the epic poem Ramayana, we find the words "*Vathu Nataka Sanghanam*" which means either dramatic companies of women or men or a dramatic company called Vathu drama. Elsewhere in the same book we find "*Nata Nataka Sanghischa*" which means pantomimists and dancers. Any how we had dramas long before the date of our epic poems. Greater portions of our Epic-poems (Bharata and Ramayana, etc.,) are more or less dramas as they are full of dialogues, and the dialogues often form the first step towards drama. Treatises containing rules for actors existed even at the time of Panini, the original compiler of Sanscrit Grammar. He mentions two authors of Nata Sutras (Silalin and Krisasva) in his book. "Patanjali, the greatest commentator on Grammar, refers to the dramas—"the slaying of Kamsa" and the "Binding of Bali" as having been represented on the stage both by mimic action and declamation. Weber, in his *Ancient History of Indian Literature*, says that the name of "Sailali" akin to Silalin of Panini occurs in Sathapatha Brahmana. Julius Eggeling, PH.D., Professor of Sanscrit, University of Edinburgh, says "judging from these allusions, theatrical entertainments in those days seem to have been very much on a level with our old religious spectacles or mysteries, though there may already have been some simple kinds of secular plays which Patanjali had no occasion to mention." In the story of the life of Mandgalyayana and Upatishya—two disciples of Buddha, representation of dramas in the presence of these individuals is said to have been mentioned. Schlegel, in his book on *Dramatic Art and Literature*, says, "among the Indians whose social institutions and mental cultivation descend unquestionably from a remote antiquity, plays were known long before they could have experienced any foreign influences." The ancient dramatists helped themselves with themes from Mythologies and from a book of stories called "Bruhatkatha." This book was, according to tradition, written originally in *Paisacha* language by a learned man named "Gunadhya." It was rendered into Sanscrit by a poet Somadeva under the direction of a learned woman Suriavati, queen of Anantadeva, king of Kashmir. This rendering must have been about 1100 years ago. Most of the plots for the ancient dramas (i. Ratnavali, ii. Malavika-Agnimitra, iii. Mudra-Ratchasa, iv. Malati-Madhava, v. Malika-Maruta, vi. Priyadarsika, vii. Nagananda) must have been taken more or less from the above book—either the original or a translation. The reading of the Hindu dramas will convey to any reader a correct idea of the manners and customs of the people of India and affords a new insight into their civilization. They also show the state of women in ancient times: how they were submissive to the will of man, how they consoled themselves with the solacing philosophy of the working of Gods, how they grieved at the afflictions of their husbands and how they prepared themselves to die with them by *Sati.* They also shew how kings both good and bad behaved towards their subjects and how Brahmins reigned supreme. The religious prejudices, the worshipping of elements, the sacrifices to the Gods, are also shown in the plays. The old Hindu dramas take the careful reader into the inner life of ancient times. They also show how the palaces of the kings and the rich people were built and how the poor lived.

Mruchakatica.

THE oldest drama extant is *Mruchakatica or Mud-carriage* written by king Sudraka about 2000 years ago. It is a drama of ten acts. It is a story of the home-life of a Brahmin trader and a virtuous dancing girl. It depicts home-life, manners, customs, the height of gambling, and also of the wicked influence of kings' brothers-in-law at that time. "The main story is interwoven with a political under-plot resulting in a change of dynasty." Social manners of the time are well described. Mr. Frazer, LL.B., in his "Literary History of India", says, "this drama was played only a few years ago at the Royal Court Theatre in Berlin as well as at the Court Theatre at Munich, where it roused enthusiasm sufficient to recall the actors eight times before the curtain fell."

Kalidasa and his dramas.

WE have our Shakespeare and Ben Jonson in the person of our immortal Kalidasa. He lived and flourished in the court of Vikramaditya a century before the Christian era. He has been and will ever be enshrined in the hearts of all. "He is a masterly describer of the influence which nature exercises upon the mind of a lover. Tenderness in the expression of feeling and richness of creative fancy have designed to him his lofty place among the poets." His work "Sakuntala" stands a valuable gem in dramatic literature. His other dramas "Vikrama-Oorvasi" and "Malavika-Agnimitra" also evidence the poet's ability. The heroes in Sakuntala and Vikrama-Oorvasi are powerful kings of the lunar race and the heroines are the nymphs of heaven (Sakuntala is the daughter of a nymph of heaven and the sage Viswamitra). Both relate to love affairs with varied incidents to connect the action with the desired end. The drama of Sakuntala is known throughout Europe by the translations of Sir William Jones. The play is highly praised by Goethe, Schlegal and Humboldt. The drama is translated in verse by Professor Monier Williams. His Malavika-Agnimitra, though historical, is interwoven with the love, virtue and envy of rival wives of a Hindu king. The wit and humour in this drama are far more keen than in the other two. In the prologue to Malavika-Agnimitra, mention is made of the existence of ancient dramas of repute hy Bhasa Sawmilla and Kaviputra and others before the time of Kalidasa. The incident about the discovery of the 'lost ring' in the drama of Sakuntala is similar to an incident told by Herodotus in his story of Polycrates "the too fortunate tyrant of Samos, who casts into the sea his most costly and highly prized ring to propitiate the deity, by a voluntary sacrifice, and sees it reappear the same night at his table cut out of the body of a huge fish presented to him by the fisherman as too fine for any but the royal board." This incident is identical in both the stories but in the Sanscrit drama it is woven into a love story. The drama of Vikrama-Oorvasi resembles the story of "Eros and Psyche." In the Greek legend, the lover is a divine being and the woman a mortal; and the understanding between them is that she should not behold his face or form. Curiosity tempts her to behold him which is the cause of separation as in the Sanscrit drama. She wanders and seeks for the lost one to whom she is re-united

Sakuntala and Vikrama-Oorvasi.

Vikrama-Oorvasi.

in the end, instead of the lover seeking for her and re-uniting as in the Sanscrit drama.

Sree Harsha and his dramas. Ratnavali.

DURING the seventh century, Sree Harsha Deva, king of Kanouj, wrote three dramas. (1) Ratnavali. It is a graceful drama of genteel domestic manners. Love forms the centre of the plot. It is about the love between king Vatsa and a beautiful maiden of Ceylon by name Sagarica. The jealousy of the king's already wedded wife Vasavadatta and subsequent reconciliation form the incidents for action. The clandestine wooing is well represented here.

Priyadarsika.

(2) Priyadarsika is another drama of Sree Harsha. It is again the story of the love of Vatsa for Priyadarsika.

Naganandа.

(3) The third drama of Sree Harsha is Nagananda. Jeemootavahana, the king of Vidyadharas, weds Malavati. The self-sacrifice of the king and the love of Malavati towards him are well depicted. This "drama begins with a benedictory stanza to Buddha and concludes with one to Gouri—the wife of Siva." The piece is therefore "intended as a compromise between the Brahminical Siva and Buddhistic doctrines." Some say that the above pieces were written by Bana and some attribute them to Dhavaka. Sree Harsha is reputed to be a king of learning and there is no reason to doubt his authorship.

Bhavabhooti and his dramas. Oottara-rama-charitra. Malati-Madhava.

WE have also the greatest man of learning as a dramatist who might be well compared to our immortal Kalidasa. He is Bhavabhooti or Sreekantha. His drama, the lovely "Oottara-rama-charitra," in seven acts, contains the history of the hero of the epic poem, Ramayana. His "Malati-Madhava" is a domestic drama of ten acts. The pure manners of the Hindus of the age are well woven round the love affair between Malati and Madhava. The main plot which results in the marriage of Malati and Madhava is intermixed with a minor plot ending in the marriage of Makaranda with Madayantica. Two Buddhistic nuns Kamandaki and Kapila Kundala possessing learning and magical power skilfully avert the catastrophies from befalling the lovers.

Bhatta Narayana Veni Samhara.

WE have a heroic drama taken from the epic poem of Bharata. It is "Veni Samhara" or braiding the hair, by the author Bhatta Narayana written in or about the eighth century. It is a terror-striking representation. Though the author has a reputation for good thoughts and classical expressions, he has spoilt the end by introducing as a variety, an episode which is very absurd and impertinent, as Professor Wilson puts it.

Raja Sekhara Viddha Salabhanjica.

WE have also a drama of domestic intrigue in a Royal family. It is *Viddha Salabhanjica* by Raja Sekhara written probably in the eleventh or the twelfth century. It tell us how Royal princes while away their time in their harems. In it a beautiful maiden passes off as a boy. The plot is made very complicated by the author. It is wanting in spirit and elegance of expression. Raja Sekhara is also the author of two more dramas—*viz.*, "Prachanda Pandava" and "Bala Ramayana." The first is a drama of two acts containing the marriage of Droupathi, the insulting treatment she received from Dussasana, and the departure of the Pandavas to the forest. Professor Wilson says "the author has not hesitated to represent in action the circumstance of Droupathi's being dragged by the hair, almost naked into the public assembly, an insult, in revenge for which Bhima vowed to slay Dussasana and drink his blood and ultimately fulfilled his vow."

Prachanda Pandava and Bala Ramayana.

Damodara Misra
Hanuman Nataka.

"HANUMAN Nataka or Maha Nataka" is a drama of fourteen acts containing the story of the epic poem Ramayana. Though the authorship of this drama is attributed to the great monkey-God Hanuman, Professor Wilson proves by evidence of language and other facts that it is the work of Damodar Misra or others who lived in the tenth century. The language is mostly undramatical.

Dhanunjaya Vijaya
by
Kanchana Acharya.

"THE Dhanunjaya Vijaya" of Kanchana Acharya is a drama of one act written in the twelfth century containing the story of Arjuna's recovering the cattle of Virata from the Kuru princes.

Murari
Prasanna Raghavam
Nataka.

A man of letters and a Grammarian by name Murari composed in the thirteenth or the fourteenth century, a drama known as "Prasanna Raghavam" or the story of Rama. This book has no dramatical merit. His description of things is crooked and unusual. Though learned men read the drama for its literary merit, they style the author a poet having crooked ways. The prologue to this drama is to the effect that an actor of ordinary ability is not fit for its performance and therefore Kalaha Kandala, a professor of extraordinary talents, has undertaken to represent it.

Kalaha Kandala
(actor).

Visakadhatta and his
Mudra Ratchasa.

WE have purely a historical drama in "Mudraratchsa" of Visakadhatta. Here a Brahmin, by name Chanikya, shows all his powers of statesmanship to bring about a reconciliation between Ratchasa, an offended minister of the murdered king Nanda, and the subjects of the state by whom the king was murdered. The plot is very well worked out. A panorama describing the terrors of hell and the tortures to which the wicked are subjected, is mentioned here. The snake charmers' art is also exhibited. In fact it is a capital drama of the eleventh or the twelfth century.

THERE are many other dramas since written by learned men. They are not worth noticing. To expose and refute the ideas of Buddhists, Charwakas, Jains, etc., to awaken in people a spirit of enquiry into the principles of Vedantic Philosophy, a truly philosophical drama was written by a great scholar and philosopher Krishna-Misra of Maithila in the twelfth century. It is known as Prabodha Chandrodaya. It is said that it became so popular that it attracted the king of Magadha who with his pandits and courtiers travelled to Maithila to witness the representation.

Krishna-Misra Prabodha Chandrodaya.

LEGITIMATE and pure dramas ceased with the end of the thirteenth century. Our old dramatists taxed the imagination of their audience too much by the absence of scenery. Sir Philip Sydney in his '*Apology for Poetry*' writes "Now three ladies walk to gather flowers and then we must believe the stage to be a garden; by and by we hear news of ship-wreck in the same place and then we are to blame if we accept it not for a rock; upon the back of that comes out a hideous monster and then the miserable beholders are bound to take it for a cave; while in the meantime two armies fly in, represented with four swords and buckles and then what hard heart will not receive it for a pitched field." Mr. Collier however is of opinion that "if the old poets had been obliged to confine themselves merely to the changes that could at that early date have been exhibited by the removal of painted canvass or boarding, we should have lost much of that boundless diversity of situation and character allowed by this happy absence of restraint."

Absence of Scenes, etc.

FROM the thirteenth century downwards we have had no real dramas but only apologies for dramas. From this period there have come into existence other kinds of dramas known as Bhanas or monologues which were not very common before. Here a man assuming the characters of a gallant will describe his

Bhanas.

love adventures in rather a questionable form in some respects. He carries on a dialogue with the imaginary ladies of his loves in different tones. He describes the beauties of women and their love adventures and sometimes speaks of men in a satirical manner. (1) *Sringara Bhushana*, (2) *Mukundananda*, (3) *Sarada Tilaka*, (4) *Panchayudha Prapancha*, (5) *Vasanta Tilaka*, (6) *Panchayudha Vijaya*, *etc.*, are examples of this sort. They no doubt describe the manners, the customs, the rites and the religious differences of different classes of people, but they only show the dark side. Of the many Bhanas above named, Sringara Bhushana is attributed to the well known ancient poet "Vamanabhatta." The scene of action is a well known place known as "*Virupatcha*," the place where the greatest commentator Vidyaranya lived and where the greatest kings of Vijayanagaram reigned, and the time of action is the beautiful beginning of summer when the car-festival takes place there in honour of "Siva." I shall here show what these monologues are and how the dramatists indulged in ribaldry and in inconceivable indecencies. In a Bhana, the Manager, who is known in Sanscrit as "Sutradhara," addresses the audience in terms to the following effect. "The assembly consists of men who are masters of the science of Venus (God of Love) and who can rhetorically converse on the philosophy of that science and who are the geniuses of this art." Its subject matter is not pure love but the animal passion which the hero feels for the harlots he is supposed to have met in the course of his love-adventures. The essential qualifications of a 'Bhana' according to the rules of dramaturgy are that the story should be the outcome of a poet's own imagination, the hero should be a gallant, the action should relate to his love-adventure and should be finished in one act. It is also essential that the hero should himself carry on a dialogue by questions and answers.

Sringara Bhushana Bhana by Vamanabhatta.

The way in which this kind of dialogue is to be carried on by one man is shown below. In Vasantatilaka Bhana in which the scene is laid in Conjeevaram and the hero named Sringara Sekhara enters describing the pleasant morning sun, smells the sweet scent of a flower, describes the season in glowing terms and also the street where harlots live, listens to their music, then thinks of his friend's wife, a beautiful lady by name Chitralekha, wishes to pay a visit to her, goes, sees her while she is drying her hair after bathing, in the morning sun, describes her posture, approaches her and wishes success to her beauty—by addressing her as "complete treasure of the God of Love." (Here I must say that the lady described is not before the audience but the hero acts as if he saw the lady and talked to her). The hero then questions himself by interrogation "what does she say?" He himself repeats her reply thus:—(Most probably in a lady's voice). "You are happy in your connection with the lady Nava Malika. Why do you flatter me here?" Then the hero says in reply that "his words are no flattery and then describes her neck, eye-brows, her face, her eyes, her cheeks, her lips and concludes that he who drinks the sweet honey in her lips is a happy man. Then he questions himself "what does she say in reply?" She says "Go—Go, you are very learned in worldly affairs." Then the hero replies to her "I am always thinking of the happiness I enjoyed in your union, how we mutually kissed each other's lips, how we embraced, etc. This description greatly curtailed here on account of its indecency is detailed in the book. The hero goes to some other lady and talks to her in the same strain. To change the monotony of speech, a variety of subjects is introduced. If the dramatist wishes to describe the snake-charmer's art, he introduces him and describes his art in detail and while there, he pretends he is seeing another lady of his love, or listening to her. He

Vasantatilaka Bhana.

then says "let me approach her." Moving a few paces forward he pretends to talk to her.

Prahasanas or Farces.

THERE are also farces or satires known as Prahasanas "Dhurta Nataka," "Dhurta Samagama," "Hasyarnava," "Kautuka Sarvaswa," are examples. Of the different kinds of Hindu dramas Ehamruga is one. I came across a drama of this kind written recently. The language in it is ornate and not poetical. It is full of scandalous matter.

WE have thus in Sanscrit, domestic, pastoral and love-plays. Love, separation and union after undergoing a series of ordeals by the pair are mostly the harmless themes of the dramatists. They did not know the difference between a tragedy and a comedy. That neither a fight nor a death should take place on the stage is a stringent rule in Indian dramaturgy. Then the dramatists looked upon the stage as a temple and place of reverence. They commenced their performances with prayers to the God "Nandi" (a musical prelude which disposes the mind of the audience to the reception of the play) and concluded them with the offering of thanks to the Almighty. The old English moralities and moral plays "usually concluded with an epilogue in which prayers were offered up by the actors for the king, queen, clergy and sometimes for the commons." The same is the case even now in Indian dramas. This is technically known as "Bharata Vakya." This form of epilogue in English dramas is changed into asking pardon of the audience for defects, etc. :—

Prologue & Epilogue.

"The end of epilogues is to enquire
The censure of the play or to desire
Pardon for what is amiss."

Subsequently the English authors thought there was no use of epilogues :—

"Why there should be an epilogue to a play
I know no cause. The old and the usual way

For which they were made was to entreat the grace
Of such as were spectators. In this place
And time 'tis no purpose; for I know
What you resolve already to bestow
Will not be altered, whatsoever I say
In the behalf of us and of the play;
Only to quit our doubts, if you think fit
You may cry it up or silence it." (BEAUMONT & FLETCHER).

It is now settled that a tragedy should not be followed by any epilogue much less a comic epilogue. In an epilogue by Home to his tragedy *Douglas* the actor is made to repeat the following lines :—

"An epilogue I ask, but not one word
Our bard will write. He vows 'tis most absurd
With comic wit to contradict the strain
Of tragedy and make your sorrows vain.
Sadly he says that pity is the best
And noblest passion of human breast
For when its sacred streams the heart o'er flow
In gushes pleasure with tide of woe
And when its waves retire, like those of Nile
They leave behind them such a golden soil
That there the virtues without culture grow
There the sweet blossoms of affection blow
These were his words; void of delusive art.
I felt them, for, he spoke them from his heart;
Nor will I now attempt with witty folly
To chase away celestial melancholy."

Indian epilogues have not undergone any change; for the Indian dramas have no tragedies ending in death. Though up to the last of the play the tragic strain is continued the very last scene converts the tragedy into a cheerful end and prayers are offered to the Almighty invoking blessings on all. Of late Indian authors are deducing moral lessons from their plays and these are termed epilogues.

THE ten kinds of varied dramas, and eighteen kinds of auxiliary dramas with their multifarious divisions with various duties performed by the characters, the conduct of the plot and the various objects of dramatic representations, convey a satisfactory proof of the extent to which dramatic literature was once cultivated by the Hindus. Such a complicated sub-division in details implies considerable ingenuity employed by the Hindu dramatists in the *construction of their plots.* The royal buffoon was a necessary adjunct in a performance and his humour was harmless and his wit very keen and fine. Call him a harlequin or clown, our Indian buffoon answers the description given below. "Harlequin's part is made up of blunders and absurdities; he is to mistake one name for another, to forget his errands and to run his head against every post that appears in his way." (Addison). "His character is a mixture of ignorance, simplicity, cleverness, stupidity and grace; he is a kind of sketch of a man, a tall child, yet with gleams of reason and wit and all whose mistakes and follies have something arch about them. The true mode of representing him is to give him suppleness, agility, the playfulness of a kitten with a certain grossness of appearance which renders his conduct more absurd, his part is that of a patient, faithful valet always in love, always in hot water either on his master's or his own account, troubled and consoled as a child, and whose grief is as entertaining as his joy." (Marmontel).

Buffoon.

FOR humour of a delicate kind Indian dramas are famous. Neither the dramatists nor the actors offend any. The Directors of the stage were usually men of high learning and morality. They commanded respect both from royalty and society. The Honourable Mountstuart Elphinstone, in his *History of India*, says "though there are no tragedies in Indian dramas, none at least that terminate unhappily, yet these plays exhibit a variety not surpassed on any other stage,

Variety of dramas.

Besides the different classes of dramas, farces, moralities and interludes, the diversity arising from the subjects seems to have been almost unlimited."

Decline of Indian dramas.

WITH the decline of the Hindu power its dramatic and classical literature also fell into disuse. The classical epical poems have been translated into the different vernaculars of the country. Much of the charm of the language bestowed by a careful attention to harmony in the original, is lost in the translations. The facility of forming compounds and the elasticity and the condensing nature of the verbs that added richness to the Sanscrit language, only served to stiffen and lengthen the translations. Sanscrit scholars commenced to write dramas to please the audience whose former proverbial morality was already vitiated by the advent of Mahomaden rulers. It is during this period that the minor dramatical works classified as Bhanas, Prahasanas, Ehamrugas and such like were produced. These more or less resemble the comedies, farces and satires of the Restoration. Authors pandered to the taste of sensual people who relished only illicit love and intrigue. The study of classical literature fell out of vogue, and the few proficients therein had to write in a manner that would suit the understanding and taste of the ignorant. This accounts for the coarseness and indelicacy of language found in the dramas written between the thirteenth and the seventeenth centuries. The subsequent generations found the study of Sanscrit unprofitable and representations in Sanscrit became therefore few and far between. This was the first step towards the decline of dramatical art in India.

Dramatical companies.

DURING the Mahomaden period when Brahmins were left penniless they began to eke out their livelihood in all possible ways. Those who had a special aptitude for dramatic performances formed themselves into companies, gave performances before the chiefs and the officials. The company, consisting of learned people, pleased the educated and the uneducated equally. A company of learned men, it is said, once gave forty different plays from the Mahabharata (the war between the Pandus and the Kurus) in about ninety days. The peculiarity in them was that they were able to exhibit any play from any of the vast epic poems within twenty-four hours' notice, with songs, speeches and verses. These may be compared to the improvisers of the Grecian tragedies. Society in general appreciated their merit and was eager to see their performances, but stigmatized them as professionals prostituting their learning for pecuniary benefit. It is a rigid principle with Brahmins (not followed in practice but serving for criticism) that no gain of a temporal kind should tempt a Brahmin to do a work which gives him food. In imitation of them, many companies consisting mostly of illiterate men commenced to give performances in the different vernaculars of India, of stories, coarse in language, indecent in action and immoral in general.

Illiterate companies.

A FEW out of very many of their themes, I here give. (*a*) "Tara Sasankam" . . . . Here a pious teacher's wife successfully seduced his student. A child was the result of their illicit union. Disputes having arisen between the teacher and the student about the fathership of the boy and the Gods even expressing their inability to decide the issue, the teacher's wife (the delinquent) herself had to decide that the boy was born to the student. The story is in itself immoral and the language heightens the indecency. (*b*) "Bilhaneeyamu" . . . Here the father (king) told a downright lie to his daughter to the effect that the teacher engaged by him to give her lessons was a man born blind and also told the teacher a falsehood that his daughter was a leper. It was a vow of

Subsequent dramas not classical.

Tara Sasankam.

Bilhaneeyemu.

the daughter not to see a blind man and it was likewise a vow of the teacher not to see a leper. A curtain was therefore hung between the teacher and the fair student. On a certain night when the moon-light was bright, the teacher described the glory of the moon in glowing terms. The fair student was astonished, broke her vow, removed the curtain and saw the beautiful poet before her. The result was a clandestine union. The king when he got scent of it ordered the teacher to be beheaded. The teacher sent him a verse threatening him with curses. The king being afraid, made him his son-in-law. This is another loose and immoral story made more so by the actors in the matter of the clandestine union.

Komara Rama Charitra and Sarangadhara Charitra.

(*c*) and (*d*) "Komara Rama Charitra" and "Sarangadhara Charitra." . . . Both resembling each other, are full of improprieties and are repulsive to the feelings of any man of refined taste. The main issue of the plot may have a lesson for people of culture, but the details are so interwoven with immoralities, that the eventual effect tends to demoralize the ignorant in society. The story in Sarangadhara is that the father of Sarangadhara, a king old in age, wanted to marry his only son to a beautiful maiden. He sent his minister with his son's picture, in search of a fair girl. The minister returned with a picture of a beautiful girl named Chitrangi. The old king seeing the picture wished to marry the girl himself. According to a custom with the warrior race, the king's sword was sent and the marriage was celebrated between the sword and the maid. The bride was brought and sent into the *Zenana*. To her disappointment and sorrow she saw an old man was to be her husband but could not help becoming his wife. One day in the absence of the king, the step-mother tempted his son in vain to illicit love. He resisted the temptation. This resistence provoked the step-mother to wreak vengeance upon him, and when the king returned home she complained that his son had ravished her forcibly. In wrath the old man ordered his only son to be mercilessly beheaded. His legs were cut off, when, some godly man interfered, revealed the truth and caused the death of the fair villain and saved the son, who regained his legs by a miracle but became an ascetic. In this story the animal passions of an old man were put before the audience, and the worst part is that a step-mother who is considered by the Hindus as a real mother, was brought into the play with all her animal instinct and made much of by the actors to please the audience. These two stories are full of improprieties and are not found in any of the ancient epics, but the authors claim antiquity also for such indecent stories. Another story resembling the above in every respect is current in Rajasthan. I read the story some years ago in the manuscripts of the library in the Theosophical Society in Madras. These are stories of imagination. In Grecian legends there is the story of Hippolytus. His father Theseus after the death of Antiope, (the mother of Hippolytus) married Phaedra who fell in love with her step-son. When Hippolytus resisted her advances, she accused him of having attempted her virtue. Theseus in a rage had him killed. This subject forms a tragic play of Euripides. But how far it is pleasing to the refined feeling of civilized moderns is a question to be decided by the readers. We may as well perform before the public the story of the origin of the birth of Theseus. He is the son of his grand-father by his mother. The tragedy of Phaedra is found in Greek, Latin, French and English. One Edmund Smith wrote this tragedy in English. It was played in 1708. Dr. Johnson praised it highly. Notwithstanding this high eulogium, however, Phaedra is now forgotten. In English you see a similar and a still worse tragedy. It is *Don Carlos* of Otway. Don Carlos opposing his father by an undaunted statement that he loved his step-mother is highly repulsive to an

Indian taste. Such stories, I think, are found in every nation, but it is my sincere opinion that they are not to be exhibited to the public view on the stage. (*e*) "Droupathi Vastrapaharana." . . . Here in the midst of spectators in the king's hall when the five husbands of Droupathi and all her relations, males and females, were assembled, Dussasana, the brother of Duryodhana, wants to make the virtuous lady (Droupathi) stand naked by attempting to remove her tying cloth. He went on untying her cloth. He did not succeed it is true. That the story is found in the most religious epic poem cannot be denied, but to display to the public gaze what might have happened years ago is not wisdom, when it serves no useful, moral or historical purpose but only raised a revulsion of feeling in men of refined taste.

MANY such stories formed the themes of exhibitions—the actors being dead to moral feeling. Kissing, embracing and the heroine sitting on the lap of the hero and many such indecent actions were freely permitted on the stage. The actors never took even a common sense view whether such an action could or could not have taken place in public. They did many enormities, having no one to guide or restrain them. This was the second step towards the decline of the Hindu stage.

Puppet-shows.

STROLLING companies commenced to give performances with songs with wooden puppets as actors and actresses. These were as well dressed as the characters required and the string-puller caused the puppets to act, himself singing the songs containing the story and making the necessary speeches when wanted, he himself being hidden behind a curtain. These were known as "Puppet Plays" and were once relished by the lower order of people. These puppet-plays, a certain Historian says, were being performed in Java and Sumatra. In imitation of these wooden puppet plays, intelligent men from the lowest class of people commenced to give performances by means of leather-puppets (known as *Tholu Bommalu* in the Telugu language). These plays were always indecent and immoral. They resemble the description given of "Karagheuz" and the stage in Turkey by Richard Davey and published in the "Theatre" of November 1896. Reference is also made to the puppet theatres by Charles Dickens in one of his letters from Alboro to his friend as existing in that town. W. C. Sydney writes in his book on "Social life in England," that Italian puppet shows or *Marionettes* were not excluded from the Court of Charles II. The puppet-show was long in high favour at the Court." The people in general condemned them but could not prohibit them. The reckless and the sensual under the Mahomaden Government encouraged them with their presence and with their gifts, sometimes of villages.

Day-characters.

WE had also a class of men who took up the impersonation of character and went to each and every house to beg in the day-time with discordant musical accompaniments and the coarsest songs and speeches. These were known as day-characters. These also sometimes pleased the Mahomedan rulers and obtained Jaghirs, now in the enjoyment of their heirs.

Dancing-girls.

THE professional dancing girls also formed themselves into companies and with the aid of a man of letters (who is sometimes the paramour) gave performances of Krishna's vagaries with the nymphs (the Gopikas). The age in which they appeared was such that the moral courage of no honest man could prevent them. Though the performances given by these dancing girls were not so obscene as the "leather puppet plays" still the atmosphere of the stage was infected with immorality.

Pageants.

SIDE by side with these performances we had also "pageants" in almost all big towns. A local versifier without any knowledge of dramaturgy or rules of grammer but looked upon in his own place by the ignorant as the *Kalidasa* or the *Shakespeare*, wrote songs and speeches and taught the illiterate actors, as people generally teach their pet parrots to speak, and the actors thus trained were made to act on temporary stages built for the day. These actors were mostly men with no apparent means of livelihood. Crabb's description of strolling actors of his time fully applies to these Indian actors also :—

> "Of various men these marching troups are made
> Pen-spurning clerks and lads contemning trade
> Waiters and servants by confinement teased
> And youths of wealth by dissipation ceased
> With feeling nymphs, who such resource at hand
> Scorn to obey the rigour of command."

The following description of Churchill is also applicable to the then actors :—

> "The strolling tribe a despicable race,
> Like wandering Arabs shift from place to place,
> Vagrants by law to justice open laid
> They tremble of the beadle's lash afraid
> And fawning, cringe for wretched means of life
> To Madame Mayoress or his worship's wife."

Society had no regard for them and would not admit them into their midst. People wanting amusement in one shape or another encouraged them by their presence as audience. Subscriptions sufficient for the expenses of the night were raised in the town by the actors themselves and performances were given from ten at night till six in the morning. Torches served as lights and clothes from the washerman were borrowed for the occasion. Faces were smeared with some indegenous colouring powder. The wooden crown as heavy as one could bear was kept on the head of the actor, the strings being fastened under the neck. The actor under such a burden had to cry out to make his speech audible to the audience who were seated, some even at the distance of a furlong or so, amidst the noise of the chorus that stood behind the actors. The inevitable buffoon raised the laughter of the audience by his foolish and coarse simian behaviour. The description given by R. W. Frazer of the Indian stage does not represent the ancient stage of India. It is the state of the stage in a village where men wanting both in intellect and learning are actors or authors. Addison in his *Spectator* denounces the method of aggrandizing persons in a tragedy. He refers to the plumes of feathers worn by the hero of the tragedy rising "so very high that there is often a greater length from his chin to the top of the head than to the sole of his foot. One would believe that we thought a great man and a tall man the same thing. . . . Notwithstanding any anxiety which he pretends for his mistress, his country or his friends, one may see by his action that his greatest care and concern is to keep the plume of feathers from falling off his head." In speaking of the heroine he says "the broad sweeping train that follows her in all her motions finds constant employment for a boy who stands behind her to open and spread it to advantage. I do not know how others are affected at the sight but I must confess my eyes are wholly taken up with the page's part; and as for the mien I am not as attentive to anything she speaks as to the right adjusting of her train lest it should chance to trip up her heels or incommode her as she walks to and fro upon the stage. It is in my opinion a very odd spectacle to see a queen venting her passion in a discarded motion and a little boy taking care all the while that they do not ruffle the tail of her gown. The parts that the two persons act on the stage are very different; the princess is afraid she should incur the displeasure of the king, her father, or lose the hero, her lover, whilst her attendant is only concerned lest she should entangle her feet in her petti-coat." Similar absurdities are also common in India.

THESE and various other causes amongst which the immoral conduct of an actor or an actress played an important part, have completed the decline of the Indian stage. I should have said that the Indian stage was irrecoverably lost had it not been for the recent attempts made by English knowing people to reform the stage after the English fashion. When everything concerning the stage tended to the decline of literature in general and the demoralization of the people in particular, could any orthodox Brahmin, who his considered to be the guardian of virtue in India, hold his tongue? He could not prohibit these obscenities, because the Mahomedan rulers who were fond of amusement encouraged every sort of indecency. He could not ex-communicate the actors from society, because they bought the allegiance of their respective religious priests with money; where the lower and the lowest class represented the higher classes on the stage and insulted them with taunts, the Mahomedans were pleased, and the Brahmins had to bend their heads and to pretend sometimes to be pleased, in order to please their Mahomedan rulers. Sometimes they had to write something against themselves. The Mahomedan conquests introduced into Hindu society, vices of all sorts, amongst which the viciousness of the stage was one. The Brahmins could not publicly denounce the actors, but quietly treated them as not fit for society. They were justified in their treatment of the old time actors. Devoid of education of any sort and bereft of all moral feeling, the actors pandered to the prurient taste of the people of a licentious age. Hardly any woman could with decency witness the performance.

THUS from the perusal of the past history of India, we see that which was known as the dark age in Europe was a golden age in India as far as literature was concerned.

When learning revived in Europe, India was immersed in ignorance as if learning and ignorance changed places during certain periods of time. During the thirteenth and the fourteenth centuries we see already in India that the facilities of education had been lessened. Sanscrit literature had been neglected. The few eminent scholars did not find sufficient remuneration for their learning, and society in general had no respect for the educated few and could not appreciate their merit. In this connection I remember the following lines :—

"I pity those, who in these latter days,
Do write, when bounty has shut up her gate
Where day and night in vain good writers knock
And for their labor, have but a mock."

THE Indian kings who encouraged learning by giving titles and gifts in ancient times, were during this period kings without kingdoms or were vassals under the Mahomedans. The Mahomedan kings took great pride in conversions and not in spreading learning amongst their subjects.

Present attempt.

THESE dark days for the dramas continued up to the middle of the nineteenth century. The substance of the old dramas was lost and only the shadow remained. When English education spread itself throughout the length and breadth of India and the English knowing public saw the marvellous effects produced by the English stage and its wonderful scenic performances, the Indians opened their eyes and commenced to enquire what their ancient dramas were like. The spirit of enquiry into their past dramatic history contained in a few Sanscrit dramas that remained to them and in the unwritten traditional lore, convinced them that dramatic amusement existed during the time of their Hindu kings and that the stigma attached to dramatic performances was of recent date. The ever enterprising Parsees, the pleasure seeking Mahomedans, and the talented Mahrattas have commenced performances in their own vernaculars. The Parsee and Mahomedan managers care more for costumes, scenery and music than for literary merit. Masses are led away by outward splendour. It pleases only boys and sight-seers.

Parsee and Mahomedan theatres.

These Parsee and Mahomedan theatres sometimes please us with their music and gross buffoonery. They spend enormous sums for scenic effects. Most of the actors are professional strolling players. Some of them in the mofussils perforn artless, formless and aimless plays as the musical comedies are termed by Stanley Jones. From these we could hardly expect any improvement to the national literature. They have borrowed from the English stage all that they can conveniently and usefully borrow. Others have followed their example. Regular theatres are built in large towns. Temporary pandals are erected in some places. Progress is now so rapid that India can boast of a dramatic company in each and every town containing a population of ten thousand. These movements are started by a few enterprising people. The unfortunate Indians who have forgotten all about the existence in ancient times of stage performances, shudder at the idea of this enterprise, and commence to dissuade the members of the movement by the oft-quoted trite expression of modern times that actors are not fit members of society. Sometimes these discussions have created hostilities, and split the societies into factions. For some time the orthodox, even the English knowing orthodox people, being averse to stage performances, never visited dramatic representations, nor even sent their anxious children, lest they should be morally contaminated. This is due to the ignorance of the people. Sir Henry Irving in a lecture puts himself the question "May there be moral contamination from what is performed on the stage"? and answers it in the following words. "Well, there may be. But so there is from books. So there may be at lawn-tennis clubs. So there may be at dances. So there may be in connection with everything in civilized life and society. But do we therefore bury ourselves? The anchorites secluded themselves in hermitages. The Puritans isolated themselves in constant abstinence from everything that anybody else did. And there are people now who think that they can keep their children and those children will keep themselves in after-life, in cotton-wool, so as to avoid all temptation of body and mind and be saved nine-tenth's of the responsibility of self-control. All this is mere phantasy. You must be in the world, though you need not be of it, and the best way to make the world a better community to be in and not so bad a place to be off, is not to shun but to bring public opinion to bear, upon its pursuits and its relaxations."

CHAPTER IX.

CHINA.

THE Chinese had a written language either alphabets or hieroglyphics, so long ago as 2700 B.C., not taking into account another statement which carries back the invention of letters to 3200 B.C. The book of Oodes written at or ahout the twelfth century B.C., is a sufficient proof of the existence of letters, music and poetry long before that date. We read in the history of the country, that ballads and pantomimes were being performed long before the seventh century A.D. The Chinese attribute primitive antiquity to the origin of their dramas, but before the sixth century they had no regular dramas. Like the Indian dramas and those of ancient Europe, the Chinese dramas also arose from the union of the arts of music, dancing and mimicry. Of all the nations of the world, the Chinese are most gifted with the art of imitation which is necessary for the development of dramatic performances. The Chinese are very fond of music and they had vocal as well as instrumental music in a rude form before 720 A.D., when the Emperor Heun Tsung reformed music radically. We hear first a species of heroic dramas about extraordinary events. There was no music in them or rather no dramatical actor sang on the stage. This condition of the stage lasted till the tenth century. In the eleventh century a sort of reformation was brought about inasmuch as they introduced music into the stage. Even then, the principal personage only had to sing and none others. Regular dramas were actually brought into existence in the twelfth century. Various subjects formed themes for dramas. Between the twelfth and the fourteenth centuries, there were eighty-five authors and five hundred and sixty-four dramas, besides those that escaped the notice of historians. There were tragedies, pastoral dramas, love dramas and farces during this period.

The *Pi-pa-Ki* is a domestic drama of sentiment, possessing, it is said, a very extraordinary merit, and is "regarded as a monument of morality and as a master-piece of the Chinese theatre." The Chinese dramas before *Pi-pa-Ki* were immoral to a degree and this famous drama was composed with the special object of reforming the stage. It is said a Chinese drama known as "*Tchao-chi-en-sul*" (the little orphan of the house of Tchao) was taken by Voltaire of France as a theme for his tragedy.

BEFORE the seventeenth century the Chinese dramas declined. Farces and satires couched in ignoble language and dramas with coarse dialogues ruled the stage. Although attempts are made to reform the state of late, dramas cannot attain to the height to which they rose before the seventeenth century. Chinese like other nations, did not care for the unities of time and place. There is no restriction as to what might or might not, be represented on the stage. Though there is a rule that every play should have a good moral, this is mostly honoured in its breach. It is also a great peculiarity in the Chinese drama that every character should announce his name and his genealogy and also recapitulate the previous course of plot. This practice is still found in India amongst the old fashioned strolling players. The authors of these street plays in India take special pains to write the genealogy of the principal characters in thundering classical pedantic language in prose with different kinds of rhymes and alliterations. One should hear it to know what this form of speech really is. All sorts of metaphors, similies and other figures of speech which the language knows are forcibly introduced into it. An ordinary student of literature cannot fluently read it unless he knows it by heart. In China, women were allowed on the stage formerly, but when the emperor Khien-Long took an actress among his concubines, the practice of allowing them on the stage was stopped and boys play the female parts. The performance of a single play continues in some cases for more than a day. It is said by some that the Chinese have no real dramatic poetry. Short lyrical pieces here and there are inserted in their dramas. Most of the dramas abound in love. If bulk is taken into consideration the Chinese can boast of their dramas. If taken for quality, it is said that except a few pieces written during the thirteenth and the fourteenth centuries, the rest are of a very ordinary kind. Their plots are very simple but their acting is said to be very good as they are actors by nature. "There is perhaps not a people in the world who carry so far their taste and passion for theatrical entertainments as the Chinese. These men have minds and bodies endowed with so much suppleness and elasticity, that they can transform themselves at will, and express by turns the most opposite passions." The incidents of the plots are true to life. The Chinese dramas are not devoid of humour. Dramatic performances in the Chinese are known as pleasures of peace and prosperity.

ALL the towns big or small, and all the villages rich or poor, have got theatres in their midst. Men high or low, rich or poor, are passionately addicted to stage plays. The actors play night and day. It is said that people ever find some pretext for getting up a play. A good crop to a ryot, a large profit to a merchant, a good promotion to an official are occasions for dramatical performances. To avert a danger, or cessation of famine or to invoke rain, a dramatical representation is inevitable. Sometimes the heads of a town or a village order that there should be dramatic amusements for a specified number of days. People then subscribe the amount required and have the plays. A man's generosity is also tested by the number of plays he contributes for the amusement of the people. In contracts between traders about the sale and purchase of goods, a dramatic performance, sometimes is one of the items to be carried out by him who is profitted by the bargain, and the arbiters decide in case of disputes arising about the performance of this condition. The poor are admitted free. People go sometimes five or six miles walking to witness a performance. "The spectators are always in the open air and the place assigned to them has no special limit. Every one chooses the best post he can find in the street, upon the roof of a house or upon a tree, so that the clamour and confusion prevailing in these. assemblies may be imagined. The whole audience eats, drinks, smokes and talks as much as it pleases." This description of spectators resembles completely that of the audience in India in the street plays. When an actor on the stage inflames the passions of the audience with his eloquent speech, a few of the worthy spectators horrify the audience with their riotous rhetoric till the police silence them in the house of correction or an influential strong man awakes his whip to play on their back. There will be thus a break of five or ten minutes both to the actor and the audience and the effect of the play is often thus lost.

JAPAN.

IN Japan the art of music, has been for many centuries past, an important element of civilization. An extract from the *Music and Manners*, written by W. Beaty Kingston and dedicted to Sir Henry Irving—the greatest actor of the day—is worth perusal. The author says that music "plays a leading part in all public ceremonies of a religious, official and social character. It is the favourite private recreation of all classes from prince to peasant. Its invention and development are attributed to the Gods and it is organised as a science upon a system of extraordinary complexity and comprehensiveness". The historians of Japan attribute the origin of this music to a goddess of extraordinary beauty. There is a story connected with this origin. The Japanese say that "music has the power of making heaven descend to earth. It inspires human beings with the love of virtue and the practice of duty". Music, dancing, songs, legendary and historic narratives and pantomimes are the elements which Japan can call its own, but the drama was imported from China.

THE history of Japan gives the name of a poet called Hada Kawastu (probably of a Chinese origin) who wrote thirty-three plays and performed them for the benefit of the country in the sixth century. There is a dance called *Sambaso* performed as a prelude to every representation. The same was the case in Indian representation for some time. The object must be to prepare the minds of the audience to the proper reception of the intended performance. A poetess by name Issno-Zanzi wrote many plays. It is said that she was a good dancer and was acting in male attire. She flourished in the twelfth century. Regular dramas were introduced into Japan in the seventeenth century. A regular theatre was built in Yeddo in 1624. Nobles of Japan who were disinclined to go to theatres and sit there along with ordinary people have the dramas performed in private in their houses. There are a species of operas in the performances of which the sons of noblemen take part. These operas generally treat of patriotic legends. In Yeddo there is a court-theatre where performances are given. M. Le Baron Hubner in his *Ramble round the World* says that in Yeddo he attended a theatre, and remarks that though the subject of the play was loose and the execution very free, yet the intrigue was well carried on and the actors were perfect. He says "I have seen in the Palais Royal many "*Vandivellas*" acted with far less spirit and with quite as equivocal a tendency; with this difference, however, that with us everything is said, and here in Japan everything is done, on the stage." The same author says that in Osaka there is a street called "Of the Theatres." "Pictures representing the scenes, especially in historic dramas are hung above the gallery. At the doors there is a dense crowd of all ages and both sexes struggling for admission." The peculiar feature of the Japanese performance is that it is commenced at sun-rise and ended at sun-set. Though Japanese dramas are historical, the names of the real persons are changed for imaginary ones. They have also comedies which indicate their manners. It is said that there are in Japan many domestic dramas of a realistic kind. Though there is a rule that no intrigue against a married woman is to be represented on the stage, they are freely performed in one shape or other, in a highly improper way in some cases. Women are allowed on the stage in the performance of ballets and not generally in other representations.

IN Japan, there is a professional class known as *Gaishas* which trains girls for public dance and singing. The following description of *Gaisha* class of woman taken from the "*Tit-bits*" of 22th September 1906 is an interesting reading to the Indians as they have also in their midst another professional class of females known as "*Dancing-girls*" or "*Vasias*" who were originally intended to cultivate music and dance for being performed before the idols of the temple. "How many of the hundreds of thousands of people in the United Kingdom who have seen that charming musical comedy, "*The Gaisha*," performed on the stage have any idea of the long and arduous preparation a Japanese girl has to go through before she is fitted to embark upon her career as a public singer and dancer? Probably not one in a thousand, for the most of the writers on Japan have only dealt with the Gaisha as she appears before the public. Before attaining the skill in her profession necessary for such an appearance, however, she has to endure years of hardship and laborious exercise which would prove too much for any one to bear who was not blessed with the strongest constitution. The Gaisha class is recruited from the humblest ranks in the Japanese social scale. If a poor man has too many daughters, he sells one of them when she is very young, if a good price is offered for her. It is lucky for her if she is purchased by an Agent of a Gaisha establishment, for in that case her future will at least be free from degredation. There are very common but erroneous opinions in Europe and America about the Japanese Gaisha. She, as any Jap will tell you, is an eminently respectable and hard working girl whose private life, as a rule, is above reproach. When she leaves her home the future Gaisha is sent to a house where she is instructed in the arts of singing, dancing, music, polite speech, and social etiquette. No pains are spared to make her thoroughly proficient in all these accomplishments, and as she is in reality a slave bound to serve her masters for a certain number of years in return for maintenance, and, later on, a salary scaled according to her popularity, she is forced to perform every task that is set her without a murmer. She first makes her public appearance at entertainments as a drum beater. The drum is a small instrument played with two sticks and the young performer sits down to play it behind the dancers. After she has acquired the mastery of the drum she appears at entertainment each day sometimes playing at five or six different functions before she can retire to rest in the small hours of the morning. But her work in the other branches of her profession is by no means relaxed on that account. She has to perfect herself in playing the samisen, an instrument somewhat similar to our guitar and also practice her voice incessantly at all hours of the day and night. It is very rare for a Japanese Gaisha to disappoint an audience through a cold or affection of the throat from any cause, and the reason for this is a remarkable one. In the days of her tutelage she is compelled to sit out in all weathers for hours together and practice her notes. It does not matter if it is the coldest winter night, the duty has still to be performed. At first the results of these constant exposures are violent colds and illnesses, but by and by the Gaisha has a voice which no change of weather can affect and until she has this desideratum she is not considered a safe investment by her owners. It is the same in social life. At most of the entertainment the Gaisha is in the habit of attending, much sake, or pale wine, is consumed and the guests keep very late hours. An experienced Gaisha-and no Gaisha who is not experienced, however young she be, ever appears at one of these functions-must be able to drink all the wine and eat all the sweetmeats offered to her by admiring guests without showing any ill effects. To refuse the proffered gifts would be impolite, an unpardonable offence in Japanese society, especially where a hired entertainer is concerned, and so she has, with gracious smiles and courtesies, to drink cup after cup of sake and keep a cool head until her engagement is at an end. By the time she is sixteen or seventeen years of age the Gaisha is generally an adept in her calling and standing at the threshold of her career. This generally lasts eight or ten years, during the whole of which time she is one of the hardest worked persons in Japan. If she is popular and a favourite with the public the costliest dresses are purchased for her and she is treated by her owners with fitting deference. She has perhaps the privilege of dancing and singing before Royalty and is rewarded with many valuable presents of money and jewelry which are her own perquisites. In this way she frequently becomes very wealthy and at the end of her period of service is regarded as a desirable party by many of the gilded youths of Japanese cities. But more often still she becomes an instructress to the younger generation of Gaishas, or lapses into a serving woman at the revels in the houses where at one time she was admired and applauded by young and old. Four or six Gaishas appear, as a rule, at an ordinary entertainment, but when a banquet is held at which notable personages appear it is customary for the number to be increased. Thus, when Prince Arthur of Connaught was recently in Japan as the guest of the Japanese Emperor and nation it was no uncommon thing for him to attend an entertainment at which as many as thirty or forty of the cleverest and prettiest Gaishas in the country were present. When the great Generals of Japan returned home from Manchuria there were one hundered Gaishas present at a reception held in their honour in Tokio. There was also a specially large galaxy of the fair damsels selected from the principal cities of Japan to entertain Admiral Togo at the big dinner given by the Enperor to signalize the gallant sailor's safe return home."

JORURI-BON or Gidayu-bon contain dramatical literature of Japan. They have many dialogues which can be sung. These dramas were intended originally for marionatte theatres. When experienced singers sitting in a corner sing the songs therein, the morionettes were played on the stage with action. These have no literary value. In the book called "Japan by the Japanese." Baron Suyematsu says that in the Joruri-bon and other books there are many parts which display high literary merits and which may be sung by men and women of the highest classes without any shame before any audience. He says that "my wife herself is a tolerable chanter of the kind, she having first been recommended by a medical man of high reputation to make good use of her voise for the sake of her health, and this kind of singing was selected for her." He asserts that the Japan of to day was mostly due to the above books of dramas, the stages and the heroic stories and the influence exercised by them can never be overlooked. The The reasons given by the author are quoted below :—

"In Japan the idea of the encouragement of what is good and the chastisement of what is bad has always been kept in view in writing works of fiction or in preparing dramatic books and plays. . . . Some kind of reward or chastisement is generally meted out to the fictitious characters introduced in the scenes and these representations either in books or on the stage, are carried out to such a pitch as to leave some sort of profound impression on the minds of the readers or of the audience. Whatever the other remaining parts may be, these features always remain uppermost in the minds of the reader or of the theatre goer. The prominent point thus produced is generally a transcendent loyalty, such as a loyal servant would feel for his master; the great fortitude and perseverance which one exhibits in the cause of justice and righteousness; severe suffering for the sake of a dear friend; the devotion of parents and their self-sacrifice; of a wife for her husband, or of a mother for her son to enable the fulfilment of duty to the lord and master. I can myself remember many times shedding tears when reading works of fiction, or when listening to the singing of dramatic songs, or while witnessing dramatic performances. This peculiarity seems to be wanting on the western stage."

ALICE MABEL BACON in her book "Japanese girls and women" gives a vivid description of how the character of the Japanese girls is formed by their frequenting the theatres. She observes that the Japanese girls catch the spirit of passionate loyalty that belonged to the ancient days, forms her ideals of what a noble Japanese woman should be willing to do for parents or husband and comes away taught, as she could be by no other teaching, what the spirit was that aminated her ancestors,—what spirit must animate her, should she wish to be a worthy descendant of the women of old."

THE No dance is a dramatical amusement of the nobility. "This No dance is an ancient Japanese theatrical performance, more, perhaps, like the Greek drama than anything in our modern life."

ARABIA, PERSIA AND TURKEY.

IN countries of Europe and Asia where Mahomedans were rulers, the dramatic art could not have flourished as the existence of the Zenana system was a hindrance to their bringing actresses on the stage with propriety. Mathew Arnold's essays in criticism mention the introduction during the last century of a passion play on theatres known as "Tekyas." The actors are men and boys, the parts of angels and women being filled by boys. It appears that all the principal families of Teheran send their children to the theatres, to act as children there and to bring blessings on themselves and their parents. The theatre is managed by a sacred personage who is respected everywhere. In Persia dramatical literature sprang up only in the ninteenth century. They had from the beginning of the fifth century excellent music, and poets too were not rare, but regular dramas like those which India and Europe had, were very scarce. Like the mysteries and miracle plays of ancient Europe, the Persians have been for centuries performing these religious dramas during the first ten days of the Mohurram. These are mere "recitals of mournful lamentations in memory of the tragic fate of the house of the Caliph 'Ali.' Most of these passion plays deal with the slaughter of Ali's son, Hosain and his family in the battle of Kerbela." Of late many dramas (Biblical stories and even christian legends) are brought on the stage and at present we see many kinds of dramas being performed with the best European stage scenery. In Arabia, music occupied a pre-eminent position and the art reached a great height once. Along with it poetry assumed also a very high position but dramatic art did not take its root in the hearts of the people.

MUSIC had been absolutely prohibited by the Prophet. "To hear music is to sin against law and to perform music is to sin against religion ; to enjoy music is to be guilty of infidelity." Even in such a regid religion, the Muezzins chanted call to prayer and a hymn of the pilgrims at Mekka round Haggard's supposed well are sung. Still among the Moors of Spain music had been highly cultivated and it is said that musical literature on the elements of music, on composition, singing, instruments and accompaniments, is found in works written in Arabic.

RICHARD DAVEY in his book "The Sultan and his subjects" Vol. I describes the sort of theatrical entertainment he saw in the month of Ramzan in Turkey. It is the performance of "*Karagheuz.*" It is nothing but a pupet show with which both Europe and Asia are familiar. Besides the entertainment of Karagheuz, the author of the above work says that Armenians and Greeks have an orchestra and there they give dramatical performahces. At present there are many theatres and music halls and there is also a Royal theatre.

CEYLON.

FA-HIAN the Chinese traveller who visited Ceylon about the fourth century says "Strange miracle plays were enacted representing the chief events of Buddhist life with appropriate sceneries and costumes and introducing figures of elephants and stags so delicately coloured as to be scarcely descernible from life." It is strange to see these curious religious plays in favour well nigh two thousand years ago. Tamil and Sanskrit plays are freely performed in Ceylon. C. F. Gordon Cumming in his book "Two happy years in Ceylon" stated that during his stay there a dramatic company came from Jaffna and performed a Sanscrit drama called Harischendra, and also he witnessed a tamil play in Trincomalee.

CHAPTER X.

AFRICA.

Music.

THE Egyptians looked upon music as an important science. They permitted the flute, the harp and vocal music, in the sacred rites of their gods. In ancient times the rural population of Egypt went in procession, singing songs in praise of their god Osiris-the vivifying power. They had no chorus as we found in Greece. Their celebrations resembled more closely the processions in honour of Bacchus with phallic songs. Ancient Egypt, ancient Greece and ancient and present India have this custom in common. I do not know which nation claims the first place for having invented this rude form of merriment. With dancing and music, pantomimes commenced. Wanton baffoonery and mimicry prevailed also on festive occasions among the lower orders of the poeple.

Pantomimists.

Caracalla.

When that bloody monster Caracalla, Roman Emperor, visited its once capital Alexandria in 215 A.D., many satires it is said were performed and in one the emperor was indirectly mocked at. Taking offence at it the mad emperor put all the inhabitants to death. Again when this capital revived, it could boast of a number of theatres. In 616 A.D., when the Arabian chief Amru took its capital it is said that that town contained four-hundered theatres. At present we are not able to trace any dramatical art in Egypt.

Amru.

E. W. Lane in his book called "Manners and Customs of Egyptians" observes that "the Egyptians are often amused by players of low and ridiculous farces, who are called "Mohabbazeen." These frequently perform at the festivals prior to weddings and circumcisions at the houses of the great; and sometimes attract rings of auditors and spectators in the public places in Cairo; it is chiefly by vulgar jests and indecent actions that they amuse and obtain applause. The actors are only men and boys, the part of a woman being always performed by a man or a boy in a female attire."

Mohabbazeen.

"SOMETIMES farces were played before Ba'sha with the view of opening his eyes to the conduct of those persons to whom was committed the office of collecting the taxes."

"KARA-GYOOZ" puppet shows were introduced into Egypt by Turks and they are played in the Turkish language. The performances are extremely indecent. These are exhibited at night.

IN South Africa, before the Dutch settlement in the seventeenth century, the Zulus had excellent pantomimes and possessed the great dramatical art and humour. They occasionally gave a set dance with precision. It is said that without the trouble of re-hearsals thousands of Zulus would "go through complex evolutions with the regularity of clock-work without word of command." They had also vocal and instrumental music. After the Dutch settled there, they imported dramas into Cape Colony and theatres were built. The dramatic companies from the different countries of Europe helped the progress of dramatic art there. It is said that in every large town in South Africa there are regularly built theatres where performances are given frequently.

AUSTRALIA

ABOUT the dramatic art in Australia and the South Sea Islands little definite information is procurable. However from a book published by John N. Dalton it is seen that music, dancing and pantomimes existed as amusements among the people of Australia. In the Fijian Islands several kinds of dances known as *Mekeys* are performed. The description is worth reading as affording materials for the inference that a nation in the primitive stages of development amused itself with different kinds of walks, struts, jumps, gesticulations, and vocal sounds, which subsequently being systematized and codified became regulations for guidance. It is stated in the book above quoted that the Mekeys consisted of native songs and dances combined, and are dramatic, religious, comical, warlike and sometimes romantic in turn. The dance consists of many varied figures, most of which are full of vigorous action, while the non-dancers squat in the middle, some clapping hands in time and others beating time on the ground. Each district and clan has a dance peculiar to itself. "The rapidity of their movements and the flexibility of their bodies is something marvellous. It seems as if every muscle was in action and all the postures are graceful."

AMERICA.

THE description of the present state of dramas in Europe is a sufficient description of that in America. America seems to possess no history of ancient indigenous dramas. The present dramatic activity of a century or two in that continent is more or less the influence of England. In America the taste for the legitimate drama was in the ascendant but that taste has degenerated since as could be seen from the following extract from a New York paper "The World." The drinking saloons exhibit gross and vulgar performances on their stages from night to midnight; and the visitor may get comfortably drunk in his seat if he desires. There are attendant Hebes too, in the shape of pretty waiters; girls who will bring him any variety of drink. Thus he may booze in peace, have his intellect improved, his taste chastened and his spiritual faculties exalted by Ethiopic colloquy, noisy vocal and instrumental strains, pantomimic mummery, mysterious disappearances, sudden tricks, rope swinging, miserable dancing and more miserable singing, hashtrash and every sort of buffoonery in order to attract the silly and weak minded." "The absorption of the public mind in the Civil War has allowed these evils to flourish for a season; but the time will come to demand this removal under the penalty of such punishment as shall deter a repetition of such degrading exhibitions."

Mexico.

IN the history of Mexico it is found that during the reign of Nezuhuileogotl poets were encouraged but subsequently the country became rude and education backward. However there were companies of singers and dancers for amusement. Solemn and gay dances were frequent even in ancient times. Mexico under the Spanish Viceroys had some rude theatrical performances. In the "Ramble round the World" written by Hubner and translated by Lady Herbert, I find that in Salt Lake City the theatre is far more popular. This theatre must have been erected in the eighteenth or the nineteenth century.

IN Peru it is said that an Inca drama called Appuollantay was being performed. When this drama was written is not known. It is said that it is a historical play containing a sweet lyric poem.

It is said that the first drama that was performed in Boston was in 1750. "The novelty made such a crowd and so much disturbance that the Legislature passed a law prohibiting theatrical entertainments as tending to unnecessary expense, the increase of impiety, a contempt for religion." Subsequently, however, the authorities were brought to their senses and the theatrical entertainments were freely performed.

J. M. ROBERTSON in the appendix to his book called "Pagan Christs" gives a description of passion play in new Mexico and said that the play was introduced in that country by the Spaniards in 1540.

IN the book styled "The Nineteenth Century" Radken Towse observes of modern actors as follows :—"Our modern actors have no such educational advantages and rather affect to despise them. Their object is no longer interpretation but adaptation, the adaptation, that is, of author's ideal to their own personalities, and so incapable are they, as a rule, of any originality or invention, that the chief employment of most of our dramatists is a sort of dramatic tailoring—the cutting and trimming of theatrical suits to display to the best advantage the meagre proportions of our stage exquisites, who vainly imagine that their individual peculiarities of voice and manner constitute a formula for the expression of eve. y mood or passion known to human nature." It is recorded in the above book that one Thomas Abthrope Cooper played one hundied and seventy-six leading characters. He was said to be "one of the most versatile, graceful, powerful and fascinating actors that ever lived." He played between 1800 and 1835. Between 1715 and 1830, there were about one hundred and fifty American authors of plays amongst whom William Demlap was most conspicuous. He is called the father of the American theatre. "He was a man of varied accomplishments who earned for himself a niche in the temple of fame as an admirable writer on art and as the founder of the National Academy of Design." He wrote many plays. The first notable tragedy that was played on American stage was "Brutus" by Howard Payne in 1820. This author wrote about sixty plays. The author concludes by a remark that "only in the luxury, not always in the good taste, of our stage appointments do we equal or excel all rivals. Without tragedians, without comedians, without playwrights, the American theatre as a separate entity, is a pitful illustration of the ill-effects of the destruction of competition by a greedy monopoly."

CHAPTER XI.

CONCLUSION.

READERS, I do not presume that I have exhausted my subject, for, the description of minute details of the dramas of different countries is not possible. I have, however, tried my level best to gather all information I could possibly get and place it before you, my Indian Readers, to judge for yourselves if the elements that constitute a drama are not permanent and if they could be completely eradicated from the face of the earth.

WITH the birth of man is born his voice and with his growth grows his art of imitation. "Imitation," says Aristotle, "is instinctive in man from his infancy." Gesture and voice are the means of imitation common to all human beings. Development of imitation is action or in other words drama. It is a natural desire of every man to express himself, his feelings and impressions as impressively as he can. The face and eyes speak sometimes—such as the steady look of veracity, the averted glances of falsehood, the side long glances of love, the fiery view of rage, the half closed eye of contemplation, and the wide open eye of admiration. Lord Bacon says that "The lineaments of the body disclose the disposition and inclination of the mind in general; but the motions of the countenance do *not only so,* but do further disclose the present humour and state of the mind and will." Though we are not here prepared to investigate the causes of reciprocal action of mind and body physiologically and psychologically, yet we can say for certain that the mind and body act and react upon each other. This action and reaction is due to the strong mental and physical impulses and influences. It becomes, therefore, necessary for an actor to develope not only the faculty of speech by the modulation of his voice but also the faculty of expressing ideas by the face and eyes. Emotions of pain and pleasure may be read on the colour and distortions of the face. Sympathy, pity, anxiety and vexation may be expressed without the help of words. Such expressions of passions being universal are understood with the help of gesture language written on the heart of every man and responded to by a similar mute action denoting approval or disapproval. That gesture action precedes words is established by human experience, for the reason that immediately after a thought is formed, it gives an electric shock to the limbs before the tongue gives expression to it. The process of thinking is carried on without words and sometimes people use words without thinking. Thinking and its expression by words are independent of each other; but when the former is at work it shows itself in expression of face and other cognate physical movements. George Harris, in his "Philosophical Treatise on the nature and constitution of Man," observes "that portion of man's language which is the most expressive and the most powerful and affecting is that which is inarticulate, consisting of signs and the modulation of the voice, and of gesticulation through the members of the body and it is the proper application of this branch of language that constitutes acting; and it is in its due use that the most important element in the attainment of eloquence, which is termed action, also consists." I think that the only language which is common to all nations civilized and uncivilized is the gesture language and that Voltaire's assertion that the French Jesuits made most converts in the countries where their language was not understood must have been based upon this gesture language. Cicero, in his "De Oratore," says that "every passion of the heart has its appropriate look and tone and gesture and the whole body of man and his whole countenance and all the voices he uttered re-echo, like the strings of a harp, to the touch of every emotion of the soul." By facial expression, a man may sometimes belie his words even. By a certain peculiar intonation or expression a man may express what he does not really mean or something contrary to what he means by his words. Human tempers give rise to various features in his form and act upon his voice by a peculiar process of nature. The voice is changed and the colour of the face also. You see a man in rage and observe tears in his burning eyes, his lips quivering, his voice shaky, his face red and his body shivering. Here the man's features express his temper. Thus without the help of words a man has in him sufficient unwritten language to express his temper. In a similar way he can express what his desires are without words by means of some gestures. This is known as gesture action or pantomime. This gesture action is reduced in India to a science known as "Abhinaya Sastra" by sage *Bharatha.*

Music.

THE modulation of voice and the vibrations of sound resulting from the different emotions of man give rise to several tunes. Emotions of mind caused by the feeling and love of the subject in communion with the heart produce many musical notes which being developed have become a musical science.

Poetry.

Prosody.

Savages in their rude state chanted their chants in irregular prose which took a definite form as the age advanced and harmony required. Prosody was the result of the said development. The measuring of chants either by syllables or by accents was the first process in the formation of poetry. This leads us to infer that the verses are so many ancient chants regulated with reference to the rules of prosody with the object of improving their harmony. This will also lead us to infer that these verses required to be sung rather than to be recited as prose. Our ancient hymns in the Vedas are in regular metres and they are sung. Our *Sama Veda* is full of musical chants. I refrain myself from going into the details of metres, and content myself with a mere statement that metre affords facility for remembrance and imparts interest and gracefulness to a prose narrative; and it was why our ancients preferred metrical verses to prose even in the treatment of very common subjects. In the musical recital of verses, sense is concealed in sound, and the reciters in their efforts to bring out the sense of the verse take the help of gesture action. Thus the gesture action and the musical voice are the most important elements for a man to express his feelings and ideas in an impressive and harmonious way.

OUR Indian authors classify passions under eight headings such as (1) Srungara, (2) Veera (2) Karuna (4) Adbhuta (5) Hassia (6) Bhayanaka (7) Bheebutcha (8) Roudra. Aaron Hill classifies them under ten headings, *i.e.*, (1) Joy (2) Grief (3) Fear (4) Anger (5) Pity (6) Scorn (7) Hatred (8) Jealousy (9) Wonder (10) Love.

How men generally express the said passions in gesture actions is described below.

"*Joy* is to be expressed by the clapping of hands, by exulting looks—the eyes wide opened and upraised, the countenance smiling—the voice rising from time to time to the very highest pitch.

Grief is represented by beating the head, tearing the hair, suspending the breath; also by screaming, weeping, stamping with the foot, hurrying hither and thither and lifting the eyes to heaven.

Fear opens wide the eyes and mouth, contracts the brows, draws back the elbows, lifts up the hands, the palms open towards the dreaded object as shields opposed to it. The body shrinks and trembles, yet assumes a fighting posture, the heart beats violently, the breath is quick and short and the voice weak and agitated.

Anger expressed itself with rapidity and interruption; rant, harshness and trepidation. The neck is out-stretched, the head nods and shakes in a menacing manner, the eyes alternatively stare and roll, the brows frown the forehead is wrinkled, the nostrils are dilated, every muscle is strained. Clenched fists are shaken, the whole body is violently agitated, the open mouth is drawn on each side towards the ear, the teeth gnash and the feet stamp.

Pity—(a combination of love and grief) lifts its hands and looks down upon the object of compassions with lowered brows, parted lips and features drawn together; the voice is frequently interrupted with sighs and the hand is occasionally employed in wiping the eyes.

Hatred of which scorn is a sort of small and mild edition, shrinks back in avoidance of an odious object, the hands are out-spread as though to keep it off, the eyes look angrily and asquint, the upper lip curled, the teeth set, the voice loud, the tone chiding, unequal, surly, vehement.

Jealousy is restless, peevish, anxious, absent, absorbed. Now it gives way to piteous weeping and complaining; now a gleam of hope that all is well, lights up the countenance into a momentary smile. The gloom clouds the face again and the mind is over-cast with frightful suspicions, horrible imaginations. The arms are folded, the fists clenched, the rolling eyes dart fury. Violent agitations succeed.

Wonder opens the eyes, the mouth, the hands; the body is fixed in a contracted stooping posture, the face has the look of fear but without its wildness.

Love lights up the face with smiles, smooths and enlarges the forehead, parts the lips, arches the eye brows. The expression is eager and wistful, but with an air of satisfaction and repose. The eyes languish half closed, the tone is persuasive, flattering, pathetic, soft, winning, musical, rapturous. The body bends forward; sometimes both the hands are pressed to the bosom in all supplicant passions—kneeling often necessary."

IF a man conceives a passion and really feels, the impressive springs of his mind produce involuntarily all the outward changes in features and expressions mentioned above. Approbation, exhortation, enquiry, modesty, shame, submission, pride, obstinacy, command, prohibition, affirmation, demand, commission, dismissal, reproof, condemnation, menace, curiosity, complaint, etc., require appropriate gesture-action to be learnt by study, observation and experience; as also the expression of mirth, madness, sloth, fatigue, sickness, fainting, intoxication, etc. When a man is mad "he rolls the eyes, distorts the features, rushes in and out furiously at every entrance and exit and appears all agitation." Sloth yawns, dozes, snores and drawls. Dutton Cook quotes Thespian Preceptor's instructions in his book "On the Stage". I am sorry I could not get at the original book which fully treats the subject.

Drama.

GRANTED a man is gifted with the said elements he is naturally inclined to exhibit his gifted powers. Such exhibitions have taken the form of dramatic performances. These from their ancient origin have formed the integral part of the life of the nation and no rigid rule can break its continuity. We cannot ask nations not to love dramas. That love will not die till nation's life perishes. This national love of dramas has improved also the divine art of poetry. Drama appears to be a favourite entertainment to nations considerably advanced in refinement and culture. Indians have got innate dramatic instinct in them. The compositions of Kalidasa and Bhavabhoothi instill into their heart emotion of joy and enhance their love for dramatic performances. Their works have become the essential part of Indian literature. The noble poetic art consists in dramatic poetry. Our ancients must have had this in view when they said that he only is a scholar who has read dramas. Even now the indispensable adjunct of classical scholarship is thoroughness of study of dramatic literature. This noble dramatic art animated our ancient poets to compose the mightiest and sweetest poems. A great literary scholar said of England that "the greatest glory of England is her literature and the greatest glory of her literature is her drama".

National pride for literature.

It was the wealth of India that many centuries ago attracted the foreigners to our land. It is India's philosophical and dramatical wealth that now attracts the attention of foreign nations. If India, at present, has lost her literary dramatic splendour it is not for dearth of dramatic genius in Indians but it is owing to extraneous circumstances which throw a thick veil over it. Though deprived of the noble dramatic entertainment, Indians even now are proud of their having once had this unrivalled literary amusement amongst their ancestors. This is naturally a national pride.

Englishman's just pride.

One is naturally proud of one's own country, one's own language, customs, and manners, and one's own national wit. In 1738, sometime after the Licensing Bill in England was passed, the Hay-market theatre was closed against English actors. Lord Chamberlain however gave a license to a French company to open it and a comedy was announced. The English audience could not bear it and was unruly. It defied the authority of the judge and did not care for the bayonets of the Military guard. They indignantly asked why an arbitrary act should suppress native talent, and encourage and patronage foreign adventurers. That the English people felt it keenly is but natural. People are not devoid of patriotic feeling—a feeling for their native literature, native manners, native customs aud native dramas.

The English people are proud of their dramas because they have their immortal Shakespeare always before them. Similarly the Indians are proud as they have their immortal Kalidasa before them. These two living nations must naturally therefore be proud of their dramatic literature and they cannot afford to lose the pleasure derivable from their dramas. In 1859 when an ovation was paid to Charles Kean, son of Edmund Kean, the Duke of New Castle, the gifted Colonial minister said "In the days of ancient Greece the theatre and the drama were the most effective instruments in forming the character of that remarkable people and even at this moment it is an undoubted index to the social status of the people. I have referred to ancient Greece in which the actor was deemed worthy of the highest honours in the state. It is strange, in this land of literature and art, while poets, sculptors and painters receive some portion of the approbation—it is strange that that branch of art, the most difficult to arrive at excellence in, should be cast in the shade and treated with obloquy, or at any rate, with indifference. Honour then to the man who has raised the stage from what it was when he entered upon it to what it is now. And therefore I will only say that I now ask you to drink to the health of one whose public virtues and whose private character have raised up around him a wide circle of admiring friends; to one whose zeal for his profession, amounting almost to enthusiasm had led him to prove that the theatre may be made not a mere vehicle of frivolous amusement, or what is worse dissipation; but that it may be erected into a gigantic instrument of education for the instruction of the young and edification as well as amusement of those of mature age." In 1862, in a meeting at St. James Hall, the Chancellor of Exchequer, W. E. Gladstone, presided and delivered the following eloquent speech :—"We cannot treat the drama as among the light amusements of

Opinion of the Duke of New Castle.

Opinion of W. E. Gladstone.

the world. It belongs to no particular age, to no particular country, to no particular race and to no particular form of religion. It has gone through all races, all countries, all ages and all forms of religion; and even religion herself has not always disdained to find in it a direct hand-maid for the attainment of her own purposes. Whether that connection be direct or indirect, its social and its moral effects must always be of the greatest importance. No student of human nature, no observer of society, no historian that tells the events of the world and aims to give a true picture of mankind, ever can omit it from his view. If it be true that the drama has thus been characteristic of the whole history of man, most certainly it is not in this country where we can assign to it a secondary place when we recollect that the land to which we belong, and the land in which we live has given birth to the greatest dramatist of the whole world." We may safely take the opinion of the above gentleman as a representative opinion of the English nation and they are proud of their dramatist and their dramas.

Natural inclination for drama.

GROWING out of nature, the merry elements are strong in man which, combined with intellectual tendencies are sure to serve as the highest kind of amusement both to the educated and to the uneducated. Thus drama becomes a delightful entertainment to one and all. Amongst the humanity on the face of the earth, very few are those who belong to the society of Quakers. Men in general do not, like Quakers, discourage gaiety and merriment. They do not desire to lead the life of hermits and say that everything that tends to exhilaration or enjoyment has in it a taint of criminality. Man cannot be always serious and solemn and contemplative. He cannot make up his mind to mortify himself in this world for the happiness in the other world when he fully knows that without this tormenting test he could try to reach the other world by leading his life in a manner more satisfactory than that of a Quaker. Man cannot, like a Quaker, deny himself the pleasures of theatre and music with a seeming reason that they are useless and that they divert him from the important duties of life and that they give rise to silly vanity. The prophet of Arabia following the rule of Quakers prohibited music, and yet in Arabia itself, and mostly among the votaries of Mahomad, music developed into science.

Professor Blakie's opinion.

PROFESSOR BLAKIE said that "in the heathen times it (theatre) was the pulpit, and undoubtedly the stage was the natural pulpit—the most intellectual of all pulpits. In spite of all the clergy in the world I will go to the theatre. A number of people object to a theatre not because they were too pious but because they were too stupid. There is no amusement that requires more talent and intellect or has more elegant kind of work mixed up with it than the representative character."

Harmlessness of Indian dramas.

I wonder how the stage, especially the Indian stage, can corrupt the people when so many Indian epic poems from which the themes are selected do not corrupt their moral. Some of the epic poems contain so many horribly indecent stories that one would shudder at reading them. The dramatists at the present day avoid immoral themes and select such of the subjects as would incline the mind of the audience to what is good and righteous. Even the indecent representations of the strolling street players I mentioned previously, have in them the ultimate objecf of teachiug a good lesson to the people. Vice is never victorious in Indian dramas. It is teased, tortured and compelled to submit to virtue. As far as I can see, leaving out of consideration the individual conduct of any particular actor in a badly conducted play-house, the stage has nothing in it intrinsically to lower the national morality. On the other hand it has, if properly understood, an elevating influence in a practical way on the conduct of man. A performance that is submitted to the judicious opinion of the public and not to the arbitrary will of an individual is sure to possess the qualities that will be approved by the general public. If such qualities are present in a drama, how can there be moral contamination from the stage? The Indians, even some of the highly English-educated Indians, do not seem to bear in mind the sources which improved the thought, taste and culture of the European nations. Sir Henry Irving in one of his lectures says "the stage is intellectually and morally, to all who have recourse to it, the source of some of the finest and best influences of which they are respectively susceptible. To the thoughtful and reading man it brings the life, the fire, the colour, and the vivid instinct which are beyond the reach of study. To the common indifferent man, immersed, as a rule, in the business and socialities of daily life, it brings visions of glory and adventure of emotion and of broad human interest. It gives him glimpses of the heights and depths of character and experience, setting him thinking and wondering even in the midst of amusement. To the most torpid and unobservant it exhibits the humours in life and the sparkle and finesse of language which in dull ordinary existence is stupidly shut out of knowledge or omitted from particular notice." Thus we see that the drama is an important element in literature, and its practical lessons tend to improve both the learned and the illiterate.

Sir H. Irving's opinion.

The opinion of the Orthodox Hindus.

THE orthodox Indians, some of them at any rate remembering the traditional reputation of the stage during the licentious Mahomadan period, are still carried away by those now imaginary impressions and stigmatise the stage as immoral. We cannot but admit that the stage was once very indecent, when the people were deeply immersed in immorality.

With grief I admit that many of the theatres not conducted by educated men are even now in the stage in which theatres were in the Mahomaden period. This is deplorable. The indifference of educated men has been the cause of this regrettable state. Were not the stages of the European nations once in the same plight as ours? A Scotch clergyman remarked as follows :- "The objectionable part of the theatre is that it is not only a distinctively wordly institution, but it is distinctively devilish one. The theatres are mere houses of assignation where rich and bloated men meet their mistresses and harlots. The whole stage reeks with vice. . . Oh, the harm those wolves in sheep's clothing are doing among the flocks of God. The theatre is the very porch of the pit; it is the vestibule of hell." It was so, and the clergy were justified in their remarks. What is the state of the stage now in England? It is the very vestibule of heaven. Mme Sarah Barnhardt one day entered a Protestant Church in America and heard the minister there denouncing her as an "imp of darkness, a female demon sent from the Modern Babylon to corrupt the New World." That very day she wrote the following reply to the clergyman: "Why attack me so violently? *Actors ought not to be hard on one another*".

Clergyman's opinion of old English stage.

Reformation absolutely necessary.—Why not the Indians —the educated Indians—try heartily to regenerate the dramatic art and the stage? Do they not think seriously that, if left in its present state, the stage will descend to the lowest depth of immorality, and any attempt on the part of the educated to revive it then would be too late? Do they think that their indifference or their condemnation will destroy the stage? No. The love for the theatre is so deeply rooted in man, especially in an Indian, that it is in-eradicable from his heart. "The stage will never lose its hold over the intellectual and moral sympathies of the people" is the correct saying of an Englishman. The English clergy even when they were the worst enemies of the stage were shrewd enough to know the inborn taste of mankind for the dramatic performance and got up therefore mysteries and miracle plays as a means of disseminating religious knowledge among the people hardly accessible in any other way. With the apparent reason of pleasing the children but with the real intention of exhibiting them, the ecclesiastics wrote many mythological, quasi-historical, allegorical and satirical comedies. Therefore I say once more that the love for dramas is in-eradicable.

Educated men to be actors.

A mighty inherent strength is needed to reform the stage and to ensure to it the vitality required for the success. The educated people who have a special knack for dramatic art need not shrink from taking up characters. "The noblest literary man of all times, the finest and yet most prolific writer, the greatest student of man and the greatest master of man's highest gift of language,——the greatest man in whose presence divines would falter and hesitate, lest their knowledge of the book should seem poor by the side of his, and at whom even queenly royalty would look askance with an oppressive sense that here was one to whose omnipotent and true imagination, the hearts of kings and queens and peoples had always been an open page"—*the immortal Shakespeare,* was an actor. *Edward Alleyn,* the founder of Dulwich College was an actor in the admirals company. "He was a man of excellent capacity, a cheerful temper, a tenacious memory, a sweet elocution and in his person of a stately port and aspect." Ben-Jonson wrote the following lines in praise of him :—

"If Rome so great and in her wisest age
Feared not to boast the glories of her stage
A skilful Roscius and great Æsop, men
Yet crowned with honours as with riches then
Who had no less a trumpet to their name
Than Cicero, whose very breath was fame

How can so great example die in me
That Alloyne, I should pause to publish thee?
Who both their graces in thyself has more
Outstript than they did all who went before
And present worth in all does so contract
As others spake but only thou dost act
Wear this renown."

The famous *Richard Burbage* was an actor in the Lord Chamberlain's Company. The ever remembered *Garrick*, a very learned man, was an actor for a long time. *Jodella*, the author of the tragedy known as "Cleopatra-captive" and other poets known as the pliads of French literature played dramas. *Francis Rabelais*, a great physician, a great botanist, a great anatomist, a great linguist and a renowned author was one of the actors in a comedy. Many of the English dramatists, men of great learning, were actors; *N. Lee, Thos. Otway, Mrs. Centlivee* and *Colley Cibber* were poets and actors. Colley Cibber, a great and famous actor, contributed largely to improvement in the decency of dramatical language. He was made poet-laureate in 1730. His son was also an actor and dramatist. *Sir Richard Steele* was a dramatist of great merit. *Livius Andronicus* who established a regular drama in Rome was said to be an actor. The seven tragic poets in the capital of the Ptolemies, known as the Pliads were said to have enacted a tragedy. *Kalahakandala* was a learned man and acted, it is said, a part in Anargharaghavam. *Thomas Sheridan*, the great educationalist, was an actor. It was he that advocated and introduced oratory on the stage. His son *Richard Brinsley Sheridan*, the greatest orator, a witty dramatist, a respected and a leading member of Parliament and a statesman of the highest genius, was an active stage-manager. *Charles Dickens*, the eminent novelist and a dramatist, was also an actor, a stage-manager, a stage-carpenter, a scene-arranger, a property man, a prompter and a band-master. In the Comedy entitled "Lingua, or the combat of the tongue and the five senses for superiority" it is said Oliver Cromwell played the part of Tactus. The following lines which he delrvered in the performances inspired him with the sentiments of ambition to wear a real crown.

In the drama Tactus "finds the crown which is the subject of contention among the various characters. He exclaims :—

"Do I not sleep and dream of this good luck, ha?
No, I am awake and feel it now :—
Mercury, all's mine own : her's none to cry half's mine
Was ever man so fortunate as I?
Roses and bays pack hence : this crown and robe
My brows and body circles and invests
How gallantly it fits me : sure the slave
Measured my head that wrought this coronet
They lie that say complexions cannot change;
My blood's ennobled, and I am transformed
Unto the sacred temper of a king
Me thinks I hear my noble parasites
Stiling me Cæsar or Great Alexander :
Licking my feet and wondering where I got
This precious ointment : how my pace is mended!
How princely do I speak! how sharp do I threaten!
Peasants, I'll curb your headstrong impudence
And make you tremble when the lion roars,
Ye earthbred worms."

The Princes of the House of Brunswick have all been partial to theatrical entertainments. Prince Frederic of Wales instructed his children to repeat moral speeches out of plays. Under the direction of the celebrated actor Quin, he made his children take up dramatic characters and perform certain plays. When George III delivered a speech from the throne, Mr. Quin was proud of his pupil and exclaimed "Ah, I taught the boy to speak! The greatest actors in England at present are men who obtained academical honours. The title of knight-hood was conferred on

Sir Henry Irving and *Sir Squire Bancroft.* I read in "The Theatre" of March 1896, that the Oxford University, has attached to it a dramatic society of graduates and under-graduates.

Aesop and Roscius.—Æsop and Roscius who lived in the first century B.C., were highly educated men and distinquished actors. Æsop was a first rate tragedian and Roscius was an equally eminent comedian. Æsop taught the art of action to the orator Cicero and through love for his student he performed many friendly services to him especially during the period of Cicero's banishment. A short extract from the life of Cicero by Revd. W. Collins, M.A., will show what wonderful effect a really good actor could produce in the minds of the people. When "Andromache" of Ennius was performed, Æsop took the principal character. "With all the force of his consummate art, he threw into Andromache's lament for her absent father, his own feelings for Cicero. The words in the part were strikingly appropriate and he did not hesitate to insert a phrase or two of his own when he came to speak of the man :—

Æsop as teacher of Cicero.

> " Who with a constant mind upheld the state,
> Stood on the people's side in perilous times,
> Ne'er recked of his own life nor spared himself."

So significant and emphatic were his tone and gesture as he addressed himself pointedly to his Roman audience that they recalled him amid a storm of plaudits and made him repeat the passage. He added to it the words, which were not set down for him.

'Best of all friends in direct strait of war' and the applause was redoubled. The actor drew courage from his success. When as the play went on, he came to speak the words—

How Æsop saved Cicero.

> "And you—you let him live a banished man
> See him driven forth and hunted from your gates ",

he pointed to the nobles, knights and commons as they sat in their respective seats in the crowded rows before him, his own voice broke him with grief and the tears even more than the applause of the whole audience bore witness alike to their feelings towards the exile and the dramatic power of the actor." "He pleaded my cause before the Roman people" says Cicero "with more weight of eloquence than I could have pleaded for myself."

How Tucki saved Delhi.

IN 1739 when Nadir Shah with his usual brutal furious spirit ordered the general massacre of the inhabitants of Delhi by shutting its gates, when famine began to rage, and when the Shah was deaf to the miseries of mankind, the public spirit of Tucki, a famous actor saved the town. He exhibited a play before Nadir Shah with which that monarch was so well pleased that he commanded Tucki to ask what he wished to be done for him. Tucki fell upon his face and said 'O, king, command the gates to be opened that the poor may not perish.' His request was granted. Thus this famous actor saved the most ancient city of India.

Prejudice against stage.

THERE is no reason, except a long-rooted sentiment, for an educated man to decline to take up a character when he has a special aptitude for the stage. Not to cultivate a charming art for art's sake is throttling it. To become a professional actor is opposed to the national idea of a respectable Hindu: but to become a member of a company formed to improve the stage must be considered as an honour by an educated Indian. The old prejudice against the stage must die away. The orthodox opinion about the stage is the outcome of prejudice and not the result of judgment and reason. If educated men, who can appreciate what is noble and reject what is indecent and vulgar, frequent the theatres, the stage will acquire a moral status, and the people in general will learn much from it. Johnson wrote in a famous prologue :—

> "The stage but echoes back the public voice
> The drama's laws the drama's patrons give
> For we that live to please must please to live."

It is certainly regrettable that the educated people of India, at any rate most of them, have taken to the amphitheatrical Exhibitions of feats of beasts. When a Roman Emperor questioned his minister as to why the legitimate Roman dramas are going to dogs, the minister wittily replied— that, when educated people commenced to go to beasts and donkeys, the dramas must necessarily go to dogs.

Good effect.—The dramatic art will, it is my sincere opinion, become one of the greatest forces for good that the world has known, and social development and social reformation will result from it, only if it is well conducted by educated men of moral stamina. It is only then that the stage will assume a real place in the life of the nation, and that the wholesome lessons to be taught therefrom are impressed on the minds of the people.

Moral effect.

THE influence of the stage upon the morals and the manners of the people is incalculable, as W. C. Sydney has observed in his book on social life in England. By means of amusement which every man by nature seeks, the theatre proves itself a moral educator. It is a correct saying that "the things seen are mightier than things heard." In a lecture given by Henry Arthur Jones at the re-opening of the City of London College, he observed that

H. A. Jone's opinion.

"wide knowledge of life and mankind is what the drama can give in a transcendent measure. No book, no other art, no more spoken address, no system of education can so instantly and vividly burn and brand the memory with the realities of life and leave them for ever stamped and pictured in the chambers of imagery as can the acted play. . . .

There on the stage in front of you is the whole drama of humanity being played out. . . . Bible and Shakespeare are everywhere allowed to be the two sovereign teachers of the English nation. But the stage is not merely the most vivid and forcible teacher of the truths and wisdom of life,—it is also the most flexible, the most humane, the most tolerant teacher. Schools and creeds, by their very nature, tend to become rigid and inadaptive to the ever changing necessities of their supporters. The drama, by its nature is the most flexible, the most adaptive, the most humane and large hearted teacher. . . Beyond giving a deep and searching knowledge of the heart of man and great truths of life, the stage has a lighter and pleasanter task in teaching good manners and the delicacies, the amenities of social intercourse."

Drama—a teacher and educator.

THE greatest divine poet, Virgil of Rome, of immortal fame, encouraged dramatic performances by his never failing presence. The noblest productions of human intellect are shown to the public through the medium of the stage. I think it may be regarded as a settled principle founded on experience that there is an inborn taste in man for wholesome and intellectual recreation. There is mental pleasure provided by the drama. "It represents life and nature in heroes and heroines and so raises, refreshes and restores the weary and depressed spirit of the world-fatigued and care-worn spectator". Sir Walter Scott said in his speech in Edinburgh that the love for dramatic representation is "an innate feeling in human nature. It was the first amusement the child had—it grew greater as he grew up and even in the decline of life nothing amused so much as when a common tale is well told. It was an enjoyment natural to

Poet Virgil.

Mental pleasure.

Sir Walter Scott on dramas.

humanity—it was implanted in our nature to take pleasure from such representations. In all ages theatrical art has kept pace with the improvement of man-kind and with the progress of letters and fine arts. In England in the time of Queen Elizabeth, the drama began to mingle deeply and wisely in the general politics of Europe, not only not receiving laws from others but giving laws to the world and vindicating the rights of man-kind."

Moral teacher.

THAT the stage might be made a great and powerful moral teacher is exemplified in England. That it has worked much moral good is a fact admitted by every Englishman, not even the clergy excepted. That the Theatre is one of the chief pleasures of men in all times and all countries is a fact borne out by the previous history of dramas.

Drama—a Divine creation.

THE drama is a divine creation, as an eminent English woman, Charlotte Cushman, reverently describes it :—

"God conceived the world,
His conception is poetry.
He formed the world,
His formation is sculpture.
He coloured the world,
His colouring is painting.
He peopled it with living beings,
This is the grand divine eternal drama."

Drama has an immortal life principle in it.

MR. DOWTON in his speech said "what inspired great minds and delighted great men 2000 years ago and did the same in Shakespeare's day must have within itself a principle of life, superior to the whim and the fashion of the hour."

SIR ARCHIBALD ALISON, the great Historian of Europe, says that the stage is a faithful mirror of public taste, and explains the taste of the national mind." We should not forget how the Greek tragedians softened, purified, and elevated the barparic mind, how the Roman players extended civilization and refinement; how the great Shakespeare improved the heart of the world with thoughts of truth, grace and beauty that can never die; how honour courage, patriotism, friendship and virtue have been described by later dramatists. George Elliot in one of her letters said "in opposition to most people who love to read Shakespeare I like to see his plays acted better than any others; his greatest tragedies thrill me, let them be acted how they may."

Alison's opinion.

Drama—a Mirror or the age.

George Elliot on dramas.

WHEN the honest English-men-of letters have the above opinion as a result of their personal experience, can we now dogmatically say that the stage is not a moral factor? Do not dramas give us the romantic side of life? Does that not make the literal more endurable? I think from my personal experience that play-goer can endure the troubles and anxieties of life with more patience and wisdom than one who naver frequents the theatre. People "who are tired of the sordid realism of the world, do really require romantic incident for their comfort." The dramatic art has the power of "stimulating thought, refreshing weary minds, diffusing alacrity of spiirit and of hallowing common life with the charm of romance." A Greek comedian expressed thus about the effect of a drama :—

Drama gives romantic side of life.

"For whensoever a man observes his fellow
Bear wrongs more grievous than himself has known
More easily he bears his own misfortunes."

Stage—a national school of elocution.

THE stage is also a national school of elocution. In the spoken drama the laws of rhetoric regulate the actor's use of speech. The law of pronunciation, modulation, accent and rythm is to be carefully observed. It is said that Cicero, the greatest orator of Rome, was on intimate terms with Aesop and Roscius, the most distinguished actors of the day, and put himself under their direction to perfect his action. Thomas Erskine, the greatest orator of the nineteenth century, confessed often that he had carefully studied Sarah Siddons' cadences and intonation and he was greatly indebted for many of his displays to the harmony of her periods and pronounciation.

Drama teaches by precepts.

DRAMAS tend to perfect the education of man by precepts and examples. Revd. W. Lucus Collins, M.A., in his life of Aristophanes, says about the Athenians of that time that "education which was received by the masses through their constant attendance at the theatre, the public deliberative assembly and the law-courts was quite as effective in sharpening their intelligence and their memory." It is also said "the Greek actors were undoubtedly among the principal and most effective agents of the spread of literary culture through a great part of the known world."

Longenity of a good actor.

IT is said also in favour of an actor after a careful scrutiny of statistics that the average actor who rises to eminence attains an advanced age. The following extract gives detailed reasons: "The old theory that the atmosphere of the theatre is unhealthy will no longer hold water, for the facts prove the contrary to be the case. He must not only rehearse his effect, but he must think them out before hand. He must study at home before he can practise in the plav house, and in the theatre, as in his own life, he is obliged, even if his own nature did not prompt him to do so, to take particular care of himself. All this conduces to health and consequently to long life. Again his very duties, his nightly appearance before the public make it imperative that he should not run to excess in eating and drinking; in short the physical necessities of his work conduce towards good health and long life; nay, more. If he is to attain the highest of his ambition as an actor, he must exert his intellectual faculties to the utmost—especially now-a-days when the race for fame is so keen so that he must look to it, that mind and body are in good order. The actor of our times takes a social rank not previously accorded him. His advantages are far greater now than ever before, and it is for himself to win the guerdon. His profession is respected; his popularity is in his own hands; so also in a great measure, is the length of his life."

Result.

THUS from the above we see that the actor is benefited physically, morally and intellectually; and "the eyes and hearts of the audience are feasted with purity, loftiness and heroism." The models of goodness tend to induce the audience to tread the paths of virtue, and greatness. "The audience nourishes and fosters the sentiments of bravery, strength, resolution and affection." By witnessing well conducted plays "perceptions are sharpened, reflections are aroused and sympathies are extended." Thus the audience is morally elevated by examples. A great literary man A. W. Ward, professor of English literature, Owens College, Manchester, writes "The time may come when it will be recognised that the progress and culture of people depends upon its diversions as well as upon its occupations, and that the interests of the national art are not unworthy the solicitude of thoughtful statesmen."

Opinion of A. W. Ward.

Opinion of Sir H. Irving:—Sir Henry Irving in his lectuse on "the stage as it is" says to the audience in the Philosophical Institution, Edinburgh "If you hold the theatre honestly, liberally, frankly and with discrimination, the stage will uphold in future, as it has in the past, the literature, the manners, the morals, the fame and the genius of our country.

IF the educated Indians continue indifferent to what passes on the theatre, and if the Indian theatre tends only to be a place of course amusement and not of noble instruction, then it is my sincere individual desire, for the sake of India that the society would try its best to put a stop to all dramatical representations. A considerate study of the above, mostly the candid opinions of the educated European nation,—will not, I hope, go in vain to influence my Indian friends towards the Reformation of the stage in India. To achieve this object, what the dramatists are to do, how the actors are to act, what to avoid and what to adopt, are matters of importance. I append below certain observations which are not entirely my own, but are, many of them, contained in the books written by the European nations. As dramas are the creations of the dramatists I commence with them.

RULES.

DRAMATISTS.

1. To convert a subject into the action or plot of the play is the entire task of dramatists. Events of real life, the facts of history and the incidents of narrative fiction may be the subjects for a play. Heroism, chivalry, chastity, self-sacrifice and such like maybe the themes.

2. To preserve unity of action is very important. Let not the dramatist pay much attention to the unities of time and place for they hamper the conduct of action. Every action must be complete in itself. It must have (*a*) opening movement or rise (*b*) growth, (*c*) height or climax and (*d*) fall or close. (I would recommend every author to read Schlegel's "*Dramatic Art and Literature*," Chapter XVII.)

3. Let the incidents of a play be probable unless the theme is mythological.

4. Let the dramatist work hard upon the invention and conduct of his characters. As regards characters designed to influence the whole of the action, let him try, as far as possible, to introduce them early; others may be brought in, in due relation to their contribution towards the course of the plot. Let the dramatist see that most of his actors at their exit leave the audience in good-humour. The ancient dramatist adorned the end of the scenes with some swelling phrases, with some jokes, and more polished lines.

5. Till the average audience is sufficiently educated and trained to the spirit of the stage, let the play be a little more narrative and descriptive than our ancient classical dramas are.

6. In comic dramas or farces, let not the dramatist display any realistic tendency in a manner to insult any family or caste or the public or any religious authority. Realistic tendency in a general way will do much good.

7. Let the dramas be true in spirit to the higher purposes of art, to the noblest tendencies of natural life and to the eternal

demands of the highest moral law. Let the dramatist remember that the spirit of an age is, in general, more completely and faithfully represented by its poetry than by any branch of prose composition and that the "drama comprehends and develops the events of human life with a force and depth which no other style of poetry can reach"

8. Let the dramatist avoid too much show, too much buffoonery and a tendency to sensual allurement. Let the claims of morality and public decency over-rule the requirements of the audience. Let him not sacrifice his taste and feeling to the fashion of the times (Schlegel says "There is an incurable vulgar side of human nature which the poet should never approach but with a certain bashfulness when he cannot allow it to be perceived"). Let the dramas be store rooms of moral maxims even though issuing out of a menial character.

9. Excepting in historical dramas, it is better not to bring about the death of a noble actor or actress, because the audience is not prepared to see the end of a good life in that way. (The ancient Greeks followed this rule).

10. Let not the dramatist exhibit on the stage actual kissing, actual embracing and any other thing of that sort. These may be love parts in a private room, but not in public, especially among the Hindus. (Greeks avoided certain exhibitions on the stage.) (*Vide History of the Literature of the Ancient Greeks* by K. O. Müller).

11. Let the dramatist look to characterization, choice of incidents, scenic effects, situation, language and dramatical points as essentials in a drama. Let the language be in harmony with the dignity of the subject.

12. It is better not to make the drama depend entirely upon a hero or a heroine or on both.

13. Let the dramatist introduce a battle or combat, if it is really unavoidable for the action. (In some 15 of his plays Shakespeare has introduced the encounter or the marshalling of hostile forces. No doubt this representation will be a mimicry, but much is to be left for the imagination of the audience. Drydon

in his *Essay on Dramatic Poesy* condemns this sort of representation. Dutton Cook, however, in his *Book of Play* says, two things were especially praised by the audience of the past :— a speech and a combat)

14. Let the dramas be scholarly, noble in pathos, passion and humour. Let the wit be of the finest quality.

15. Let the acts and scenes be so divided as to enable the actors requiring a short play to cut out any scene or act with a slight addition of speech as a connecting link.

16. Let the dramatist adopt such of the rules of Hindu dramaturgy as will make the course of his drama suit to the taste of the educated people of the present age.

17. Dramatists will do well not to attempt to adopt plots of the plays written by others. Let them do their best and leave the rest to the actors. They are not responsible if a good play is spoiled by the indifference or carelessness of actors.

18. Let the dramatist not keep his plays in manuscripts. Let his dramas be printed and thus become literary and living dramas. Our present dramas are behind times. Let some of the plays contain the ideas and the passions of the present times. Let the dramatist make strenuous attempts to produce historic, heroic and romantic dramas leaving aside the usual mystery and miracle representations. Some dramas though ably written by great poets are not fit for the stage, because these poets are not versed in dramatic language and stage tricks. They are, however, worth being printed on account of their literary character.

19. Where the appearance of ghosts on the stage is necessary for the development of action, introduce them, though in the opinion of some, it is unnecessary. (Aristotle lays down a rule that a ghost is the soul of a tragedy. The English stage still has ghost on it in spite of adverse criticism. In Shakespeare's *Henry VI, Julius Caesar, Hamlet, Macbeth, Richard III,* we see ghosts making their appearance on the stage. Otway in th ragedy of *Venice Preserved* introduces the ghosts of Jaffier a n his friend Piere as seen by Belividera (Jaffier's wife). At the ight of these ghosts, the heroine Belividera is made to die,

Fielding remarks "of all the particulars in which the Modern Stage falls short of the ancient, there is none much to be lamented as the great scarcity of ghosts. Whence this proceeds I will not presume to determine. Some are of opinion that the moderns are unequal to that sublime sort of language which a ghost ought to speak. One says ludicrously that ghosts are out of fashion; another that they are proper for comedy." Addison in his *Spectator* writes "Among the several artifices which are put in practice by the poets to fill the minds of the audience with terror, the first place is due to thunder and lightning, which are often made use of at the descending of a God, at the vanishing of a devil or at the death of a tyrant . . . . . . There may be a proper season for these several terrors and when they only come in as aids and assistances to the poet, they are not only to be excused but to be applauded.")

ACTORS.

From the dramatist I pass on to the actor, who is the interpreter of the dramatist and in whose power lies the success or failure of the play. His art is inseparable from dramatic literature. I would earnestly ask every actor to follow the advice of Mr. Irving.— "First a patient and conscientious study of the text: it is essential to understand the author's meaning. When this has been mastered you may trust to your instinct, to inspiration. Then, amongst the ideas thus discovered, you may make your selection of the good ones by a species of mental process which will enable you to reproduce them artificially at will". The actor may wish to know what action is. An author describes it as follows:— "Acting means the acquisition of Protean gifts; the concealment of the personal beneath the assumed individuality; the expression of emotions, traits and habits foreign to the actor and appropriate to the fictitious character or circumstances; the mastery of eloquent and dignified gesture, and the cultivation of the vocal resources in order to insure a facile, significant, melodious and illuminative delivery of the text". Further the qualifications necessary for the success of an actor on the stage are given by Hubert in his book *The Stage as a Career*. They are the following:—

1. A strong physique.
2. An unimpaired digestion.
3. A slender figure.
4. A marked face.

5. A carrying voice.
6. A lack of real feeling.
7. An abundance of pretended feeling.
8. Much magnetism.
9. Fascination of manner.
10. Purity of speech.
11. A general knowledge of history.
12. A good general education.
13. A general knowledge of costuming.
14. A practical knowledge of economy in dress.
15. Considerable business faculty.
16. Unflagging industry.
17. Undaunted ambition.
18. An utter lack of sensitiveness.
19. A vast capacity for taking pains.
20. An absolute and undisputed devotion to the theatre.
21. An unwedded life.
22. An ability to distinguish criticism from abuse.
23. A readiness to profit thereby.
24. Some genius at advertising.
25. Quickness at seizing opportunities.
26. A well defined specialty.
27. A good memory.
28. Good luck.
29. Talent.

Qualifications Nos. 3, 6, 14, 21, and 24 are not very necessary. 28 is a vague term. 16 and 19 are almost the same. Number one qualification includes number two. 11 and 12 may be grouped together. I think the qualifications that are really necessary for an actor are (1) Youth, (2) Good complexion, (3) strong body, *i. e.*, "Sound and capacious lungs, a vascular and fibrous throat and amplitude in the interior mouth and nasal passages", (4) Education, (5) Dramatic instinct, (6) Memory, (7) Powers of observation, (8) Power of application, (9) Pure speech and (10) Good voice. Thomas R. Gould, in his *Of The Tragidian*, says of an actor that "he is statue and picture, and poem, and music, and infuses them all with life and motion through the charm of his magnetic presence". Though action includes standing, walking, running, attitude and gesture, it is not advisable for an actor to habituate himself to long strides, the swinging of arms, the clenching of fists, the placing of hand on the hips and the shaking of one or two fingers. The actor is advised to keep "a three quarter face" to the audience so that his voice and features may have their effect. I would strongly recommend every actor to study carefully the chapter on the *Art of Acting* written by Dutton Cook in his book called

On the Stage Vol. I. It is a strong piece of advice to the actors not to mouth their speeches nor to saw the air too much with their hands. Overdoing and redundancy of action are always blamed as also the excess of movement and gesture. Employing arms and legs "with a sort of graceless and vehement diffuseness" and also ranting are equally blamed. Betterton rarely lifted up his arms higher than his trunk.

1. The actor is to know the art of acting, which possesses a theory and a technical system of its own. Its true exercise implies a creative process. Acting includes the use of gestures or bodily eloquence, *i. e.*, his bearing, walk and movement of the face and limbs with reference to the particular affections of mind. He must employ every limb and every finger to produce the desired effect. Acting is not mechanical but is the result of feeling, study and practice. The extraordinary control over the vital and involuntary functions, exercised by Junius Brutus Booth is described by an American critic in the following terms:—

"We are informed that the Actor could tremble from head to foot, or tremble in one out-stretched arm to the finger-tips while holding it in the firm grasp of the other hand. . . . . The veins of his corded and magnificent neck would swell, and the whole throat and face become suffused with crimson in a moment in the crisis of passion, to be succeeded on the ebb of feeling by an ashy paleness. To throw the blood into the face is a comparatively easy feat for a sanguine man by simply holding the breath; but for a man of pale complexion to speak passionate and thrilling words pending the suffusion is quite another thing. On the other hand, it must be observed that no amount of merely physical exertion or exercise of voice could bring colour into that pale, proud, intellectual face. . . . In a word he commanded his own pulses, as well as the pulses of his auditors with most despotic ease".

The actor is to be so thorough in his art as to express grief by outward expression, when his mind is really revelling in joy, and *vice versa*. In fact the actor should know that action is the very soul and substance of the drama. A blush, a sudden pallor, a particular quiver of the lip, distension of the nostril or the corrugation of the brow produces effect if it is consistent with the occasion. The actor's facial expression is to be full of meaning. He must have such a command over his facial expression that he should be able to blush, turn pale and perspire at will.

2. He must have a genius called dramatical instinct, *i. e.* an extraordinary inborn imaginative faculty. He must have technical training, artistic instinct and inspiration.

3. He must have the magnetic quality to identify himself with the very spirit of the man he represents on the stage; or in other words he is to forget his own individuality for the time being, and must actually believe himself to be the character he is endeavouring to represent. (Vide Edmund Kean's life)

4. He must study the many sided and the many mooded characters he assumes.

5. He must realise the full impressiveness of the drama. It is only then and not till then, that his emotions in communion with the nervous centres affect the organs of expression.

6. He must be able to interpret, not only the extremes of human passion, but also the depth and subtleties of thought.

7. He must keep his body and mind clear and should be a type of masculine worth and honour.

8. He must be able to rouse the intellect and attract the heart of the audience and thus be able to turn, even the bitterest critic into a lover. Remember the Horotian proverb rendered by Churchill thus:—"Those who would make us feel must feel themselves". Sensibility is the prime requisite of great acting. Cicero and Quintilian both observe that it is not possible "for hearer to grieve, or hate, or fear or to be moved to commiseration and tears, unless the emotions which the speaker wishes to communicate are deeply impressed and stamped on his own bosom in characters of fire. When the actor is in full grief, it "takes effect upon the organs of his voice; and the very tone of it is altered: it is broken, hoarse and indistinct" Salvini with much authority observes:—"If you do not weep in the agony of grief, if you do not blush with shame, if you do not glow with love, if you do not tremble with terror, if your eyes do not become blood-shot with

rage, if, in short, you yourself do not intimately experience whatever befits the diverse characters and passions you represent, you can never thoroughly transfuse into the hearts of your audience the sentiment of the situation." Mrs. Bancroft observed that in the matter of producing pathos, art should help nature and nature must help art. To know the subject fully, I would recomend every actor to read William Archer's book *"Masks or Faces"* or *"A Study in the Psychology of Acting."*

9. Remember that well-meditated pauses produce good effect. (Edmund Kean in the character of Sir Edward Mortimer had to say the words :—" Wilford remember' ! Kean used to pause after 'Wilford', and during the pause his face underwent a rapid succession of expressions fluently melting into each other and all tending to one climax of threat, and then the deep tones of "remember" ! came like muttered thunder".

10. Rember also, that Hamlet's advice to the tragedians of the city that they should suit the action to the word, the word to the action, applies more to the pantomimists and less to the speeches of the actor in a regular legitimate play. If the advice is interpreted literally, in a regular drama, there will be no dramatic action. The dramatic action consists in expressing by gesture the idea of the sentences in the actor's speech or in other words in the expression of passions contained in the speech. The literal meaning applies in India to "Abhinaya Science" and not to dramatic action.

One Hylas, the scholar of Pylades, who had so advanced in his art as to almost rival his master, one day played in a piece of which the last words were "The Great Agamemnon". Hylas, to express the idea of greatness, stretched out his whole body, as if he meant to indicate the measure of a very great man. Pylades cried aloud "you represent length, not grandeur". When the audience asked him to act the same part himself, he obeyed and represented Agamemnon as pensive ; since, nothing in his opinion, was so characteristic of a great king as *thought* for all."

11. He must assume grace and dignity, which will win the sympathy and admiration of the audience.

12. He must have a strong grasp of character, artistic feeling, sincerity of purpose, truthfulness to nature and attention to necessary detail.

13. He is to elaborate, to magnify and endow with life, the frame work that is given him by the poet. He is to infuse into the play life-like qualities which the author never dreamt of. He must give also due effect to the author's meaning.

14. Remember that the actor with the least vanity in his calling gives the greatest dignity to his company.

15. He must never accustom himself to the voice of the prompter. If he does so, the effect of his action is gone as he will not be master of the situation. Sometimes it will disgrace the actor and ruin the play. (Once a Manageress, by name Mrs. Baker, undertook to discharge the prompter's duty herself in a farce known as "*Who is the Dupe*". "The part of Gradus was undertaken by her leading actor Garduer, and in the scene where Gradus attempts to impose upon the gentlemen of the story by affecting to speak Greek, the performer's memory unfortunately failed him. He glanced appealingly towards the prompt side of the stage. Mrs. Baker was mute examining the play book with a puzzled air. "Give me the word Madam" whispered the actor. "It is a hard word, Jem" the lady replied. Then give me the next. "That is the harder". The performer was at a stand still; the situation was becoming desperate. "The next", cried Gardues, furiously. "Harder still" answered the prompter, and then, perplexed beyond all limit, she flung the book on the stage and exclaimed aloud "There, now you have them all; take your choice"). Thus both the performer and the play were ruined. Relying too much on the prompter is not learning a lesson but depending upon copying. Some players not getting by rote the part set for them, utter some words to suit the context and thus confuse the prompters and the fellow actors. An actor in his impersonation of Macbeth finding himself at a loss as to the

text, soon after the commencement of his second scene with Lady Macbeth, cooly observed :—"Let us retire, dearest Chuck, and con this matter over in a more sequestered spot, far from the busy haunts of men. Herè the walls and doors are spies and our every word is echoed far and near. Come, then, let us away. False heart must hide, you know, what false heart dare not show". To such an actor the prompter is useless. The other actors are confused and a good play is spoilt. Schlegel says "Of all the actors in the world, I conceive those of Paris to have their parts by heart; in this as well as in the knowledge of versification, the Germans are far inferior to them."

16. Let the actor not repeat his verses and dialogues in haste. Even the best and experienced actors are confused by haste.

(*a*). An experienced actress by name Mrs. Gibbs who took the part of Miss Stirling in "The Clandestine Marriage" said in a hurry "she has locked the key and carried away the door in her pocket".

(*b*). Mrs. Davenport as Mrs. Heidelberg said in confusion "I protest there is a candle coming along the gallery with a man in his hand."

(*c*). An actor, levelling his halberd to prevent Richard from impeding the progress of Henry's funeral, instead of saying "My lord, stand back and let the coffin pass" cried, in his hurry and confusion "My lord, stand back and let the parson cough".

(*d*). The great actor Charles Kemble when he was playing Shylock, instead of asking "Shall I lay perjury upon my soul?" overturned the text by exclaiming "Shall I lay surgery upon my poll".

17. He must cultivate distinct and powerful articulate voice and graceful action. Remember the observation of De Quincey that "certain features, it is well known, and peculiar styles of

countenance which are impressive in a drawing room become ineffective on a public stage". The following lines written by Llyod should guide the actor on the stage.

"'Tis not enough the voice be sound and clear.
"'Tis modulation that must charm the ear.

*   *   *   *

"The voice all modes of passion can express
"That marks the proper word with proper stress.
"But none emphatic can that actor call
"Who lays an equal emphasis on all
"Some o'er the tongue the laboured measures roll
"Slow and deliberate as the parting toll,
"Point every stop, mark every pause so long
"Their words like stage processions stalk along
"All affectation but creates disgust
"And e'en in speaking we may seem too just.

*   *   *   *   *

"In vain for them the pleasing measure flows
"Whose recitation runs it all to prose
"Repeating what the poet sets not down,
"The Verb disjoining from its friendly Noun
"While pause, and break, and repetition join
"To make a discord in each tuneful line
"Some placid natures fill the allotted scene
"With lifeless drone, insipid and serene
"While others thunder every couplet o'er
"And almost crack your ears with rant and roar.
"More nature oft and finest strokes are shown
"In the low whisper than tempestuous tone

"And Hamlet's hollow voice and fixed amaze
"More powerful terror to the mind conveys,
"Than he, who swollen with big impetuous rage
"Bullies the bulky phantom off the stage.

* * * *

"He who in earnest studies o'er his part
"Will find true nature cling about his heart;
"The modes of grief are not included all
"In the white handkerchief and mournful drawl
"A single look more marks the internal woe
"Than all the windings of the lengthened "oh"!
"Up to the face the quick sensation flies
"And darts its meaning from the speaking eyes
"Love, Transport, Madness, Anger, Scorn, Despair
"And all the passions, all the soul is there".

"Remember also the following advice of Aaron Hill to the players to strengthen their elocutionary powers:

"To warm, dephlegm and clarify the thorax and the windpipe by exerting, the more frequently the better, their fullest power of utterance; thereby to open and remove all hesitation and roughness or obstruction and to tune their voices by effect of such continual exercise into habitual mellowness, ease of compass and inflexion, just for the same reason why an active body is more strong and healthy than a sedentary one".

18. He must be very distinct in his delivery. A prosy manner of delivery is not dramatical. It must be a dramatical delivery fashioned by the art of oratory. To arrest the attention of audience, a man ought to be gifted with both an oratorical and imitative power. Homely conversational language is not suited for a tragedy. Let the actor remember that the sense of the verse does not in many cases end with the line or with the duration of breath.

19. He must be clever enough to prevent laughter and create silence in serious parts. Silence spells success and tittering means ruin. He should know that the rendering of grief and its kindred shades of emotion is the highest craft of an actor.

20. He must understand that even if the best plays are exhibited parrot-like, the whole effect is lost. He should know that the reproduction of passion is the actor's highest and most essential task. Changes in the face, the limbs or the organs of speech are essential for the manifestation of passion.

21. He must also know that dramatical delivery varies in soliloquy, dialogue, lyrical passages and "aside talk". (The actor will be benefited by reading Addison's Spectator No. 541). Dutton Cook says "we have soliloquies and asides, the artful delivery of which duly to secure attention and enlist sympathy, evokes the best abilities of the player, bound to invest with an air of nature and truth-seeming purely fictitious and unreasonable proceedings".

22. Know that the actor needs the guidance of healthy criticism.

23. The actor must constantly look to the protection of his own self-respect.

24. He should try to deliver a speech in such a way that he makes the audience imagine that he has not got it by heart. (J. B. Booth, in repeating the soliloquy of Richard III beginning "Now is the winter of our discontent," appeared like a man thinking out, not as if reciting from memory.

25. In singing let the words be very clear. Let not the actor display only his voice.

26. Let not false emphasis be laid on words. (Stanley Jones attacks the actors and says they "add to a villainous mispronunciation of their words a reckless disregard for the rules of syntax".

27. In side-talk let the speaker go a little distance from the character for whose ears it is not meant.

28. Let not the actor turn his back upon the front of the house.

29. If he is to leave the stage at the end of a speech let him not finish it in the centre of the stage.

30. Let not the actor appear on the stage till he thoroughly practises his part. (Edmund Kean, it is said, practised even the number of paces he had to walk on the stage) Let him not accustom himself to gag. Gag is a language introduced by an actor into his part. This is a common occurrence in a comedy. Shakespeare in his "Antony and Cleopatra" said "the quick comedians extemporally will stage us and present our Alexandrian revels". When gag becomes a fashion, the play is spoiled. Garrick said in an epilogue :

"Ye actors who act what our writers have writ
"Pray stick to your parts and spare your own wit ;
"For when with your own you unbridle your tongue
"I'll hold ten to one you are all in the wrong".

31. When the actor plays the part of violent emotion let him not calm himself at once. Let his facial appearance assume its natural shape gradually. Let the quivering muscles and altered tones be an index of the subsidence of his passion.

32. Let the actor practise the art of changing the tone to denote the cheerful, tender, melancholy or animated emotion of the mind. The primary emotions—such as grief, joy, terror, &c. one may easily express, but the actor must learn to express the more complicated and habitual secondary emotions such as love, hatred, jealousy, &c. which are the real attitudes of mind.

33. When singing, let the actor not keep time with his hands and legs.

34. Let not the actor go and take a seat in the house during the performance of the piece in which he acted after his part is over.

35. Let him study the directions of his entrance and exit.

36. Let him not be over-vehement or cold. A cold declamatory delivery is bad. He should grow warm by degrees,

37. Let the actor not lose his presence of mind when he finds that he has erred. (One Thornton was a famous actor and was a special favourite of George III. One night when representing the Biron in the tragedy of "Isabella", he died without giving the letter which unravels the plot; and as he lay prostrate in the last scene, one of the performers in the stage whispered to him, "Mr. Thornton—the letter—the letter". Thornton then rose and took the letter from his bosom and said "One thing I had forgot through a multiplicity of business. Give this letter to my father: it will explain all" and then lay down again in the arms of death).

38. Making up is difficult with an actor when he desires to look younger or older, stouter or thinner. He should practise this art assiduously. (The portraits and life of Mr. George Robey will show that by practice a man can assume varied shapes).

39. Let the actor be careful in applying paints to his face. ("There was a great laughter in the theatre one night when Stephen Kemble playing Othello for the first time with Miss Satchell as Desdemona, kissed her before smothering her, and left an ugly patch of soot upon her cheek).

40. Let the actor try his best to appear on the stage in a dress suited to his character. Let him also pay his best attention to chronological and national accuracy. Let him remember the following lines:

"To suit the dress demands the actor's art,
"Yet there are some who over dress the part,

"To some prescriptive right gives settled things,
" Black wigs to murderers, feathered to kings,
" But Michial Cassio might be drunk enough
" Though all his features were not grimmed with snuff.
" Why should Poll Peachum shine in satin clothes?
" Why every devil should dance scarlet hose?"

41. Remember that the first duty of the actor is to fit his part to the character that he personates.

42. Let him study his text, know his part by rote and leave inspiration to the spur of the moment.

43. Let the actor not speak before his interlocutor has finished a sentence.

DRAMATIC COMPANY.

To an Indian dramatic company a few words are not amiss here.

1. Never form yourself into a company from mercenary motives. A noble and *bona fide* intention to impart instruction to the general public by means of amusement, should be the guiding principle in your conduct. Commercial speculation improves the art but degrades the dignified object of the drama.

2. Know that an indifferent play will cause indifference in the audience, while an invigorating play will have a corresponding stimulating effect upon them. This will live and draw large audience and that a great deal of laughter and ridicule.

3. Bear in mind that as in the stage of life so on this mimic stage, one single error often ruins it.

4. Know that a great deal of training for actors is necessary as also intelligence and unceasing attention to details.

5. Never exhibit a play which is inadequately rehearsed. Remember that in France and England no new play is put on boards till it has been rehearsed forty to fifty times. Their performances are admitted by the public to be superior. In Germany, the play is rehearsed only from sixteen to twenty times. The actors not being ready, go to the curtains to follow the voice of the prompter. The effect of the play is therefore lost.

6. In getting up the play take the author for guide. Remember that in France the author of the play is everything to the company. The French therefore are always successful on the stage; but in Germany, the author is little or nothing. The German plays are not therefore so successful.

7. For producing the stage effect, devote to your scenery and to your arrangement, not only much money but much thought

and origiuality : for in dramas scenery and mounting play a most important part. Remember at the same time, that pleasing the eyes with gorgeous scenery and cavalcades is not as essential as pleasing the senses with legitimate dramas and good acting. Bring in the former only as accessory to the latter.

8. Never place before the audience an actor who is nervous and in-experienced.

9. Let there be the sifting and weeding of actors till you select the best. Bear in mind the lines of Lloyd :—

> " The player's province they but vainly try
> " Who want those powers—Deportment, Voice and Eye."

(Read the Life of Charles Dickens by Foster, Vol. 2, page 341) ;

10. Avoid demoralizing exhibitions.

11. Your behaviour both public and private must be such as to have the magic and magnetic effect of drawing people.

12. If you place before the audience an actor fully trained, and dramatically developed in the art of acting, the effect is simply electrical.

13. Avoid the system of engaging a trunk-maker in the gallery. (Read Addison's *Spectator* on the subject). If the audience is pleased, they will certainly approve of your actors by cheers and applauses. This play-house thunderer is a nuisance. Sometimes he may save a play, but such tricks are not worthy of a good manager. Friends and well-wishers of a company or the author undertake sometimes the duty of applauding and cheering. When Addison's "*Cato*" was performed, his friend Steel brought all his friends and they cheered the actors. But this is only an occasional "*claque*". Some are of opinion that "every dramatic or lyrical artist cannot invariably by sheer force of talent overcome the coldness, the languor or the indifference of the audience, yet

the general effect of the representation would suffer much, if all applause, including that of a premeditated and indeed purchased kind, were entirely withheld ; the timid would remain timid, talent would remain unrecognised, and therefore almost unrevealed, if no cheering were heard to reassure, to encourage, to kindle and excite ").

14. Do not introduce real horses, dogs, and other animals on the stage. (In the parody of Coleridge, in " Rejected Addresses," he condemns the appearance of animals on the stage).

" Amid the freaks that modern fashion sanctions,
It grieves much to see live animals
Brought on the stage ; Grimoldi has his rabbit,
Laurent his cat, and Braudbury his pig.
Fie on such tricks. Johnson the machinist
Of former Drury imitated life
Quite to the life. The elephant in blue beard
Stuffed by his hand, wound round his proboscis
As spruce as he who roared in Padamanabha ".

A critic remarks " as the Musalman dates his computation of years from the flight of Mohamat, so should the hordes of folly commence their triumphant register from the open flight of common sense on this memorable night, whence whole troop of horses made their first appearance in character at Covent Garden."

An author in the following lines ridiculed not only the introduction of horses upon the stage, but also the prevailing taste of morbid German dramas of Lotzebne School.

" To lull the soul by spurious strokes of art,
To wrap the genius and mislead the heart,
To make the mankind revere wives gone astray,
Some pious sons who rob on the high way

For this the foreign muses trod over stage
Commanding the German schools to be the rage.
Dear Johnny Bell, you boast much resolution
With thanks to heaven, a glorious constitution
Your taste recovered half from foreign quacks
Takes airings now on English horses back,
While every modern bard may rage his name
If not on lasting praise, on stable fame.
Think that to Germans you have given no check,
Think how each actor horsed has risked his neck
You've shown them favour. Oh, then, once more show it.
To this night's Anglo-German's horse play poet".

15. Till Hindu society is fully developed physically, greatly reformed morally, and vastly improved intellectually, do not allow a woman to become an actress. Hindu customs and manners do not allow such a course being taken. Reynolds was especially severe upon the "sin of boys wearing the dress and affecting the airs of women" and "thus unconsciously helped on a change he would have regarded as still more deplorable—the appearance of actresses on the English stage". Even the English people who treat women on a level with them felt keenly the introduction of actresses on the stage).

16. Never give up music in a drama as being unnatural. It is as natural as verses are in the place of speech, but you should remember that the artistic conditions of a music hall are not identical with those of the theatre. One attempts to show proficiency in technical music, the other attempts to please the audience by harmonious music.

17. Try to avoid enlisting as actors too many of the juvenile school-going population.

18. If you take boys as actors in your company, see that wholesome supervision is exercised over their general education.

19. Be punctual as regards time.

20. Make proper arrangements for the comforts of the audience.

21. When an actor is earnestly encored and called back, be courteous to him. (Certain calls and recalls are not worthy and sometimes absurd. "Ophelia after tripping off insane to find a watery grave, has been summoned back to the stage to acknowledge suavely enough by smiles and courtsies, the excessive applause of the spectators, greatly to the perplexity of king Claudius, Queen Gertrude, and Laertes, and seriously to the injury of the poet's design, and this is but a sample of the follies of the modern theatre in this respect").

22. Do not measure the merit of your performance by the receipts.

23. If there are two or more companies in a town let the spirit of emulation reign in your heart, and not envy.

24. Play good farces because they do immense good. In this attempt do not insult the feeling of even a single being.

25. Companies will do well and the audience will be better enlightened if no notices containing the purport of the story, scene by scene, are circulated among the spectators.

26. Avoid doubling or trebling of parts unless it be of minor characters. A minor actor may take many parts. Some actors are much inclined to undertake dual duty with a view to manifest their versatility or to surprise their admirers. The following story is written by Dutton Cook in his "Book of the Play".

"At a provincial theatre, then under his management, Elliston once tried the strange experiment of sustaining the characters of both Richard and Richmond in the same drama. The entranc of Richmond does not occur until the fifth act of the tragedy, when the scenes in which the King and the Earl occupy the stage become alternate. On making his exit as Richard, Elliston dropped his hump from his shoulder, as though it had been a knapsack, straightened his deformed limbs, slipped on certain pieces of pasteboard armour, and adorned with fresh gear, duly presented himself as the Tudor Prince. The heroic lines of Richmond delivered, the actor hurried to the side wings, to assume something of the mis-shapen aspect of Richard and then re-enter as that character. In this way the play went on until the last scene, when the combatants came face to face. How was their fight to be presented to the spectators? This omission of so popular an incident as a broad sword combat could not be thought of. The armour of Richmond was forthwith shifted on to the shoulders of a supernumerary player, who was simply enjoined to "hold his tongue and fight like a devil." Richard slain, Richmond departed. The body of the dead king was borne from the stage and Elliston was then enabled to appear as Richmond and speak the closing lines of the play". The above may not be an impossible feat to an Indian actor, but the effect on the audience will not be so impressive as two actors appearing and performing their part. Within the interval of five minutes, an Indian male character can become a female actress and perform her part, and then again assume his original male character.

27. Do not exhibit what is not fit for a well-educated and sensible young woman to listen to.

28. Let there be no long wait between the acts.

29. When a manager announces a play and the audience attends and an important actor has stopped away by some mishap, obtain the permission of the audience to read his part from the play book. (Such mishaps happened on the European stage, when Addison's "*Cato*" was performed, on account of the absence of Sheridan).

30. Let the manager see that there prevails perfect agreement among the actors, for, as Sheridan says, "when actors do agree their unanimity is wonderful". Companies or individual actors generally fall out with the critics of the day. The critics in some cases make much of insignificant defects in an actor to run him down. In an address to Garrick, a certain author said:—

"Your bucks of the pit are miracles of learning
Who point out faults to show their own discerning
And Critic-like bestriding martyred sense
Proclaim their genius and vast consequence."

In the play "*All for Love*", the author opens with the lines:—

"What flocks of critics hover here today
As vultures wait on armies for their prey
All gaping for the carcase of a play".

Another prologue begins:—

"They who write ill and they who never durst to write
Turn-critics out of mere revenge and spite.
A play house gives them a fame and up then starts
From a mean fifth rate wit, a man of parts."

CRITICS.

The actors accuse critics of want of art and education. It is therefore necessary to say a few words on the subject. From experience it can be asserted rather affirmatively that "Dramatic criticism is an art which the veriest novice in literature may handle with profit to himself and advantage to the actor". It requires neither training nor knowledge nor skill. Experience and acute observation are enough. A man broad in sympathies and fair in judgment will shine well as a critic, and his opinion will be respected. Some defects in a character or in a play are however of the kind which time and exercise of judicious self-restraint may cure. The critic need not take serious notice of such things. Many anomalies and countless unpardonable absurdities are tolerated, nay, favoured by the public. The stage not having the moral courage to discontinue them practises them to please the public. The critic will do well to refine the taste of the public rather than hit hard against the stage. The stage also will do well to take note of such criticisms and try to reform; instead of calling the critics names.

Let a company not act a play which was acted by another company in the same town. This will give the critic an opportunity to compare, and comparisons, as we all know, are odious and unpleasant and give rise to unnecessary misunderstandings.

AUDIENCE.

Last but not least is the goodness of the audience. It is the audience that teaches the actor how to play his part. Leaving aside the inner audience who are sympathetically disposed towards the players, and not saying much about the indifferent sort of gentlemen who keep silent even when an actor plays his worst, we may say a few words about that class of the audience which will not tolerate either a slight grossness or a little defect in an actor. They hiss and roar. This may be the result of a voluntary emotion on the part of the audience which will not brook the tomfoolery of the actors. Whatever the defects of the actor may be, the audience will do well not to hiss or roar, for it discourages an actor, and sometimes it may be that an incipient dramatic genius may feel himself unfit for the stage.

In 1808, the great Comedian Lewis retired from the London stage and he recommended Richard Jones to the manager of Covent Garden Theatre, to fill up his place insted of Mdvin, an actor of extraordinary ability. In a comedy called "Love a la mode", Richard Jones had to appear for the first time. Lewis attended behind scenes. When Jones appeared on the stage "he became transfixed with fear", and instead of speaking, "he was stuck dumb and became immoveable; Lewis perciving the dilemma of the new actor, roared "Yoicks-Yoicks," "the audience hearing those well-known sounds exclaimed "A second Lewis", then slapping Jones on the back he told him "to go in and win" Jones taking courage, dashed on the stage amidst the most deafening plaudits and as he passed about in his jokey-dress-thus showing off his slime tall and well formed person, minutes absolutely elapsed ere he could utter a word for the applause". His success was most complete. After he left the stage, he "devoted his latter years to pulpit elequence or giving instruction to those elevated personages intended as dignitaries of the church". If instead of being hailed with applause, Jones had been hissed by the audience he would have left the stage in disgust and the audience would have lost an ornament. In one of Dryden's plays, an actress said the following line in as moving and affecting a tone as she could :—" My wound is great, because it is so small". The Duke of Buckingham rose immediately from his seat and added in a loud ridiculous tone of voice.—" Then it would be greater, were it none at all". The audience hissed the poor woman off the stage.

2. The audience also would do well not to go late to the theatre and not to enter the hall in the middle of the scene, for, this late entrance in the middle, discomforts the rest of the audience and inconveniences the actors. Malicious members of rival companies generally cause disturbance in the play especially when a good part is being acted. They show their pretended "disguest at the performance by significant signs and indecent indications of contempt. They would laugh aloud in the most serious scenes of tragedy and sometimes rise and quit the theatre. The boistrous manifestations of dislike, however, as hisses howls, whistles, and the imitations of the mewing of a cat are common in such people". They would do well to behave like gentlemen.

3. I would advise the audience or the major portion of it to know the work nearly by heart, so that, during the representation, the whole attention may be divoted to the acting and every faulty syllable may with immediate detection be reprobated.

4. Do not be carried away by the caprice of the moment, either in the applause or denouncement of the play. Think twice before you give expression.

When Voltaire produced his tragedy of Adelaide-du Guesolin for the first time, it was hissed through every act. The play was therefore condemned. Some thirty years afterwards when the same tragedy was produced without any change, every scene was applauded. There are many instances of this sort even on the English stage.

INDEX.